GUIDED

A TRUE STORY

What People Are Saying About GUIDED

"Unwanted, unloved, and abused, baby Linda had given up on life, let go, and cried out for help. And someone answered her. Not even old enough to understand who they were, these protectors and teachers saved her life, became her best friends, and guided her through unimaginable life challenges."

Betsy Chasse, Los Angeles, CA
Co-Writer, Producer and Director of "What The Bleep Do We Know?"
Author of "Tipping Sacred Cows"

"Based on her amazing true-life story, Linda Deir has written a readable and profound book, Guided. From her abusive childhood, business successes and failures, series of husbands/ partners, troubled relationship with her daughter and grand-daughter, and astounding family secrets, she has crafted a vivid and inspirational story for open-minded, creative living, and paranormal/spiritual readers.

With gratitude, the author makes it clear in Guided that she has had the extraordinary and blessed guidance of a host of Spirit Guide Angels, or benevolent beings. From her early childhood and continuously throughout her life, they have served as her best friends and life coaches.

This book is so powerful in its plot line, mix of characters, and empowering message, I would like to see it become a film or TV series, so that it can educate and inspire many more people than today's books typically reach.

Without her guides' presence, Deir admits that she would have given up and expired long ago. She details how these guides have concretely instructed her on how to neutralize the heavy negativity and maximize the wonderful fulfillment in her life. It is a step well beyond the Beatles' reference of "a little help from my friends."

In its 28 chapters, Guided is Deir's honest and gritty tale of her living in her two intersecting worlds – the cast of good, bad and ugly people who have inhabited her life, and the other-worldly guides who have unconditionally loved, spoken to and supported her. The life she has led is indeed fascinating and uplifting. In the face of crisis after crisis, disappointment after disappointment, and tragedy after tragedy, she has achieved victory after victory. Her positive life outcomes happened because she has listened to the insights and followed the wise counsel of her guides. And her current loving life with her husband, Ray, is due largely to his bringing his own circle of guides to aspects of their golden relationship.

A practical and valuable feature of Guided is that Deir has clearly articulated the many universally applicable statements that embody how she has been guided; these are presented in the form of short Tips, Lessons, and Awareness. Not only do these highlighted inserts contribute to the uniqueness of the book's unfolding, they also comprise a system of wisdom that can be used by us readers to open up and tune into our own guides and guidance. The author took a photo of and put on the book's cover one of her paranormal guides, which can be used in accessing one's own guides through meditation-like states.

If you are seeking inspiration from a true-life story on how to overcome adversity and live in spiritual awareness, if you are eager to become wiser in your choices with timely input from source-connected guides, and if you want to live in the bracing truth-filled reality relevant to who you authentically are, then Guided is the book that you must read, underline and reflect upon. For people whose capacity to hope and grow has been diminished by life's struggles and setbacks, this book should be required reading. Thank you, Linda Deir, for telling your full story and sharing your guided and empowering wisdom – all for the benefit of your readers' consciousness evolution."

Larry J. Rosenberg, Ph.D., retired marketing professor and international business consultant

---

"Guided...an incredible, true story, of a young girl who is led by her spirit guides as she struggles to find her place in the world. I found myself cheering for her as she overcomes one adversity after another, and discovers many painful lessons, including the unbelievable revelation of her family's secret past. Feeling unloved, she repeatedly fails at love, but wins at business, as she is shown the way, in one endeavor after another, by her spirit guides.

Every woman who has suffered the agonizing pain of not being loved, but wishes to overcome the loneliness and hurt, should read this marvelous book. The 137 lessons sprinkled throughout the pages, encourages the reader to understand that it is possible to overcome even the most tragic of life's circumstances, and find true and lasting happiness."

Ben Lizardi, Pasadena, CA
President, Lizardi Communications, Inc., Advertising & Marketing

---

"This is a riveting true story that immediately draws you into Linda's life when she, only 20 months old and in a diaper, is found walking alone in the middle of a very busy freeway, looking for her father. But was she really alone? That's just the beginning of a series of hard-to-believe events that Linda was to experience throughout her life. You will shake your head in disbelief, laugh, cry, feel disappointment and triumph. You will discover how her deep connection with her Spirit Guides saved her life many times and guided her through unimaginable situations.

Linda shares the lessons she learned along the way, provides guidance on how to access your own Guides, and emphasizes the importance of paying attention to them."

Sonia Martin, Chief Editor for David R. Hawkins, M.D, Ph.D. — Sedona, AZ

"A heartfelt, authentically written story that clearly shows how important it is for each of us to learn to not only connect with the benevolent spiritual guidance that is always available to us, but also to fully trust in the inspirations we receive. The author endured numerous challenges, and yet overcame them all simply because she embraced the wisdom shared by her spirit guides instead of letting a fearful ego motivate her choices."

Jeff Maziarek, author of Spirituality Simplified and Codi's Journey

---

"I have been talking to Linda's guides for several years now, and they have consistently given love, compassion, and valuable guidance to everyone who reaches out to them. The dialogues have made me more spiritual because I feel like we are always surrounded by angels, and we can communicate with them anytime."

B. Singh, Santa Monica, CA

"From the very beginning of Guided, Linda takes you on this incredible and sometimes very painful journey of her life. We get to see her constant struggles with abusive relationships, family dynamics, and other challenges that appear along the way. No matter what happens to Linda, someone or something is always guiding her in the right direction.

In every chapter of Guided, Linda does an amazing job of sharing these valuable lessons she learned from her guides. She provides you with a wealth of knowledge, on how to strengthen your own relationship with your guides. This gives the reader plenty of opportunities for self evaluation and a chance to apply these tips to our own life experiences.

Guided is well written and easy to comprehend. If you're an open minded or spiritual individual, you will enjoy Linda's remarkable journey. Just like Linda, we all choose our own path. The question we should all ask ourselves is, are we alone for our journey or are we simply being.......guided?"

Brad Miller, Scottsdale, AZ

"Unlike another tedious self-help book, this riveting and entertaining true life story guides you effortlessly through the steps necessary to make the connection with your own Spirit Guides and Guardian Angels."

Meghan B. Austin, TX

GUIDED

Her Spirit Guide Angels Were Her Best Friends and Life Coaches

LINDA DEIR

A TRUE STORY

GUIDED Press

2675 W. Hwy 89A, PMB 1310, Sedona, Arizona 86336
www.GuidedPress.com

Published in the United States of America by Guided Press

Library of Congress Cataloging-in-Publication Data
Deir, Linda   Guided: a true story / by Linda Deir – 1st ed. p. cm.
Summary: Linda Deir has always experienced the paranormal as normal. As a small child, she discovered her *spirit guide angels* and developed a lifelong relationship with *them*. In 1994, *one* of *them* materialized right in front of her while she had a 35mm Nikon camera in hand and became the front cover of Guided.

Editor: Laren Bright, Laren Bright Words
Interior design and layout: Booknook.biz
Cover Design: George Foster, Foster Covers
Front Cover Photograph: Linda Deir

Printed in the United States of America.

Type: Non-fiction / Spiritual

First Printing, 2014

ISBN-13: 978-0692238134

TABLE OF CONTENTS

DEDICATION TO MY "GUIDES"

I dedicate this book to *those* who have Guided me, *my life coaches, my best friends, my spirit guides.* Thank you for *your* infinite wisdom, teachings, patience, *your* impeccable timing and clarity, and *your* unyielding love and support. Thanks to my *Spirit Guide Angels,* I have lived to tell my story.

Without *all of you,* I wouldn't have made it — I wouldn't have wanted to.

FOREWORD

GUIDED is the author's true story that follows her life from survival as an abused child through her escape as a teenager and into her phenomenal success as a businesswoman in a man's world by age 19 and beyond. Using her life as a template, GUIDED is a roadmap for stepping on board at any point along your life path to join forces with your own *spirit guides* to create a better life than you could have on your own. Sprinkled throughout the book are 137 universally applicable Tips, Learnings, Lessons, and Awarenesses that Linda shares directly from her life-long relationship with her *spirit guides*.

Linda Deir has always experienced the paranormal as normal. As a small child, she discovered her *spirit guide angels* and developed a life-long relationship with *them*. She had such a close connection to these *benevolent companions* that in 1994, *one of them* materialized right in front of her while she had a 35mm Nikon camera in hand. That photo became the front cover of this book.

From early childhood, Linda was unloved, threatened, and alone. These *benevolent beings* provided her with unconditional love, and through that, *they* became the most influential *teachers, life coaches, best friends* and *protectors* she could have ever had. *They* made the impossible possible throughout her life. As a result of *their* guidance, nothing has ever been out of reach for her. *They* can do this because *they* know you better than you know yourself.

These *spirit guides* are too wise to force you to learn any-thing. *They* just know when to present you with exactly what you are ready to experience at just the right time. This makes learning easy because what you learn is self-realized. That's what makes this learning so solid.

They are acutely aware that, to learn anything, the environ-ment for learning must first be established. The pressure that blocks learning must be released, and then *they* align you with what you are ready to learn at that particular time. *They* trigger you with events that ignite your passions and set you on your journey. From all this, there's nothing you can't learn, figure out, do, or have. All you have to do is step into it.

The first thing *they* insisted that Linda learn was knowing who she really was. Again, *they* realized that until you know who you are, YOU can't be present to learn anything, because the real YOU is not there. The powerful learning experiences from her *spirit guides*, starting early in her life, prevented her from having to unlearn all the wrong things later on.

At different times, this true story will touch your heart, break your heart, make you cry, and make you smile and laugh. You will find yourself cheering for this little girl, raised by *spirit guides*, who triumphed over extreme adversity.

"Life will get better for you as you get older, IF you can make it through childhood." One of her first memories, this was a prophecy from Linda's *spirit guides,* which was both a warning and a promise. It would turn out to be chillingly true.

Most of all this book will give you the hope and the help you never knew existed as you learn to detect your own *spirit guide angels*, interpret *their* messages, and take action. *They* will never let you down as you build this rapport with *them*. In the end, *they* may be the *only ones* who don't let you down.

Are you ready to get to know *them*...?

Notes from Linda Deir

About Spirit Guides

The use of italics. In addition to the *merry-go-round dream*, as you read through the book, you will notice that I have put references to *guides, your guides, spirit guides, life coaches*, etc., in italics. I did this so it would be clear that I am speaking of those *beings* that are non-physical. I hope this makes it easy for you to track what is going on as the story unfolds.

Whether we know it or not, we all have what people call "*guides*." *They* are identified by many names, among them, *spirit guides, those who stayed behind, guardian angels, angels*, and *others*. In a very real sense, I have come to consider *them* my *life coaches* and *best friends*, assisting me in maneuvering through life's adventures and avoiding many of the pitfalls that were on my path.

This book is a chronicle of my experiences with *them*, and is designed to assist you in recognizing the great value in establishing contact and building a working relationship with your own *guides*. Throughout the book you will find practical instruction for doing just that.

About the Book Cover Photograph

This is the only book ever written about *Spirit Guides* or *Angels* with a real photograph of the author's *Spirit Guide Angel.* I took this photograph in 1994 as *"her"* energy filled the room when *she* materialized right in front of me with my camera in hand (the same year my *guides* came to me in a dream, telling me I would write a book about relationships). This is what *"spirit guides"* really look like when *they* allow themselves to be seen. *They* radiate energy by harnessing the electrical current in our world to project *themselves* into our dimension so we can see *them. They* don't all have wings or look like fat little cherubs.

I've seen my *Spirit Guide Angels* my entire life, and *they* rarely look the same from one visit to the next. That is because *their energy* is always in motion, as is *their* consciousness, as well as ours. Although this is a rare occurrence, it was no accident that *she* allowed me to capture *her* magnificence that day. It was deliberate and a gift to the world to help you make contact with your own *Spirit Guide Angels.* Seeing is believing!

How to use this book — *Spirit Guide* Connection Visualization

 Sprinkled throughout this book are sections labeled **TIP, LEARNING, LESSON, AND AWARNESS**. They are an integral part of the book, coming directly from my *Spirit Guides*, and are what *they* taught me throughout my life.

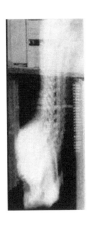

After reading each tip, learning, lesson, and awareness stop and ponder what you just read while gazing at the *Spirit Guide Angel* photograph on the front cover of this book Then, to make an even deeper connection with your *spirit guides*, place your left hand on the photo, take a breath, close your eyes, and let it work. The powerful energy this photo sends is amplified each time you touch or gaze at it.

If you follow this exercise, with a sincere intent, by the time you finish reading the entire book, you will be well on your way to establishing a lifelong connection with your own *Spirit Guide Angels.*

PART 1: RAISED BY SPIRIT GUIDES

Chapter 1: First Contact — The Merry-Go-Round Dream

While I became aware of my *guides* at a very young age, I did not always know who *they* were. I was introduced to *them* in a remarkable life-destiny dream that set the stage for my entire life. It showed me who I am, why I'm here, and that I am guided. That repetitive dream played out night after night and year after year and is the first memory I have. The dream started around the age of two and continued until my mid-thirties. In all those years it never changed. It showed me my purpose, people's intentions, and their reactions to a world to come. That was also my first contact, when I met my *old friends...*my *spirit guides.*

I call it *The Merry-Go-Round Dream.*

The Merry-Go-Round Dream

In the dream, I'm about seven years old, and I am on a merry-go-round that is mounted to the top of the inside of a gold-domed ceiling painted in renaissance designs like a cathedral. It was a centuries-old, rich architectural master-piece. I am about 75-to-100 feet above the floor riding this merry-go-round, holding on single-handedly while leaning back in total joy as the merry-go-round speeds up, going faster and faster until I feel like I'm flying. Life just doesn't get better than this!

I am having so much fun, as "everyone I know in the whole wide world" is riding on this merry-go-round with me. As it speeds up, the other people start to get scared. Then, one by one, they begin giving up and letting go. I see them fly off the merry-go-round hitting the side walls of the domed ceiling, blood splattering everywhere. It is gruesome as they scream to their deaths in utter terror. I am in total shock as I watch each one of these people become fearful, then let go and die.

I don't understand why they are afraid and why they can't see how great this ride is. To me, it's the most exciting feeling and a freedom that surpasses anything. This feeling gets interrupted when I see everyone fearful, letting go, and dying. I'm always the only one left on this merry-go-round.

Over time I came to understand how that dream was showing me the theme for my life. It showed me that my experiences in this life would be very different from those of other people – sometimes the exact opposite. It was that single repetitive dream that made me realize that more was going on than anyone was telling me, or that they understood themselves.

In the beginning, I loved having that dream. However, as it persisted, the suffering of the people started dominating it. I was having the dream three to four times a night, and it got so I dreaded going to sleep. I tried to stop the dream or change it because I couldn't bear the part where everyone else got scared and died. It was horrible to see and hear. Since I couldn't stop it or change it, I starting asking "Why? Why me? Why are you showing me this over and over again?" I didn't know who I was asking, but I hoped someone was listening.

As the dream persisted, I became more and more determined to understand it. Even at a young age, I knew it was showing me what I was to experience in this lifetime. I saw that people would be reacting negatively to what was really a good thing. I understood I would need to help the ones who could be reached.

Although I could not see the entire meaning at the time, the dream left me with a very different way of looking at things. I was able to clearly see through the intentions of people without their ever knowing it. From what I experienced in that dream, I realized several things: many or maybe most people were naturally fear-based, they didn't really have a strong will to live, they didn't want things to change and speed up, many people weren't going to reach their desired destinies, and I wasn't going to be able to change their reaction to that.

The most horrifying part of that dream was that those people died with so much fear. I was not able to convince those on the ride with me that this was a good thing. They couldn't see that this could be the best time of their lives as we all ride through it together. I was haunted with the challenge of finding a way to reach them. I became aware that that was my job.

The message of that dream was my *spirit guide angels* showing me how people's fear turned into pain, and that to get out of pain, they must first get out of fear. It was fear that set it all into motion. The fear stopped the people in the dream from experiencing new things and believing in themselves. My *angels* showed me in the dream what would become the biggest tragedy of our times. This tragedy is that most people will die having lived fear-based lives.

The dream always left me feeling disappointed because I wanted all my fellow riders to enjoy this amazing life as much as I did. I was really excited to be here. It was a very sad feeling to be the only one who knew what a remarkable life this is. The other people in the dream who didn't understand this made being here in this life hard when it didn't need to be that way. It was as if I was the only happy, enthusiastic person on the planet.

As I saw that, I realized I was missing something very important, that what I knew from somewhere else didn't exist here: I missed where I came from. These clues about what was really happening in this life led me to spend most of my time alone and keep my thoughts to myself. I became an observer of others while letting them think that they had all the answers. The longing to find that elusive part that was missing consumed me. I experienced a deep loneliness that couldn't even begin to be fulfilled by anyone here in this life.

That dream shocked me into remembering what I knew before I got here and why I was here. I was not interested in the self-defeating, life-draining examples that were all around me at home and in society. They reflected a horrifying interpretation of this life. I was definitely alone in this awareness. I had a memory of a time before coming into this life. I remembered the exciting feeling about how I could do anything once I got here. That's what it feels like before we get here. It's like an urge we cannot resist. This urge is so powerful that we are blinded to the reality of actually being here.

The source of the soul's urge is so pure that it doesn't consider the folly of mankind when breaking through from the other side into this world. This is how it really is before we get here, before we are assigned our amnesia and forget.

But I remembered. And remembering is what made me different right from the start. It also opened the way for me to accept my guidance. But remembering also put me at risk because those who didn't remember would think I was crazy or a threat, or something else that might harm them, and my *spirit guides* knew that. I began to realize what a hostile place this world really could be. It was such a disappointment!

In order to live out the urge that brought me here, to come into this life, I realized I would have to go it alone. I also knew I would need solitary time to explore it. Having sorted out the people around me and becoming aware of what not to say, I realized that acting like a clueless kid and doing what they wanted me to do was all that was needed to fly under the radar. Doing that, I felt like an impostor, when in fact, with my awareness of the greater reality, I knew I was the authentic one. I also realized that nothing was wrong with me; it was those who branded me as wrong who didn't get it.

What I was experiencing and learning was normal, not paranormal. With the majority of the confusion and disappointments now behind me, I became much more accessible to the magic that was mine all along.

This was how the dream put me in touch with my true essence, and from that place, I could fearlessly enjoy my secret freedoms and the reawakened excitement of being here in this life. The dream made me see what I needed to understand in order to navigate through this life. It trained me to be detached at a very early age and see things for what they really are. It showed me a future where things would be speeding up and how people would react. Again, it showed me that it would be very hard to reach these people.

How could a preschool child learn all this, let alone comprehend it? I knew I had help. But who was it coming from?

These realizations came through very clearly. It was from "remembering," or "never forgetting," or both, that would enable me to achieve what I came here to do. All this was breaking my heart because I was longing for something that wasn't here. I had answers I couldn't explain; they were just there for me to decide if, how, and when to apply them. These answers were only good for me because I was too young to articulate them. Even if I could, there was no one to explore them with whom I could relate to. I was on my own. Or was I?

It was getting so my curiosity about *who* was helping me became bigger than the "why." At times the dream felt like a curse because it wouldn't stop. However, it was this dream that awakened and transformed me right from the start.

I came to realize that the *merry-go round dream* represented the wheel of life — the karmic cycle of what is learned in other lifetimes, and being with others who had been in those lifetimes with me. You would think that having such an advantage of knowing these things at an early age would be a great thing. I can tell you firsthand, it was just as confusing and painful as it was an advantage.

The hardest part was thinking I was alone in this awareness. Here I was having all these exciting experiences, and I had no one to share them with. I felt disappointment most of the time with regard to other people. It was as if they were living in a different reality, or I was. Little did I know that this relentless longing was the magnet, the beacon that attracted my *real friends, those who stayed behind, my life coaches... my guides*.

Many of the disciplines that made up my training as a young child are typically learned in the adult years, if they are learned at all. Of course, I did not know that at the time. What I learned also made me an outcast throughout my childhood. That was not such a bad thing because it allowed me to think for myself and have the quiet time to detect the clear messages that came from my most *trusted advisors*. And when *they* showed up, *they* brought with *them* that familiar love I was longing for.

Since the *merry-go-round dream* kept recurring and I couldn't stop it, I resigned myself to the fact that my only choice was to experiment with it, so I let it teach me. I learned to become lucid while in the dream on the chance I might change something. When that failed, I tried avoiding the dream. I set my alarm to go off every hour to wake myself up before the dream started. Nothing worked.

In the midst of all of this – the dream and the alone time — I began to see I wasn't alone; I was being guided by *someone*. I was being trained to see, but not in the typical sense. I started seeing things out of my peripheral vision that would disappear if I looked at them straight on. It didn't make sense, but it was real. That taught me to not over-analyze everything. I learned to focus, but not to expect to see any particular thing. That opened me up to seeing the unexpected. As a result, I was able to see and focus in two different ways. I was seeing two different worlds at the same time.

I practiced with this in the simplest ways. Nothing seemed out of reach as I played with it. From practicing this, I also learned to discern what people were really saying without their actually saying it. I could read their true intentions. The only requirement was a safe, alone place to experiment. Getting interrupted would stop it cold every time, especially in the beginning.

 TIP: This is how it feels in the beginning — when you know that something more is going on but you can't put your finger on it yet. Just leave your mind open to what you don't know. Don't over-think any of it.

Learning to focus and see from both a linear as well as a non-linear perspective encouraged me to try other things over the years. I would hold my breath to manifest things. This allowed me to see through my mind's eye. When holding my breath and then exhaling, two things would happen. One, this practice would release stress, and two, it would allow me to cause things to happen that were normally impossible from a linear approach. For example, from this focus, I could make people say certain things, forget what they were about to say, not see what was right before them, not remember what just happened, etc. *They* were training me to manifest through the breath.

I never talked about doing any of these things. I knew that if I told anyone, it would invite unnecessary confrontation that would interfere with my experiments. Although I kept expanding myself, I still managed to "act normal," not bringing attention to my real self. Life was boring for me most of the time as it was always filled up with a lot of unnecessary drama. I just wasn't interested in the mundane things that were the norm for everyone else. My approach was to let them think they knew what was best and leave it at that. That kept them from feeling inclined to force their beliefs onto me, which would be a complete waste of my time and distract me from more interesting things I was experimenting with. I was learning to live in two worlds.

From that m*erry-go-round dream* I learned how to manage my life and really get to know myself. Once I surrendered to that, other amazing skills showed up. Without thinking about it or analyzing it, these hidden parts of me just came to life. Learning the way I did was both endless and effortless because I had help – *their* help!

That *merry-go-round dream* taught me to be a self-thinker and figure out the dilemmas I was facing — with the training I received from *my guides. They* taught me not to fight a challenge, not to run from it. It helped me see that if you are faced with the unavoidable, the only way to benefit from it is to embrace it. Let it teach you because it's there for an important reason.

My guides also taught me that what we have to learn may not be easy. That's especially the case with the truth. This all started through the intelligent language of a dream, the self-discovery it provided, and the introduction to *my old friends*. Little did I know how important all of this early training would be in the future.

Chapter 2: Second Contact —
Torment Brings My Guides into Focus

I came into the world naturally happy and optimistic. However, before I was born, I didn't anticipate that things would be so dysfunctional here.

It started with my mother. She was hard, angry, and very strict. She hated me, and I mean that literally. Dealing with such intense negativity was such a shock that I just had to find a way out. Her anger manifested as non-stop abuse, both mental and physical. She would berate me and actually physically beat me for the smallest misbehavior.

Linda at 20 months old as her mom glares at her

My knee-jerk reaction was to escape that hostile environment. So one day, I decided I'd had enough and went to find my dad. I shook the front gate to get the latch loose (being around two years old, I wasn't tall enough to reach it), walked down the street and headed onto the expressway. I knew I was in danger and had to find my dad at work. My dad would protect me. For some reason I was sure I was going find him in the direction I was headed.

Before long, two police officers saw me, barefoot and in diapers, walking in the median of the expressway. They picked me up and asked me where I was going. I told them I was going to find my daddy because something's wrong with my mommy. Then they asked me where I lived, but I wouldn't tell them because I didn't want to go back there. So they took me to the candy store and bribed me with my favorite goodies. Then they asked me again to show them where I lived. At that point, my guard was down so I showed them how to get to my house.

I remember my mom's surprised face when she opened the door and how she immediately began covering her tracks. She was so nice to the police officers that they left reassured I was in good hands. But when she closed the door and she was sure they were gone, her demeanor changed.

She looked at me with such anger—maybe even hatred. Then she grabbed me by one arm and started swatting my bottom with what seemed like all her might. She hit me so hard and so many times that my diaper actually flew off and she was swatting my bare behind. I was shrieking, of course, mostly out of seeing my mother so out of control, and also because it hurt, but the pain I could handle. The "out of control" was another matter.

She actually beat me so badly that I passed out from exhaustion, crying myself to sleep. When I woke up, I was horrified to find myself still trapped in that situation. My mother wouldn't let up. She defended her actions to the family by saying, "I'll teach her not to make a fool of me again!" What she really meant was that she almost got caught. I saw through her even then but had no way to get away from her. I began to feel that dying would be easier.

I realized that I couldn't run away from it, so I began to ask for help, but I didn't know who I was asking. To my surprise, I received answers. Even more, I received support for the first time ever. I didn't know what this was, but I knew it was real and *they* were on my side. Finally, someone was on my side — someone was there — someone who loved me! This was the very beginning of what was to become the powerful life-coach training I would receive from my *Spirit Guide Angels* throughout the rest of my life.

Around the age of three, I began to gain a clearer sense of things in the world. At the same time, my mother began increasing my punishment. As soon as my dad left for work, she would make me go into the backyard and sit on the glider all day. She wouldn't let me go to the bathroom, eat, or do anything else. I wet myself every day because I couldn't hold it until my dad came home from work. Just before my dad was due home, she would make me clean up. She sternly warned me that the punishment would get much worse if I ever told him what she was doing.

In the beginning, I would cry to myself most of the day as I asked out loud for help from my *elusive friends*. I just wanted to be released from this world so the pain would stop once and for all. I didn't know why I was being punished, but it went on day after day, week after week.

After a while, in order to deal with it, I would just lie down on the floorboards of the glider in an attempt to shelter myself from the full intensity of the sun. I would sleep there most of the day. Then something happened. Once I stopped fighting it, my prison became a peaceful place for me. Being left alone was no longer such a trial. Now that I knew what my mother would demand of me, as soon as I got out of bed every morning, I just went out to the glider on my own. I was no longer struggling with that punishment. In fact, it was no longer punishment to me.

Lying on the floorboards and sleeping shifted me into a different space where there was no more suffering. The pain was gone and something else was going on that felt very familiar and comforting. I began to sense I wasn't alone; "*they*" were there with me all the time. I had learned to let go, but not give up.

Eventually my mother saw that I had adapted, and since it was no longer disturbing me, she stopped that form of punishment.

 LEARNING: Through that otherwise hopeless situation, I not only made the critical connection with *my guides*, I stopped reacting to my environment. Everything that would happen from this point on would only strengthen the alliance I have with my *spirit guides*.

After the glider period was behind me, I made playing outside in the sandbox my refuge. I had become accustomed to
spending the entire day alone in the yard when it was punishment, so now I chose to stay out there to avoid my mother.
Sometimes I would even sleep there. During these lengthy
periods in the sandbox, I would converse with *whoever* cared
to listen. It turned out there were many *listeners*. I also discovered that all that time in solitary confinement on the glider
was the incubation that brought my *guides* into focus. That
was where I learned to listen and detect *their* subtle messages.
Now *they* were there as I talked and cried and played in *their*
presence in the sandbox. That sandbox turned out to be my
self-help therapy refuge — my early life-coach training.

My *guides* knew that until *they* helped me release the pain and
pressure that had built up from the abuse, I couldn't begin to
learn what *they* came to present to me. So *they* created a safe
and peaceful place — both externally and internally — where I
could detect *them*. As a result, we developed a powerful communication bond. I did not know or question who *they* were.
Like everything else, this started out unexpectedly, and I used
this sacred place to express myself freely with *them*.

This is where I really learned to communicate with *them*
telepathically. What a great language, and what a contrast
to life here. Some people call these *guides* their *imaginary
friends*. But *my guides* were far from imaginary. *They* were,
and continue to be, the most real and tangible *friends, teachers* and *guides* I could have ever asked for.

Over time I built a powerful connection to *those* I had come
to know from some other place. I would not ever attempt to

explain or tell anyone about *them*. As *these listeners* came closer to me, *they* kept me from panicking about the family I found myself trapped in. I spent more time with *them* than I did with anyone in the physical world. *They* were always steady and truthful and conversing with me like an adult. *They* always knew what I needed, even when I didn't. *They* were, and still are, my *best friends*. No one here, with the possible exception of my husband Ray, has ever touched my heart like *they* have.

Once I had this solid connection with this *intelligence* from somewhere beyond the physical level, I was able to understand and experience amazing things that were not offered here in this world. It was a powerful learning experience, and I never knew what *they* would be showing me next. I was completely open, while expecting nothing. Of course, this is exactly how *they* had trained me from the beginning. That's what it takes to not only make contact, but also to discover what is possible in that intangible place.

Because of the rapport I had established with these *intelligent guides,* I saw my family from a different perspective, and they stopped feeling like a threat to me. With my *guides* as my real family, I was less dependent on my physical family and could sidestep the emotional and physical abuse my mother aimed at me. To my delight, I realized I was being raised by *spirit guides,* and because of *them,* everything made sense. More importantly, now I made sense!

I was no longer in panic mode, even though I still lived in a very hostile environment. I learned how to maneuver through the family dynamics like a ballet dancer. My emotions were no longer running my life. I no longer automatically went into reaction mode. When a troubling incident occurred, I would go off by myself and either go to sleep, lay in the twilight between sleep and wakefulness, or think it through. Or I might do all of those in order to figure out the best course of action. This created the ideal opportunity for these *helpers* to come through to provide me with the insight I needed at just the right time.

If someone were to observe this from the outside, they would have assumed things about me because I appeared to be very mature, or that I was very calm and collected under fire, and I was a well-balanced child and a deep thinker. All of these things were true. They might also assume that these behaviors were brought about from a supportive and healthy family environment, which most definitely would not be true. Strange how things appear to be, versus the way things really are.

 LEARNING: You've heard the saying, "*Integrity is doing the right things even when no one is watching.*" This is how you live your life when you have the life-coach training from *your spirit guides*. In the above case, it didn't matter how I was perceived, or what others did with my behavior. What mattered was that I stayed true to myself. This is what you can expect for yourself from the life-coach training you will receive from *your own spirit guides*.

Thanks to *my guides*, I was learning how to live around challenging people without setting them off. From this new perspective, it often seemed like I wasn't even in the troubling situation but was just observing it.

Another strategy was to act like I didn't see what was happening, no matter what was said or done. This worked most of the time. When I couldn't escape a situation, I learned how to leave mentally. For example, if my mother went after me in a moment of rage, and I went away mentally, it left little or nothing for her to engage with.

Although my mother was sick with endless rage, my father was a saint. He loved me. What a contrast! My mother hated me and my father loved me. My dad was an athlete and very adventuresome. He was a lot like me in that he did not allow the people around him to ruin his life. He never indulged in inconsequential small talk or drama, either. I could see that my dad had his share of disappointments, but he chose to focus on the present moment instead. For these reasons, my dad made sense to me, but something still didn't add up.

With all the advantages I had from the help that I received from my *guides*, I still could not see all of what was going on. Why was my mother like this? How come my dad didn't stop her? Why didn't she attack my older brother like she attacked me and my little brother? Even at pre-school age I had learned a tremendous amount from my *guides*, but there was a lot I still did not understand.

The fact that my *trusted advisors* were not saying anything about these missing pieces led me to the conclusion that I knew what I needed to know for the time being. When I needed to know more, I began to realize, it would be presented to me. I just let go of the questions that weren't getting answered, but I knew I would pursue them again sometime in the future.

TIP: I heard a man say that karma is spelled s-t-u-p-i-d. What I believe he meant is that when we are in our karma, we can't get the big picture; parts of it are hidden from us. In hindsight, that's what was going on with my family – karma, plain and simple.

When I had questions, I would ask my dad. He would always answer them as if I were an adult, which is how my *trusted advisors* always communicated with me. My dad was my hero. He believed in me, loved me, and played with me and my brothers. My dad was the eternal kid and was a lot of fun. Everything I did with my dad was easy.

My dad would say things to me like, "I would bet my last dime on you," and, "The world is your oyster." He saw my essence and my spirit and he liked me. My dad understood that kind words went a lot farther than force and rage. He understood that no one could make anyone do anything if they didn't want to do it. This is the same approach my *guides* had. *They* were never pushy or demanding. *They* were wise, similar to my dad. Although my dad was my hero, my *guides* were my *best friends,* my *real fans.*

My dad thought he was the only one in my life whom I loved, but he was wrong. I loved my dad, but I also loved my *guides* because they loved me unconditionally. *They* were always there to help me, and I knew *they* could deal with what was going on in my life and always helped me through it intelligently. *They* never pretended that things were different from what they were — *they* just kept the bar high so I could learn and really get to know myself.

LEARNING: The skills you learn as a child not only make you into the person you become, but are exactly what you need to master in order to accomplish what you came here to achieve in this particular life. In my case, I really don't think I would have made it without the support of *my guides.*

There's a statement *my guides* told me many times as a young child: "*Life will get better for you as you get older if you can make it through childhood.*" These words were an inspiration for me when they first came through, even though, later on, I would realize they were also words of warning. These words gave me the hope I needed every time things happened in the family that were overwhelming. I got through many tough times because I knew I could contact *my guides* though breathing, dreams, in the twilight sleep, and being peacefully alone. My relationship with *them* was vital to my survival.

When I was around the age of three, two things happened that caused me a lot of confusion about my mother, and I think they caused her some puzzlement about me. The first was that I started creating colorful drawings with my crayons on the inside corner of the living room walls. They were so huge that, when I couldn't reach any higher, I had to stand on chairs to finish them. There was no way I could explain why I was doing that, and I did it repeatedly even after being told to stop. My mother removed them, and I would be very upset each time she did. I remember my mother's perplexed look, like she was trying to understand why I kept doing it. She knew I was not doing it out of malice or stubbornness.

The other event involved a friend of my mother. She was unusual because my mother never had actual friends. That lady was large and had dark "energy." I could feel that something was wrong with her. I tried to muffle my reaction to her being in the house, but I just couldn't hold back.

I started crying because I didn't know how to tell my mother that something was wrong with the lady. I didn't want to hurt my mother's feelings or ruin her only friendship, but I couldn't contain myself. The crying turned into screaming as I sensed that that person was very evil. Unable to control me, my mother had no choice but to ask her to leave.

I told my mother that something was very bad about that lady. She was freaked out by my explosive reaction, but she must have seen something in me because she didn't punish me. I remember my mother looking at me with an odd sort of respect, like she saw me for the first time.

Years later my mother told me the woman had committed suicide. That wasn't what I had reacted to, though; I had felt something much worse than that. I believe my *guides* were protecting me by having me do the only thing I could to get my mother to have her friend leave.

After those incidents, I found myself puzzled about my mother. I was too young to put any rational thought into what was going on. Those two incidents were the first times my mother didn't treat me like I was deliberately being bad. Although she didn't understand me, she realized that something else was going on within me. I saw these reactions on her face and was hoping that that would end her abusive behavior toward me. Though things did change a little, they did not change that much.

One day I looked up at my mother and out of my mouth came the words, "Something is wrong with my mommy." The next thing I remember was waking up on the floor on the other side of the room. I knew I had been hit because my face was swollen and it hurt. That was the final blow, the one that taught me not to let words of truth ever slip out again. When I woke up, she acted like nothing had happened. I guess that was her way of covering up what she had done.

While I didn't really know what was going on, I perceived that my mother was becoming threatened by these truthful words and actions that came out of me time and time again. I think she felt they risked exposing her. I was guided to stay objective in order to continue moving through this situation. That meant not to take any of it personally – this was the key!

 LEARNING: When you're a small child, the truth just comes out. You came from the truth so this is to be expected. However, the people here are often shocked or offended when this happens. Because children don't see this for what it is, they begin to close down. When you make contact with your *guides* at a young age, *they* train you to see things for what they are so when this happens, you don't close down, you understand it. This is empowering beyond words.

Chapter 3: Everyone Here Lets Me Down

Even though there were incidents where my mom recognized something important was going on with me and didn't punish me, she still beat me for other things so many times I can't begin to count them. It all turned into a blur. The thing that was consistent was her saying, "You are going to do what I say or else!" One time she took me in the bedroom when my dad was home and beat me so badly that I couldn't walk. I crawled out into the living room and begged my dad to make her stop, but he turned his head the other way as my mother dragged me back into the bedroom and beat me even more.

This was astounding. I knew my father loved me, but he simply was not seeing what was going on with my mother. I have come to learn that this "willful ignorance," overlooking what's going on right in front of your eyes, is a defense mechanism people use when they can't cope with reality. But at the time, seeing my dad turn away from me broke my heart and was a turning point that drew me even closer to my *true protectors* — my *guides*.

Even so, I became aware that I was in deeper trouble than I ever imagined. I realized that my mother could kill me, and no one would stop her. As she continued to beat me, I flipped a switch and stopped struggling or crying. I am not sure how I did it; I just mentally left that hostile situation.

Again, once I stopped participating by not reacting to her beatings, she stopped. I don't know why; maybe she just lost interest in a dead subject. I don't even remember anything until the next day when I woke up shivering in total panic to find myself back in this life right where I left off — trapped in a special kind of hell. Now what do I do?

My dad, the hero that I thought could save me, apparently had no control or didn't wish to assert control over my mother. He could not or would not stop her. It was this disappointment in my dad that caused me to hit a new low. My mother had the power, and she expressed it through her rage. Realizing this, I went to a place that even I cannot describe. I was still pre-school age and trapped by my mother's fury.

I was at an age where wetting the bed was something I should have outgrown. However, I was still doing it. That made my mother even more outraged. She told me I ruined her life. No matter what I did to stop wetting the bed, I was unsuccessful, so my mother decided to take matters into her own hands. Through a mail order catalog, she bought an electrical underwear garment that she put on me before I went to bed at night. It plugged into the wall, and when I wet the bed it would severely shock me. It was terrible! It would jolt me right out of my sleep, but even that never stopped me from wetting the bed. That device left scars on my body that I have to this day. That bed-wetting was something I could not control no matter what I did, or anything my mother did.

 TIP: When you find yourself in hell, just keep walking. It sounds tough, but it's the best advice there is. Your *guides* are with you to help you through it, but it's you who came here to live it. You choose the parents you have because they can provide you what you need to learn in your unique life.

At about age four or five, I developed a sort of game. I would lie in bed on my back, lick the ends of my spring-loaded rubber darts and shoot them onto the smooth ceiling. They would stick to the ceiling, but once they dried, they would fall back down on top me. Then one day, I decided to shoot one and before it could fall back down on top of me, I went up to the ceiling and retrieved it.

I shot a dart, it stuck, and I went up to it. I actually did it on my first attempt. I didn't fly up there, of course, but I was at the ceiling. Little did I realize that I was going out of my body to do it.

I would always make sure that my bedroom door was closed before I did it again, because I knew I did not want to be caught off guard when I was experimenting this way. I did it over and over again, until at one point, I decided to look back down at my body lying on the bed while I was at the ceiling. It surprised me so much that it landed me back in my body so hard my head hurt. At that point I realized I was missing something. How could I be both here and there at the same time?

Puzzled, I went to sleep and got my answer in a dream. *They* told me *"When you go up to the ceiling to retrieve the darts, don't look back down. If you do decide to look back down, just don't question why you are in two places.*

*As long as you don't question it, you can do this as much
as you want to."*

That was the key. It was easy for me to do, and I experimented with it a lot more after that. That was my first "out-
of-body experience," but I didn't know that's what people
called it until I was in my late thirties.

The next stage in these out-of-body experiments took place in
the living room. One night when the entire family was watching Walt Disney on TV I decided to leave my body and hang
out in the corner of the living room ceiling to see if anyone
would notice I was gone. No one did, and when they would
walk by my body, they acted like everything was normal.

I observed them from the ceiling as they watched the TV and
would go back into my body when I wanted to talk or get up.
But otherwise, I would leave my body and travel around the
ceiling of the house. That was a lot more interesting than
watching TV. As I had learned the hard way, I never mentioned
this to anyone, and they never noticed anything different.

 AWARENESS and TIP: These escape techniques
were born out of trauma and turned into mind-
expanding experiments that many kids do, but they
often forget them as they grow up. Going out-of-body
teaches you how to fluidly live in two worlds. For that
reason, mastering this makes it much easier to contact
your *guides*.

One day I was playing my follow-the-dart game in my
bedroom, and my mother screamed my name. In the

out-of-body state, this was the most disruptive feeling I can describe. She always screamed our names when she wanted us for something, but this time it was much, much louder. It made my whole body hurt. I realized that my hearing had become much more sensitive and now everything was louder — not just sounds, but people's thoughts and intentions.

I also could detect my *guides* better than ever. It turned out that the out-of-body training was to heighten my sensitivity in more ways than one. However, it made being in that family even more difficult. I felt way too vulnerable, especially around my mother. I decided not to ever risk going out of my body in that house again. It was just too unsettling. There was just no peace in that house.

 TIP: Often, kids who experience this kind of thing choose to turn everything off. If you can remember it, you can reignite it now and use it as a bridge to power up your connection with your *guides*.

As I look back on those early pre-school years, despite the pain and dysfunctional family dynamic, it still was a magical learning time in my life. In fact, it was those family dynamics that forced me to discover things that would set the stage for the rest of my life.

I had so many rich experiences, but to me my discoveries were just normal. I knew who I was and that I had a *support team*... my *guides*. I knew how to get clarity and answers whenever I needed them, I understood what real freedom was, and I saw people for who they really were. Best of all, I didn't need anyone's validation.

Thanks to an early life of self-discovery and experiments that my *connections* guided me through, I had what I needed. It turns out that I was miles ahead of most people, although I didn't know that at the time.

 TIP: People you live with may think you are losing your mind as you pursue a relationship with *your guides*. It's a juggling act that you will need to learn to live in two worlds. The best advice I can give you is to keep a journal with dates of your encounters with your *guides* and your dreams. Doing this will be invaluable as it keeps you on your path to self-discovery.

I was still pre-school when my mother found new ways to add to my torment. It was more of the same, except worse.

She actually told us kids she was going to break our spirit. She said it was just the way it was going to be, and we would have no choice in the matter. Hearing that set me off. I told her she would have to kill me because I would never let her break my spirit. In my mind, what she had said was ridiculous, not to mention that she had said it to her own children.

She also took a great deal of pride in letting us know she would take all her secrets with her to her grave. She would laugh as she told us we would never know what she had done or who she was. Every year that passed, she proved to be even more vindictive and unstable. She was carried away with power. She let us know in many ways that she intended to destroy my life and that of my little brother.

My brothers were not the targets of her rage nearly as much as I was. I began to think that I was her target because my dad favored me. Plus, I was a girl. We were a "don't ask, don't tell" family. Buried in the serious dysfunction were so many lies and secrets. One secret lie had to do with my older brother, Randy. He didn't look or act like my younger brother, Larry, or me. That, along with the way my mother over-protected him, just didn't add up. He was certainly her favorite, and Randy was always granted a free-pass when it came to our mother's abuse.

I never liked Randy; he always had icky energy. That made me very protective of Larry, knowing what it was like to endure our mother's constant abuse. He was small for his age, and he could not emotionally handle her torment. He didn't have the *helpers* I did — he didn't even know *they* existed. I couldn't risk telling Larry; I knew he wouldn't understand how important it was to keep it quiet. So I just had to look out for him myself.

 LEARNING: One lesson I learned from this situation is that when your life becomes really unbearable, help someone else.

Here's how the family lined up: Randy had Mom, I had *my guides* and Dad, and Larry had me. That dynamic never changed. When Mom spanked Larry, he really went through a lot of pain. I showed him how to put books down his pants before she spanked him so it wouldn't hurt him so badly. He did that until he got caught. Larry was an ideal victim. He did everything to make an abuser feel powerful. He would cry and scream and beg Mom to stop at any cost. He would take the blame for everything just to avoid more punishment than he would otherwise have had to go through.

When going through the ranks of "Who did it," Randy rarely got spanked and I learned not to react at all, no matter what my mother did to me. So my little brother became an easy target, taking the blame for just about everything. Larry was a very sweet kid, but he was vulnerable. He became my project, and I tried to teach him not to be so afraid, how to be stronger, and how to outsmart his opponent. Larry was a year-and-a-half younger than me, and I remember how relieved my dad was that I looked out for him. When I was four years old and Randy was eight, he took me to my first game of marbles. The games were played in big circles about 12 feet in diameter. The kids, who were all older than I was, were very serious about winning. They were tough street kids who knew how to fight.

At the game, Randy pushed me into a fight with one of the kids. I didn't know how to fight so I got beat up. Randy did not defend me; he just watched and then walked back home with me, calling me a loser. He was ashamed of me. Randy wasn't much of a big brother. He felt no sense of protecting Larry or me. He had no patience with us and didn't like us bothering him. It was like he was an only child and we were intruders.

Mom was very similar in the way she treated Larry and me. I didn't care, but it really bothered him. Of course, I had my *guides* and as far as I was concerned, *they* were superior to anyone here. Because of that, I was strong enough to take care of both Larry and myself without any problem.

One day, Randy was lying down in the living room while Larry and I were chasing each other through the house. I was in front, and I started to close the glass door behind me to slow him down. But he was closer than I thought and as I closed the door, we collided and crashed through the glass. We were both bleeding profusely.

I screamed for Randy to come help us. He never even bothered getting up. So I wrapped Larry's cut hand and my cut wrists before we both fell asleep in puddles of blood. The next thing I knew, I was awakened by our parents screaming at Randy for not doing anything. For once Randy crossed the line of my parent's tolerance. That was one time mom couldn't cover for him.

It was around that same time that Randy fondled me. I was four and he was eight years old. He told me I was dirty and needed cleaning and gave me a quarter. He put soap on my private spot and told me I was bad because I took the quarter.

I knew that was wrong and told my mom what Randy had done. She freaked out but still defended him, asking me if I thought that was the worst thing that would ever happen to me. Then, terrified that Dad would find out, she threatened me with all kinds of punishment if I ever told him. Randy never did it again, so I suspect Mom let him know that wasn't going to fly.

Being younger than me, Larry was on his own with mom when I started school. I wasn't there to guide him or protect him. I knew Mom didn't want to be burdened with us kids, and he was the last one holding her back. He heard about that pretty much on a daily basis. Those two years between when I started school and Larry finally did are years that he could have done without.

Mom resented both Larry and me, and she made it clear that she hadn't wanted either one of us. I was forced onto her as a condition from my dad, but it was a condition she had not willingly accepted. Larry was an "accident" and had not been planned by either my mom or dad. Unfortunately, he always knew it, which made me even more protective of him.

 LEARNING: Family is not an accident of birth. You actually picked your family before you were born to help you deal with your own shortcomings and provide you with the opportunities you need to learn. In my case, the family I picked made life so unbearable, that I was able to break through to the other side and gain full access to my real family — my *guides*. Don't expect your earth family to fulfill the meaning of your life.

Chapter 4: School Exposes Me as an Oddball

When I started school, I thought it would bring freedom — at least from my mom. Instead, school became a challenging necessity of life for me. I was disappointed because what I had discovered from my inner world, from my *guides*, had no value there. School was all about achieving outer-world learning and experiences, and it took me some time to wrap my head around that.

Until school, I had been in an exciting, rigorous, self-expansive place of learning and discovery. That was much more challenging and interesting than that school stuff, which I found mostly boring.

The forced approach to learning I encountered at school was a ridiculous way to teach anything to anyone. I saw right through it because I already had superior *teachers — brilliant ones,* not from this world. *Their* training was much more rigorous. *They* taught me complicated lessons that *they* made easy to learn, which also encouraged me to know myself. Being in that school environment required that I dumb myself down. I really was an oddball now.

I was only starting school and my life already felt long and drawn out. Having friends was not important to me, because I already had the *best friends* anyone could possibly ask for, and *they* were as real to me as anyone I had ever met here. Because of that, I never settled for friends just because that's what they called themselves. I found that most kids didn't know what having a real friend was like. What's more, I found that the kids in school didn't even know who they were. They thought they were who they were taught to be by their parents. I knew they were much more than that, but they didn't.

I was only five, but I already had a mind of my own. I didn't do the things the other kids did, like cry for the smallest reasons let alone bigger ones. I didn't blindly do everything the teacher told us to do in an attempt to be liked or to fit in. I saw doing that as a game of manipulation for the land of lost souls. I did what I loved to do no matter what the other kids said about me. Because of that, of course, they were always judging me.

Even so, the social part of school was easy for me because I wasn't invested in making friends. I was open to having friends, but I wasn't going out of my way to please anyone.

The part of school that was hard for me was doing everything the way they told us to do it — no exceptions. I found school to be a very rigid place that went against my way of learning. I felt like a soldier, not a person, and I found that humiliating.

The other kids complied with the rules and control because they were afraid and didn't want to get in trouble. They would do anything to make the kids and teacher like them. I saw that fear was what motivated them to buy into these control tactics. I saw that as a total sell-out — but I was the only one who saw it. "Aha," I thought, "these are the fear-based people in the *merry-go-round dream.*"

Some may have considered me rebellious, but I was just seeing through all the politics around the kids and the teachers. It didn't take me long to size up the school situation. Everyone had a motive for wanting us to do things or act a certain way. It wasn't what was best for us; it was what was best for them. Everyone was doing what they were told to do. Before entering school, I was accustomed to seeing things for what they really were. I also saw my place in it. This would have never been possible without the training I received from my *guides*.

 LEARNING: The life-coach training you receive from your *guides* can make you appear to be an oddball. After all, you see everything for what it is, and you conduct your life from the truth. Society's politics and threats just don't work on you when you pay attention to your *guides*.

Every day there was play time in the kindergarten classroom. The kids had to rotate each activity so everyone would have equal time to learn and play. My project of choice was the building blocks. They were large wooden blocks of different shapes and sizes. I loved them so much that I had to have them every day. I would give the other kids my lunch, toys, candy, or money to get them to give me their turn at the building blocks. I was obsessed. I didn't understand it then, but that was no accident. It would prove to fit into my calling later in life.

Being in the classroom day after day felt like being stuck in a slow-motion movie. Most of the time, I was bored out of my mind and could hardly stay awake. I was used to learning through self-discovery with the support of *my guides*. When something interesting did occasionally happen in class, I would usually miss it. Later, my grades would suffer because of that. I just couldn't connect with that ponderous mode of learning.

I quickly became frustrated with school and vented my frustration on the tether-ball court. I skipped lunch so I could play tether ball. Before long, no one challenged my place on the tether-ball court because no one could beat me. I have a very strong will, and I found that when I wanted something, I got it. Working out my frustrations through my passions and exercise became a real saving grace for me.

Throughout kindergarten I was mostly left alone by the kids and teachers. Even so, I kept my eyes open and occasionally saw teachers abusing their positions. I think it was just from frustration with the kids. I remember one teacher who dug her fingernails into a boy's arm so hard it made him bleed. I saw that she was a lot like my mother attempting to control us kids through force rather than reason. I had no respect for her, and I pretty much questioned everything she told us to do.

The other kids just went along with the agenda and accepted what she did. They didn't seem bored like I was. They could stay focused in class, and they played well in groups trying to be liked. I was the opposite because none of that appealed to me. My behavior drew a line between me and them early on. I was being me, and they were being who they were programmed to be; it was the only thing they knew.

From my experiences in kindergarten, I realized how different I was. Until then I was just secretly holding my ground, as I was learning even more about myself, my real self, with the loving support of my *guides*. It was because of *them* that I had such a strong sense of who I was so early in my life.

 LEARNING: Getting to know who you are is the most important thing you can do. Without that, you will never find your place in this life. You've seen people who don't do that; they are fear-based, always floundering and needing to be told what to do. They need constant validation. When you are learning from your *guides*, getting to know who you are is the strongest part of *their* curriculum.

Once in school, it didn't take me long to realize I was a tomboy. I liked sports, but not the team kind. I liked the games where I could rely on my own abilities. Thanks to my dad, all of us kids were seasoned water skiers before we started kindergarten. We also had our own gasoline-powered mini-bikes before we were even in school. My dad built our backyard like it was an amusement park, with larger-than-life slides, swings, slip-and-slides, pogo sticks, and stilts so tall you had get on them from the top horizontal rail of the eight-foot-high fence. Every kid wanted to play in our backyard.

By today's standards, that would have been a colossal legal liability, but those were the days before we became so litigious. My dad was so much fun. He worked hard and played hard, and what he couldn't afford to buy he built. There wasn't anything my dad couldn't do, or anything we couldn't have. This is where my dad excelled.

My dad did have an unusual quirk, though. The only way I can describe it is that it seemed like excessive energy would build up in him, and he would have to release it from time to time. He did it by rubbing his hands together very fast while he held his breath. When he exhaled, the release would come in one big rush. He would only do it for about 30 seconds or so and then his energy was balanced again.

I remembered doing a similar breathing technique to release my stress when I was being trained by my *guides* to see things that couldn't be seen with linear vision.

 TIP: Your *guides* know you better than anyone else. *They* are masters at aligning you with exactly what you are ready to learn at just the right time in your life. That's why *they* don't think of you as being too young or too old to learn anything — to *them* your age has nothing to do with it.

I knew my inner life was different from that of most kids', but I didn't realize that was true of my outer life also. I learned that one day at school during "show and tell." I told the class about an excursion my dad and mom had taken us on the previous weekend. It involved hiking up a roaring waterfall and grabbing a big vine, and swinging out over the chasm created by the falls. Before I could finish, the teacher told me to sit down and stop lying.

She might not have believed me, but every word was true. In addition to going water skiing two to three times a week, my dad and mom took us on white-water-rafting trips, and we traveled to remote places on our motorized mini-bikes. In the incident with the waterfall that I had tried to relate, when I impulsively swung on the vine, my dad freaked out at first, but he quickly got into the spirit of the occasion when he saw I was fine. Having paved the way, everyone else wanted to do it, too. I was always the fearless one because that's what I was encouraged to be from my *guides*.

We traveled to places where we would discover Indian ruins with their original primitive tools still laying around. This was one area where my mother excelled. She was a researcher and would map out exotic, hard-to-get to sites to see if we could actually find these places on our weekend outings. We were always going on adventures to discover mysterious locations.

One place was about 75 feet above an ice-cold-crystal-clear, calm river. The water was so clear that there was no way to determine how deep it was. My dad dared us to dive into water and retrieve a dead snake at the bottom. I dove in and still remember the head-pounding feeling of that ice-cold water. Despite the cold, I went deeper and deeper until I finally got the snake and brought it back up. Dad smirked — he knew I would always be the one who took the dare.

My mom and dad were also treasure hunters and we were thrill-seekers long before they started making TV shows and documentaries about people like that. Extreme living is what we did, but because I had no basis of comparison, it was all just normal to me. Until the teacher told me to stop lying in "show and tell" that day, I didn't know just how different my life was.

With that incident, I realized that I had even less in common with that school reality than I thought. Unlike the other girls, I had no interest in Brownies and Girl Scouts. I was living fully immersed in the things that these organizations only provided a taste of. I was beginning to realize I was living a very different reality from most people I knew in school. Like the *merry-go-round dream* showed me, many times I would be the complete opposite of others.

My first experience with how things worked in society came in the first grade. The kids in my class had already learned to play peer-pressure politics in kindergarten, and had picked the friends who would best serve them in that. They were well into the process of becoming experienced manipulators.

One of the most effective methods of asserting control they had learned was bullying, and in the first grade, the bullies were out in full force. It all came as a shock to me. I may not have liked school up until then, but I really didn't want to be there when I saw that.

On top of that, my first-grade teacher was even worse than the one I had had in kindergarten. I was really having problems wrapping my head around all the dysfunction. I had never taken this stuff seriously, but now it needed to be dealt with. It was becoming institutionalized. The kids were no longer innocent and open; they were clearly on a mission. They had decided who fit in with them and who didn't. Guess who didn't fit in with any of them.

My parents started hearing about my nonconformity at teacher-parent meetings. They decided one way to deal with it was to give me more homework, and my mother was supposed to help me with it. This made me somewhat independent, and I did better when I didn't have the kids around me so much.

My resistance was strong, but I knew that resisting would only make things harder for me. So, to combat the school politics, I decided to focus all my attention on the academics and turn my back on everything else. The first grade was a difficult adjustment for me, but I got it worked out so I was able to get passing grades. But living in two worlds was what I was really perfecting.

I also began to experience what it was like being at odds with both the teachers and the bullies. I was tolerating it acceptably well until I saw what the mean kids did to the other kids who were outside their group. That was <u>not</u> okay with me, and I started to stick up for the underdogs. It began with warning the bullies not to pick on the other kids. That didn't go over so well, so my fighting career began.

I always let the bullies hit me first because I couldn't really fight until I got mad. Once they hit me, though, I rarely lost a fight. I learned to fight without any real training; I think it came naturally to me because it came from the heart. I could not stand by and let bullies pick on the nice kids. I was never the instigator, but I was always there to finish something a bully had started.

With my new fighting career came a revolving door of school suspension and re-admittance. Without seeing the big picture, adults just viewed me as a really bad kid. But I knew I wasn't. It was another calling. Until I went to school, I did not realize this part of me existed. I found I was almost compelled to protect those who couldn't protect themselves. Before I started school, Larry had been my "project" as I showed him how to overcome his fears and defeat his opponent in smart ways. But I hadn't known this would extend to people outside my family.

Looking back, a lot of my life has been filled with balancing injustices and confronting bullies.

 TIP: Never let a bully slide. The sooner a bully is confronted, the faster you put him or her out of commission. Schoolyard bullies are a festering sickness in our society because they grow up to be monsters.

As time went on, much to my surprise I discovered that I actually did fit in after all. The school and neighborhood I grew up in was mostly African-American with a fair number of Latinos. Next came the Asians and Caucasians who were always in the minority. I'm Caucasian, but I found I fit in best with the African-American kids. It was the late 1950s, and my African-American friends liked and disliked the same things I did.

They liked dancing and the same music that I liked. They disliked the bullies and white kids who flaunted their privilege. They didn't like my mother (I'm sure they could feel her racial biases). They liked chasing me on my mini-bike and fighting with me. They were the best fighters, athletes, and dancers — just like me. They also were the funniest and most real people I had ever met; they told me things that I knew were the truth.

I had a special affinity for my African-American friends because of the injustices they all faced. It was almost like society was a big bully toward them. I think that was the single most important reason I favored them. The white kids I knew were not nearly as classy and poised as my African-American friends and their families.

Case in point: I would stop by my white British friend Rita's house to walk to school with her. Her dad would be walking around the house in his underwear right in front of me, while he shouted at clients on the phone. On the other hand, I would stop by my African-American friend Norrie's house to walk to school with her. Her mother would have me sit in the living room, turn on the cartoons and serve me breakfast. She would close the doors to the living room so the family could get ready for school and work in privacy. They were very polite, modest, decent people.

As I settled in at school and started having friends, my life began making a little more sense. However, my mother, who was not fond of black people in general, didn't approve of my choices. Of course, that did not affect me one bit. She just used my choice of friends to justify her deeper resentment of me. She became more intense as the years went by. I began to see she was like the school bullies in that she would abuse her power. I was disturbed to see this and was ashamed of her.

I was hoping that my African-American friends would never find out what a bigot my mother was, but they were smart and very intuitive, so I'm sure they knew. I was the only white kid with African-American friends (it being the 1950s after all), but I didn't think about it at the time. I just knew what made sense to me, so that's what I did.

 TIP: Since your *guides* always show you everything for what it is — the truth — what works for you may not fit society's idea of what's acceptable. That doesn't mean it's not right for you; maybe society is wrong. They certainly were wrong in my case when I, a white kid, chose African-American kids as my friends of choice.

Chapter 5: Consequences of My Choices

By the end of the first grade, I had adjusted pretty well to school. I had found friends who saw things a lot like me. I had become used to getting kicked out of school, sometimes weekly, when I got into the fights and beat up yet another bully. Most of the teachers didn't like me and I didn't like them. For my money, they didn't deserve to be liked or respected when they treated the kids the way they did.

I thought the kids I hung out with were funny. They made me laugh all the time despite continually threatening to beat me up. I felt confident I could handle them – and I proved it.

For example, one day I was told I was going to get beat up after school. So I ran home and got my German Shepherd, Teddy. When my would-be attackers showed up, I pretended to be struggling to hold back my snarling monster of a dog and said I was ready to fight now. They climbed up trees, jumped on top of the cars, hopped over the fences, and some just ran down the street.

While my response may sound extreme, the fact is, these threats were not empty. Some of these kids had actually beaten me up more than once. It wasn't fun for me, but it made me a better and smarter fighter.

They were constantly testing me because I was white. I always knew that, but I liked them anyway. I understood that there would always be an edge on our relationship because of the racial tension that persisted all around us – it was the 1950s, and things were not at all like they are today. However, that didn't stop us from liking and respecting each other, even if we fought from time to time. There were no pretenses; our relationships were truthful. That is also what I was used to from my *guides*.

 TIP: To many, the truth appears to be coarse. That's why the phrase "politically correct" became so popular. That's how the coddling of society began. It's no longer okay to speak the truth.

Your *guides* don't follow any of this. *They* don't have to. The whole point in having input from your *guides* is to get the truth. So, if you are offended by the truth, there will be times when you won't like what your *guides* have to tell you, but that doesn't mean you don't need to hear it.

At school, the white kids would play boy-chase-girl games. That's where the boys would chase the girls to try to kiss them. The girls would run into the bathroom so the boys couldn't catch them, but they really wanted them to. In my opinion, this was really stupid. I told those boys who tried chasing me not to do it to me. I would not run away from them.

One boy would not stop going after me. I would slug him, but he persisted. One day my mom pinned a flower on my dress with a long florist pin. When that boy came after me that day on the playground, I pulled the pin out of my shirt and stuck him in the butt with it. He freaked out. I got kicked out of school again, and he moved to a different school. The good news is that the boys never tried that with me again. These boys would pull on my ponytail and I would slug them, but that was different from trying to get me to play their submissive kiss-and-run games.

At some point, though, I did start wondering what it felt like to be submissive like the other girls? They were all that way, and I was the only different one. I also noticed how these girls would not raise their hands in class when the teachers asked who knew the answer to a problem. They didn't want to appear too smart in front of the boys. I didn't understand that at all. Because I wouldn't play that phony game was another reason I was not accepted by the girls or the boys in my class. Even the teacher thought I was obnoxious. It was a social stigma to be your real self if you were a girl.

However, one day at school I decided to experiment. I decided not to participate in the class when the teacher asked us for answers. I wanted to see, first, what it would feel like to act like these submissive girls, and second, how they would respond differently to me. The outcome was ridiculous. It felt like I was in a void where I couldn't breathe — I was totally stifled. I could also feel resentment. I don't know what the other kids thought of my behaving like the pack; I didn't give the experiment that much time to work. That day I learned that being nonauthentic was not for me.

From my perspective, all the girls I knew had sold out. The boys thought they were in charge because the girls were so coy. I could see that the setup had already begun — the boys were given the job of taking care of the girls, and the girls pretended not to be as smart or as capable as the boys. That was surely not going to work for me.

I was not concerned with whether the boys or girls liked me. They didn't like me because they thought I was stupid, that I didn't get it. The teachers saw it the same way. That just created more alienation between me and all of them. Once I understood what was really lying beneath the surface of the boy-girl dynamic, I was clear about what was right for me, and I never questioned it again.

I started to see even more reasons why my African-American friends were my friends of choice. They were more real with me — and with everyone else, for that matter. They didn't play these games with each other. They were a lot like me, but for some reason they didn't hang out with me at school or after school; we just walked to and from school together.

 TIP: Your *guides* like it when you experiment. It seems to open a doorway for *them* to chime in when you need *them*. You need to listen and learn from *them* because there is much more going on than what you are focused on. *They* have great input.

When I was in the second grade, my younger brother started kindergarten. He was a lot smaller than the other boys. I had already taught him to fight, but he was still not a strong or confident fighter. He was mostly sweet and didn't have the heart for fighting. In our neighborhood and at school, there was no way you could survive without learning to defend yourself. I looked out for Larry while letting him find his own way, although I would step in when he couldn't defend himself. The kids knew that he had an older sister who pro-tected him so they were not as aggressive with him as they otherwise would have been.

But there was one girl in my grade who started picking on him. She gave him black eyes, bruises, and scrapes all the time. It went on for months. It got so that Larry was afraid to go to school. I'm pretty sure it was her way of calling me out for a fight. I told this girl to leave him alone, or she would be dealing with me. She didn't listen and just got more aggressive and mean.

One day she really hurt Larry. So the next day I told him to meet me after school, and we hid behind a bush waiting for her. When she showed up I stopped her and asked her why she kept beating up my little brother. She was snotty and said she just felt like doing it. She added that I couldn't stop her. She was a big white girl, bigger than me and a lot bigger than he was.

I provoked her so she would hit me first so I would be mad enough to beat her up. She did hit me and I did beat her up. When it was over, I told her that if she ever hurt my little brother, I would come after her again. This time she understood. I made her apologize to Larry, and he felt a lot better knowing she wouldn't be hurting him anymore. He also kind of liked that she had gotten a taste of her own medicine.

Later that night the doorbell rang at our house. My dad answered it, and there was the girl bully with her father. She looked terrible. Her father told my dad that I had done that to his little girl. My dad called me to the door and asked me if I had done it. I told him that I did it because she would not stop beating up Larry, and I had to stop her. My dad looked back at the father and said he hoped she learned her lesson because she had it coming. Dad closed the door and patted me on the back saying I had done the right thing by looking out for my brother. And that was the end of that.

Larry wasn't the only kid to get picked on. There was a fat girl the kids made fun of all the time. I knew that wasn't right, and I made that girl my friend. When I did that, the bullies knew that I would stick up for her if they continued to pick on her. Of course, it was just a matter of time before one of them started up with her, and I was in another series of fights.

This time, though, my African-American friends stepped in to help me fight the bullies. On the way home from school, we cornered all of them and beat them up. These bullies were many and hard to stop, so I was relieved when my only earthly friends stepped in to help me. These friends knew what I was about and they liked me for it. They were there whenever I needed their support. I was there when they needed mine.

 LEARNING: Bullies are a big problem. Even to this day, they are everywhere. If you or someone you know is being assaulted or threatened by a bully, take it seriously because letting bullies get away with it only strengthens them. Bullies also are cowards so they are sneaky. Being exposed and outsmarted are their two biggest fears, so consult with your *guides* and figure out how to do that effectively. They can be stopped.

My dad took me aside and talked to me about my energy. He said that I needed to learn to harness that energy or it would become my downfall. Dad understood because he also had this pent-up energy. I didn't see my energy as extraordinary or anything unusual; to me it was normal. But Dad knew the burden it was to him when it controlled his better judgment from time to time, and he was concerned about how I would deal with this in my life.

Once Larry started school, I began to take him with me wherever I went: the archery range, the zoo, the amusement park, bowling, swimming at the YMCA, to play basketball, skateboarding and roller skating, and to the movies. He learned a lot and he learned fast, and he had fun and felt protected. I always had enough money to pay our way from the money I made as a fly hunter. Dad would pay me a penny per fly, and I quickly became Linda the fly hunter. I would kill more flies in a day than my dad wanted to count, sometimes earning ten dollars in one day.

At home we used to gear up our mini-bikes so they would go really fast. We would ride them on our street and the kids would try to catch us, but they never could. That was so much fun and Larry loved it too.

Home life when Dad wasn't around was sketchy even though we were older and not stuck in the house as we had been when we were younger. We never knew when Mom was going to find fault with one of us and beat us. Larry was taking on more of her wrath now that he was older. It was just better not to be around, so he and I were gone whenever we could be.

Mom was never affectionate with either of us. She liked being left alone so she could read her books on the Old West. She was fascinated with anything related to that era, and her dream was to explore Arizona. We never had friends over to the house; it simply was not an option because of Mom. We knew our family was weird, but we didn't dwell on it. On the other hand, we also had amazing adventures, we were awesome athletes, and we had the coolest things as kids all because of our dad.

Larry was beginning to get the hang of navigating through family stuff, and he was learning how to steer clear of Mom. As a result, he stopped feeling so scared all the time. Without telling him anything about how I learned any of this, I was teaching him what I learned from my *guides*.

 TIP: Helping Larry was the project that eased my own suffering. It helped me overcome the threat that was so monumental at the time. When you reach out to help someone else, you do things for them that you never thought of doing for yourself. In a way, you become their guide.

My bully mother at 27 years old

Our mother would gossip and talk badly about people all the time. Dad would tell her that if she couldn't say anything nice, to say nothing at all. She never listened to him; she was stubborn. She'd let him know not to tell her what to do; she'd do whatever she damn well pleased! It became apparent that Dad could not stop her negative behavior. That continued throughout their lives together. My mother would have been happier without any of us, except for Randy. That was a strange and unexplainable relationship. All this just made Larry and me closer than ever as we worked out ways to maneuver around Mom's constant rage.

There came a time when I started thinking about the day I would be able to go out on my own and have this part of my life behind me. I was still wetting the bed, and I couldn't understand why I couldn't stop doing that. I tried everything. I set my alarm clock every hour to go to the bathroom, and it still happened. My mother used the bed-wetting as yet another reason to resent me. She punished me all the time for doing it, but I still couldn't stop. The *merry-go-round dream* continued exactly the same way it started. So, between that dream and wetting the bed, I really dreaded going to sleep at night although I had no trouble falling asleep.

Randy and Mom were constantly calling me names and tormenting me because of my bed-wetting. As a ritual, my mom would make me stand on the kitchen table and instruct each family member to take turns at saying hateful things to me. This was designed to make me feel like I had no value and to convince me that no one in the family wanted me around.

In response, I moved into a somber demeanor to deflect their assaults. My mother made them all tell me I was stupid and ugly. My mother started calling me her "Ugly Duckling." That exercise in demeaning me became an undeclared battle of the wills between my mother and me.

Around the time my mother instituted that mental abuse, I started sleepwalking. Once it began, I did it all the time. It was first discovered when my parents saw me walking through the living room and right out the front door one night. When they told me to get back in the house and I just kept walking, they realized that I was asleep. I would wake up in the morning and find my things missing. I would look around the house and sometimes find them. When I did find them, they would appear in the most unlikely places. Even in my sleep, I was trying to escape that family environment.

 LEARNING: Under such abusive conditions, going into fight-or-flight mode is a natural response. It becomes survival. Being guided when suffering like this will bring you very close to your *guides*. So, while you are being depleted in one area of your life, you are being blessed in another. You are never alone as you walk through this life – never!

Our parents were very stereotypical in what they taught us kids. My dad was a building contractor who did concrete foundation work for other home builders. He would take Randy and Larry out on his job sites to teach them the trade. Not me. Being a girl, I was taught how to cook, clean, and sew. I didn't think about any of this; it was just the way things were back then.

I actually liked learning what I was taught. I mostly liked sewing my clothes, testing different fabrics and customizing the patterns. I liked experimenting and coming up with my own designs.

One day I asked my dad for materials to build a car out of wood. Although he was a little surprised, he gave me what I asked for. Each day after school, I would work on that car. Dad really liked it and helped me with it after he got home from work. Once it was done, Larry and I would pull it with our mini-bikes. It looked like the Flintstone's car, and he and I had a lot of fun towing it around. We would give our friends rides in it and they loved it. It's interesting that although they could see I was different, my parents didn't take me seriously. Their stereotypical thinking was either stronger or easier than what was obvious.

From time to time, I would ask my mom and dad when their wedding anniversary was. They would never answer me. Mom would look at Dad and he would walk away. Mom would say it was sometime in June, but that was as specific as she got. I wanted to know so I could do something special for them. I finally stopped asking because I knew something was fishy. I wouldn't learn the truth for many years.

In addition to his adventurous nature, my dad loved playing musical instruments. Dad and I played music all the time on the weekends, just the two of us. I learned to play the organ and bongos really well. Dad played the Hawaiian slide guitar, the violin, the harmonica, and the accordion. For me, though, the coolest things he played were spoons. Dad played spoons so fast and musically, it was mind-blowing to listen to him play the spoons.

My dad and me 1960

My dad and I would also watch the Friday-night fights together, and on Saturday nights we would watch vampire movies together. No one else was around; it was just Dad and me. We would eat Melba toast and tomato soup. We really got along, and it was very natural doing things with him. I thought when I grew up I would marry a man just like my dad. I really believed that it would be that easy. People called my dad a leprechaun and me a pixie. We were a lot alike and had a very strong bond.

One day I asked my dad about religion. I asked him if he believed in God. He said that from his perspective, religion was filled with hypocrites. He suggested that I would find my own way. This came from a man who had been groomed to be a priest from the time he was a boy. Both Mom and Dad were disgusted with the church, and I sensed that Dad had been abused in some way, but he never talked about it.

Later in life I did marry two men who believed in me and were proud of me, but they both lacked confidence. These two marriages ended in divorce because I couldn't compromise. Come to think of it, my dad also lacked confidence or he might have been successful in steering my mom away from her abusive ways.

 TIP: Having a good relationship with your dad is critical to the relationships you will have with men in your life. This same fact applies to your relationship with your mother. If they are both great parents, you will likely be a balanced person throughout your life — but the opposite is also true. So, no matter which way it goes, work through it by understanding what's really going on. The life-coach training you will receive from your *guides* will prove to be a huge value with that.

Chapter 6: Reaching a Boiling Point

My mother seemed to be content with Dad and me doing things together. Maybe she enjoyed the break from Dad. I know she was always glad to have a break from me. As far as I was concerned, life was good because I was away from my mother's abuse; I was in school or out playing or hanging with Dad. But then, she introduced some new rules. If I did something she thought was deserving of a spanking, she would wait for my dad to come home from work and order him to spank me instead of her doing it. Dad couldn't talk any sense into her; if that's the way Mom saw it, then that was the law — period.

Linda at 10 years old, watching her back and holding her ground

Dad would take me into the bedroom and close the door and tell me to cry each time he hit the bed. That seemed to work for a while, but somehow my mom caught on and would stand there to watch so he would really have to hit me. I think she did that for a couple of reasons: first, she was tired of being the bad guy who delivered the punishment all the time, and second, she wanted to break the bond between my dad and me.

My mother generally didn't like me, especially as I got older. I didn't agree with her thinking or ways of doing things. She was very angry all the time, frequently rude to people and, as I indicated earlier, was racially prejudiced. She talked about everyone behind their back and spent a lot of time gossiping. She was hard, angry, and cruel. She always said that she didn't have a jealous bone in her body, but I often saw evidence of jealousy.

Most of all, she was unpredictable, and she took a great deal of pride in that. She bragged about how she loved catching us off guard. She claimed to be smarter than everyone else and that no one would ever figure her out. However, I'm pretty sure I had her figured out — I just didn't let her or anyone else know it.

What I took from all of this, based on advice from my *guides*, was seeing what power looked like in the wrong hands, in the hands of a bully. Dealing with people like my mother would become very easy for me later on in life. Of course, I didn't know that was what I was being trained for at that time, but my *guides* knew because *they* could see my entire life.

LEARNING: Are you beginning to see how this works? It doesn't matter how those around you behave; you aren't them. However, you become like those you associate with, so hang around with your *guides*. *They're* always honest and act with the highest good in mind. If you want to become like someone, become like *them*.

Mom told us stories about her brother, Bobby, a marine who died in WWII. She also talked about her Aunt Agnes, whom Mom just hated. She told us about the time she threw Aunt Agnes down a full flight of stairs, calling her a mean bitch. Mom said her dad was a drunk, but she said they understood each other. She would go to the bar where he hung out in order to get the money their mother needed to buy food. Mom said she was the only one who could get money from him. She said that she got used to going to the bar by the age of six or so. The patrons would make rude and inappropriate comments, but she thought it was funny; she got a kick out of it.

She said even though her dad was a drunk and would hit her at times, she was not afraid of him. She said she was more afraid of her mom for some reason, even though her mom was gentle and never hit her. Mom told us kids that we had no living grandparents, or relatives. She would tell us stories about how they died and what a terrible life she had as a kid. She told us another story about how she met dad when he worked for her father. That was the family history — according to Mom.

Over the years I learned not to believe her at all. In fact, as time went by, I didn't even bother listening to any of her exaggerations or lies. As I would learn much later in life, this was a wise choice on my part.

Now and then my mom would say things that exposed her secrets. She would say she grew up too fast, that people didn't realize how precious childhood was, and that she had been robbed of hers. She said she lost her innocence at an early age because she had a hard life. Experiencing my mother's swings between instances of truth and complete and total lies taught me to become acutely aware of how to detect both in others. This turned out to be a critical life skill I was guided to learn that I would need in adulthood.

The rest of our family just accepted her the way she was because they never wondered about those things like I did. Unlike the family, I just went about my business and ignored her. That is exactly how I handle people to this day. I have no use for people who say ridiculous things, or make ludicrous claims, or, worst of all, attempt to push their beliefs on me. I don't say anything, I just walk away.

 TIP: Your *guides* will encourage you not to engage with people who attempt to make you believe what they believe. In fact, *they* will help show you how to avoid them, leave them with their opinions, and just walk away. Your *guides* are very smooth!

I always had to keep my guard up and be several steps ahead of my mother to steer clear of her outbursts of rage. Because of this, I learned early in life how to know what someone was thinking before they ever said or acted on it. I became a master at it. I would take a nap and just before fully waking up, I would bask in that twilight between here and there. This was my way of tip-toeing back into this reality so I wouldn't be caught off guard.

The warnings that I received in this state between sleep and waking were invaluable. These messages were coming from my *guides* who worked with me to keep me out of harm's way. Mastering this became another one of those critical life skills that supported me in adulthood.

Beside the dreams and twilight times between sleep and waking, I became more intuitively alert in my waking hours. I started using this intuitive awareness at school. I began to know if there was going to be a fight on the playground before one broke out. I knew when I would have a good day or bad day before the day started, and I knew why. When I got home from school, I also knew what I was walking into before I even opened the door. I was like a human radar detector.

This skill was necessary because both school and home were environments where I was required to continually watch my back. It never ceased. But one night I had a dream where I was at the vacant land behind our house, and the kids who wanted to beat me up were trying to gang up on me. Suddenly I was inside a bubble, floating directly above them. They hit the bubble with sticks and stones, but it gently floated a little higher and out of their reach. I recognized that I'll always be protected. This was just another important message from *those who walked through this life with me, my guides.*

After the bubble dream, I start writing down all my dreams. I also started recording my thoughts, the unexplainable things that happened all the time, including the things I knew before they ever took place. I never told anyone what I was writing; it just helped me understand what was really going on.

No external person brought me this kind of clarity. It only came from my dreams, journaling, and the inspiration and guidance I always received from my *guides*. By this time in my life, I realized that no one outside of me would understand any of this. In fact, if they glimpsed what I was experiencing, they would probably lock me up.

 LEARNING: Dreams like the bubble dream really make it clear that your *guides* are with you and are serious about looking out for you. It doesn't get any clearer than this.

Looking back to when I was three years old, my mother saw firsthand some of the strange things I did, and she observed my reactions. That caused her to know more about me than anyone else knew. Because of what she saw or deduced then, she now attempted to talk my dad into getting rid of me. I heard her screaming at him about this, demanding that he agree with her. Even at that early age, I could figure out that she didn't want me around. She didn't want me at all.

There were periods when my mother and father fought all the time. However, that was the one time I heard my dad put his foot down, and I never heard her bring up the subject again. Even so, one day when my dad was at work, she grabbed my doll suitcase, opened it on my bed, and told me to pack my stuff and get out. When I had my stuff packed, she pushed me out the door. Knowing this wasn't going to fly with my dad, she got in car and chased me down. I often thought that she was playing out something on me that happened to her when she was a kid.

I remember times when she would sleep all morning after dad went to work. I knew my mom was depressed and had nowhere to turn. Larry and I would be playing in the living room, and I would go into the bedroom and pet mom's head. I knew something was wrong with her. I felt so sorry for her and I wanted to help her. Unfortunately, she felt I was getting too close to her, and it just caused more tension between us. There's that *merry-go-round dream* again: some people won't be able to be reached.

 TIP: In spite of how difficult or dangerous your environment is, it doesn't help to panic. This is when your *guides* become critical to your wellbeing and sometimes survival. Lean on *them;* that's why *they're* there.

I reached the third grade and found school remained as lame as it had been in first and second grades. But home was also no place I wanted to be either, so I became reclusive. I learned to focus my energy on doing schoolwork and going places with Larry. My life became all about lying low, real low. I didn't hate my mother, but I knew she was dangerous.

Eventually, I decided I was done trying to tiptoe around Mom's mood swings. Nothing came as a shock to me anymore. I was just counting down the days until I could get out of there, remembering what my *guides* told me: "*Life will get better for you as you get older — if you can make it through childhood."*

It had been about five years since *they* first started telling me that. I reached a point where I was beginning to experience more of what it really meant. And for the first time, I was beginning to get concerned about whether I was actually going to make it through childhood.

It didn't get easier as the years went by; in fact, it was wearing me down. I was really tired of constantly deflecting my mother's next round of attacks. She didn't work, so she had all the time in the world to think up new ways to make my life hell. Larry and I (especially me) were outlets for her anger and rage. I was getting warning signs from my *guides* letting me know that the time was coming closer when something with my mother was going to play out. *They* didn't show me what it was going to be, but I knew it was tied into *their* warning about making it through childhood.

 TIP: When you get reminders, you may think of them as hunches, or feelings. These are coming directly from your *guides*. It's important to learn to recognize these warnings, as in the case I mentioned above, you feel it coming closer and it is.

Just before completing the third grade, my mother went to the principal demanding that they hold me back. They told my mother that wasn't necessary, that my grades were satisfactory, but she insisted. So I ended up repeating the third grade. Mom's explanation to me was that I would learn what it felt like to be humiliated when I returned to school in the fall. Dad was really upset with her, but once again he couldn't stop her. I realized that lying low wasn't enough anymore. Mom was determined to deliver a new punishment to me that she hoped would be more effective: humiliating me in front of my peer group.

That summer, when I was nine years old, my dad's brother, Uncle Charlie, and his wife and her sister came out to visit us. That was the first time Larry or I met any of our parents' family members. I remember how concerned my parents seemed to be before they arrived. Something wasn't right. I sensed that my parents were worried that some secret might be revealed.

I found these relatives to be very nice and genuine people. I was at such a low spot at the time that I imagined asking Uncle Charlie and his wife to take me home with them. That was the first time I felt like I could have devised a way out of my home situation. Perhaps, like in the movies when someone passes a secret note saying they are in danger, mine could say, "Help, please get me out of here... she's trying to destroy me!" After all, I'd already been warned by my *guides*. But I knew it would not have worked in real life, and that all it would have done is expose the serious dysfunction in my family and cause even more devastating assaults from my mother.

I never brought it up, and they left without any dark family secrets coming to light. While I was definitely right that my mother and father were hiding something, I wouldn't discover how dark their secrets really were for decades to come.

My mother had been right: returning to school to repeat the third grade was humiliating. It was a dismal year for me.

I adapted by becoming even more reclusive. I had never depended on friendships anyway, so it wasn't much of a transition. That experience just allowed me to see the behavior from the kids in both grades, the one I would have graduated into and the one I was stuck in. No big surprises, though; the kids were pretty predictable. To them, and to the teachers, it just proved that they were right when they judged me as stupid.

This converted me into the ultimate observer. That was yet another layer of being alone that brought me even closer to my *guides*. I may have been alone, but I was not lonely. I was learning much more from *them* than I could ever have learned in school.

So, over the next few years, I got even more deeply involved in my own projects and activities outside of school. I just wasn't meant to be one of the soldiers playing the games that would qualify me for the roles the kids and their politics offered. I had better things going on and *real friends,* my *guides,* who were with me every step of the way, even if I couldn't see the whole picture.

 TIP: Overcoming things like ostracism and humiliation will make you wiser and clearer. Learning to do this is a skill you will use throughout your life. It can only happen when you observe and don't take things personally. You are never alone, your *guides* are there to help and believe in you.

Eventually, I managed to reach the sixth grade and the completion of grade school. School had been literally one fight after another, in one form or another. It was at the start of the sixth grade that I secretly decided to see if I could get straight A's. After all, it's the sixth grade that demonstrates how well a student has learned in all the previous years. This was my own personal test, and I passed it with flying colors: I got an A in every subject.

Once I accomplished that and had proved to myself I was keeping things together, I returned to being totally bored with school. I understood what it took to get straight A's and that it was not hard for me to do. I just wanted to spend that energy on something that really intrigued me, like the things I learned from my *guides*, not just on test scores.

My family situation got so much harder to live in as the years went by. Aside from the support from my *guides,* there was no one in this world to turn to who could help or get me out of there.

Just before I hit puberty my mother's Gestapo tactics went too far. I was completely out of energy to fight her off any-more. I attempted suicide. My mother was taking some sort of pills called Cope, and coping was not something I could do any longer. So I swallowed all the pills one day in the school bathroom where I was alone. That's where they found me: passed out on the floor in a bathroom stall.

Although this appears to have been premeditated, it wasn't. I just woke up that morning, empty of this world. I had no feelings, no fear, and I never questioned that I wouldn't carry this out. From the moment I took the bottle of pills out of the medicine cabinet, I no longer had a connection to this world.

It was like I was already gone. It's interesting to describe how I felt when I didn't feel anything at all.

All I remember is waking up in the hospital. The first thing I saw and heard was my dad holding my mom back from swinging at me as she yelled out over and over again that it wasn't her fault. She was crazed with anger and rage. Dad had his hands full, and it was all he could do to hang onto her to keep her from hitting me. I had taken another shot at escaping this life only to find myself right back where I left off. Again, my lesson was to not run from any of this. Just keep walking through it.

After I was released from the hospital, my mom stopped the constant torment and abuse. It just all stopped. Nothing was ever said about the incident, not why I did it, no words from my mom or dad or brothers. The "Don't ask, don't tell" family policy was in full force.

But they all knew why I had done what I did and that Mom too often had gone too far with me. I remember thinking that I must have passed a milestone when *they* told me, "*Life will get better for you as you get older if you can make it through childhood.*" I almost didn't make it through childhood, but *they* knew this was a possibility when I first came into this life. That's why that was the first thing *they* warned me about.

 TIP: Your *spirit guides* know everything about the life you entered when you first came here. It's like a movie that's playing out. In my case, *they* saw that this moment in time could be where my life could be cut short because the obstacles were so great. It was *my guides'* job to see that I made it past that milestone. *They* had *their* hands full. When you try to leave this world and *they* insist on keeping you here, you know that your life has a higher purpose.

By now racial tensions were rising up in our neighborhood and at school. It was the 1960s, after all. My African-American friends started fighting with me and accusing me of saying things I never said. I knew that this was the end of our friendship because the racial tension was clouding the reality of our relationship.

I believe they had no choice; it was their time to fight back. I understood that they had been discriminated against for far too long, and they were sick of it. I imagined I would have done the same thing had I been them. However, this made it more dangerous to walk to and from school. I was in less danger than other kids because they really knew me, and we used to be friends. They knew I was not a racist — but I was still white.

On November 22, 1963, President Kennedy was assassinated. I was at school when it was announced, and everyone went into shock. It was like we were bombed or something. My knee-jerk reaction was to be an observer. I could not join them in the mass confusion and shock because something just wasn't right about all that. Everyone was in a hypnotic stupor; they were like lemmings following each other off the emotional cliff.

I was so removed from the mass hysteria that people thought something was wrong with me. It wasn't that I didn't have feelings or didn't care about our President; I just refused to be part of the hysteria and couldn't wait for school to get out that day. When I got home, my mom was really capitalizing on the event. It so happened that it was my mother's birthday, and she relished the fact that President Kennedy was murdered on that particular day. I had left the school's mass hysteria to come home to another bizarre situation.

Day after day our house was filled with TV coverage speculating on what happened. Then came the funeral. It was underscored with Mom's notion that her birthday would forever be special now. Watching this and the people's reactions was mind numbing. To me, the African-Americans were rightfully feeling a big setback from the loss of this President, as he was on their side in their fight for equal rights. I understood that. But everyone else was just feeding off everyone else's emotions as it compounded. I wasn't being sucked into the mass emotionality, and I found myself even more of an outcast at school and at home.

A few months after the assassination, the Beatles came to America for the first time. It was called an invasion, but it was really a cult happening. The reaction from my generation was weird. It was so intense that it actually scared me. I was very defiant toward it. I was not a Beatle's fan, I was an observer as I saw the kids get into drugs, lose their minds, and become followers. I became even more isolated from the lost souls of my generation. To them I was a dork, but I was comfortable with myself and didn't need them in my life. I wasn't inclined to get involved with their mindless cult behavior. My music of choice was Motown music, and that wasn't a cult or an invasion, it was a movement.

TIP: Be cautious when you see people getting caught up in the drama or excitement of events. They don't think for themselves; they just get herded along like sheep. It's not even real to them; it's entertainment. Observe and sit quietly by yourself to tune into what's really happening. That's where you will find your *guides,* and *they* will help keep things in perspective.

When I was 13 years old, one of the high-end department stores asked me to model for their Bobby Brooks line of clothing. That was my first job and I did very well. They liked my modeling work, and they provided training on how to walk and properly exhibit the clothes. It was great; I was making some money, got my school clothes for free, and felt good about myself. Naturally, it was too good to last.

Out of nowhere, my mom stopped it all. She told the store that I would not be able to do it anymore, and that was the end of it. I still don't know why she did that because it was very lucrative and I was feeling so good about myself. (Oh, wait...I was having success and feeling good about myself. That would explain it.)

Just about that time, I came home from school one day and found all my Aretha Franklin records broken in half. My mom admitted doing it, calling me racial names because I liked the soul singers and had African-American friends. After a fairly long period of backing off, my mom was back at it again. The break from her abuse had been nice while it lasted.

 TIP: The worst thing about someone taking something away from you is when they won't tell you why they did it. It's because they aren't playing fair. At least you got to experience and learn from it. It's all about the experience and not dwelling on what could have been, especially when you have no control over it. Take the good stuff, leave the rest, and keep walking.

The Way-Out-House was a Baptist church in the neighborhood that held dances every Friday night. I loved going there and learned to dance from the best dancers: the African-American kids. It became the highlight of my week. There were never any problems there. I always had a ride home, so it was a perfect time to still have fun with my old friends who, being in church, seemed to be willing to ignore the racial tensions that were building. That was a great time in my life. Getting older agreed with me; my real power was starting to emerge. I was just beginning to feel something I hadn't felt before and it felt great.

One day when I was in the eighth grade, I was attacked by a gang of Mexican girls on the school basketball court. They wore razor blades in their ratted-up hair dos. They knocked me down on the ground and pulled the blades out of their hair to carve up my face. A lone teacher interrupted what was going on by screaming at those tough girls, telling them to stop. He saved me. Those girls were put in juvenile detention until they turned 18 years old. It was this incident that finally alerted my parents to get me out of that neighborhood and that school.

My dad was in the process of building a house for us in the foothills about 30 miles from our home in the inner-city. Building the house was a real killer for my dad because it was such hard work on top of his regular job. I was very worried about him, but he pulled it off. He knew the neighborhood we lived in had become too dangerous and that he had to get us out of there. I remember how nonchalant my mom was when he first came to her about building a new house and getting us out of that neighborhood. She didn't want to be bothered with all the work it was going to take. She didn't care. It wasn't affecting her, and she wasn't going out of her way for anyone.

Not long after we moved, the old neighborhood completely exploded with riots, burnings, and killings. Within three years, you couldn't even drive down that street for fear of getting shot.

It was a valuable lesson in learning when to hold'em and fold'em, walk away, or run. It gave me a heightened sense of timing. From the pre-explosive times when racial tensions were building to the actual explosions, I learned the warning signs all along the way. Like the dream of me in the bubble that was out of their reach, I was not meant to be a casualty of that situation. However, I was supposed to experience all of it. Yet again, I was being guided all the way by my *protectors*.

 LEARNING: What's learned from your challenges lasts a lifetime. It's all about the experiences. Once you have them, it's like a treasure chest of valuable riches for you to pull out just when you need them. This story is filled with examples of the many ways I applied these early experiences in my adult life that turned out to be critical to my many successes that were on the horizon.

Chapter 7: A Tsunami of Change

We moved in the middle of my eighth-grade school year. Randy was finishing high school, and Larry was in his last year of grade school. Randy stayed behind to finish the last semester before graduating, then moved to the family home in the foothills.

For me the new school was totally different, and so were the kids. There was no fighting or gangs, but the kids had the same peer-pressure politics going on. Their behavior was very similar to that of the white kids in my old neighborhood. I didn't like what the white kids did back there, and I didn't like what the white kids were doing here. That was the last year before starting high school, so I was hoping that it would somehow change in the fall, like hitting a big re-set button.

The summer before high school was lonely. I walked to Folsom Lake with my dog a few times a week. I sewed my clothes for school. My dad would come home from work very tired from the big push building the new house. My mom was lost in Star Trek. Larry was building a dune buggy. Randy was just lying around the house. It was an uneventful summer.

The kids from the old school did not stay in touch with me, the racial tensions having taken over. I understood it; the friends I liked had to discard me as they focused on their fight for civil rights.

I stepped out of the racially explosive environment of inner-city Sacramento and into the drug-addled culture of semi-rural El Dorado Hills, California. The new kids were experimenting with everything they could get their hands on. They were going off the deep end with their first exposure to these mind-altering recreational drugs.

By the middle of my freshman year, everyone was taking them. Not me — I was the outcast. I knew that these drugs were not a good choice for me. When the kids asked me why I didn't take them, I told them I was going to need my mind. I had no desire to do drugs anyway. Kids were dying, getting hurt, and becoming addicts, although a few actually did have mind-altering experiences and came through it understanding themselves better. But mostly, it was about getting high and not mind expanding at all.

It was 1966 and even our art teacher gave the kids marijuana when he took us out for nature walks. He was experimenting with how much more creative the students could be when they were stoned. To me, most everyone seemed lost and just drifting around.

 LEARNING: Had these kids been in touch with their *guides,* much of this would have never happened. What they didn't realize when taking those mind-altering drugs was that they were reaching for their *guides;* they knew something was missing. But they didn't know how to find their *guides* through the haze so they ended up just using drugs to escape reality. That was why I was never inclined to take drugs; I already had what these kids sought. For me, nothing was missing because I had a great connection with my *guides.*

Then one day I met a girl who had moved from Pleasant Hills, near San Francisco. Like me, she was used to city life with its variety, diverse cultures, and choices. But her experience was even vaster than mine. I liked her. I was 14 and she was 15, but she looked much older, which was cool then. She had a boyfriend who drove up from San Francisco to see her on the weekends. He had a Ford Woody and she would ride in the front seat with him while three of us girls would ride in the back seat as her tag-along girlfriends.

We would be quietly laughing at how she had him wrapped around her finger. He was about seven years older than she was. She played so many games on him and he would react, falling right into her trap. It was fun as they played the kind of music I was used to and liked.

He took us everywhere with them. She loved showing off for us. I remember when I would go over to her house and how angry her father was with her. I think they moved to get her away from the San Francisco influence. Her father never let up on her, calling her terrible names and insulting her for the way she wore her hair, makeup, and the way she dressed. She smoked, but didn't take drugs. She was far from perfect, but I understood why she was the way she was.

Even though I wasn't really friends with the local kids, they would invite me to their parties. I would show up and see everyone drinking and taking drugs. I would leave right away. This had nothing to do with what my parents would think if I indulged, it was my call. I just wasn't interested. Because of that, I was considered a dork. But I shook my head as I watched them getting more lost than they already were. I knew I was reserving myself for another calling that just hadn't shown itself yet. After all, I had made it this far with the support of my *guides*. I knew who I was; I just didn't know where I was going yet. Fortunately for me, my *guides* did, and soon life as I had known it would be changed forever.

While I hadn't been much into the social scene, there was an older boy who liked me. He wanted me to be his girlfriend and consistently pursued me. I wasn't interested in him, but he would not give up. One day he gave me a present that I opened when I got home. It was a marijuana cigarette and some other things. I showed it to my parents, and they asked me where it came from. I told them and pointed out that I wasn't about to smoke it. I could see they were pretty angry and asked them not to say anything to the boy's parents. But they didn't listen to me. They contacted the guy's parents and told them I wasn't interested in their son. They also said to tell him not to contact me again.

The boy was so devastated by all of this that he attempted suicide. When I heard about what he'd done, it really shocked me because I never considered that anything like that could ever happen. I learned two things from that: first, to never trust my parents again, and second, to never be so insensitive with someone's heart.

The school work at the new school was also a lot easier than what I had been doing in Sacramento. I had already learned most of that stuff, and it seemed that everything was behind the times and slower there. As a result, I was really bored so I spent my time swimming, sewing school clothes, and doing all the cooking and most of the cleaning at home. My mom had it made. I was doing all of that because that's what it took to manage everything on the domestic front. Before long I learned why.

Near the end of my freshman year I meet a boy named Alex Smith. He was a "bad boy" and had a reputation in school for minor run-ins with the law. I saw him as someone who knew how to get things done. He liked having money to get what he needed and wanted, and he knew how to get it.

His parents were both raging alcoholics, and he was seriously ashamed of both of them. He was so ashamed of them that he said they weren't his real parents and that he was adopted — which I discovered later was not true.

He was physically abused so badly as a young child by his alcoholic mother that he was cross-eyed before the age of five as the result of her having hit him in the head with beer bottles. Somehow he got the medical attention he needed to correct his eyes sometime around the age of eight, but he started school with that stigma, which only added to his shame. Crossed eyes are symbolic of not wanting to see what's out there. In his case, he didn't want to see his alcoholic parents and the dismal world he grew up in.

I could relate to him and how his childhood experiences made him different, sort of like mine did to me. His early life was rough, and his family was extremely poor. He was really ashamed about having lived in poverty, and I really felt bad for him.

Coming from the "other side of the tracks," he viewed me as if I had come from royalty. He treated me with respect and maybe a little awe. I like to think I had a positive influence on him because it was pretty clear he knew he was heading down the wrong road in life and needed a big change.

When we met, he was in his sophomore year and working two jobs that kept him busy until 3:00 a.m. School was so easy for me that I took on his homework along with my own so he wouldn't get behind. We started dating and right from the get go, we began doing what it took to build a life together.

Several days a week, he would drive 30 miles one way just to pick me up at 7:00 a.m. for school. He didn't come to my house, of course; my mother would have found a way to sabotage our relationship had she known about it, so he would pick me up at the school bus stop.

One time on a date, a cop started following us. Alex became very nervous, so I asked him what was wrong. He didn't answer me, but told me to get out of the car if he stopped and don't ask any questions. After the cop finally turned off, I asked him what that was all about. It turns out that he had stolen the car we were in. He stole a car for a date?! I realized that I was with a wild and crazy guy. I opened the glove compartment, and it was filled with packs of cigarettes.

Since Alex didn't smoke, I asked him what that was all about and he said he sold them to make money. I never knew where he got the cigarettes; for all I knew, he stole them. He was on his own early in his life, so he had learned to survive.

I knew my mom and dad would never approve of Alex — I could hardly accept all of what he did myself. But somehow I knew that he had what it took to take on life, just like I did. We were ready to move on and get out of the environments we were in. We had some real core connections.

One evening Alex came to my house to pick me up to go to the drive-in movies. Although he was respectful and polite, my parents could sense his rough energy. They were always leery of him. My mom and dad, as many parents are, were pretty wise about that kind of thing.

Alex and I were together every chance we could get. We never talked about anything long-term. We just did things, went places, and had fun together. We didn't have friends to do things with because we had nothing in common with most of the people we knew. The more time we spent together, the more my mother disliked Alex. He didn't like her either, but he was composed about it.

In the summer of 1968, when I was 16, I decided to make the break from my family. By October I was pregnant. I can't say that this was an accident because I was ready to get on with my life no matter what the consequences were. Alex and I were running on pure instincts. He wasn't afraid and neither was I. We were thinking through our plan about what to do next. I could never tell my parents because they would have reacted explosively. This was way off track for them, so I felt I had no choice but to run.

Alex took me to a very remote place he knew about where I could stay. I didn't go to school, or tell anyone where I was. I was on the run. After several days of being gone, Alex started seeking advice from some people he worked with. Based on what they said, we decided that I would have to go back home and just tell my parents that I ran away. So that's what I did.

 LEARNING: There are times when taking a risk doesn't feel like one. That's because you are living a bigger risk than the risk you are taking. Fear of what people's opinions and reactions will be have no place here. If you allow any of that to determine your fate, you will wind up living a life of compromise.

Though I hadn't said anything about being pregnant, my mom took me to the doctor for a pregnancy test. No big surprise, the results came out positive. At least I didn't have to tell her. I'm sure that not coming home for several nights sort of tipped them off, so they had time to react without me being there.

When my dad found out, he got his loaded shotgun out and took off to find Alex. They thought they were in control of everything. My dad did not handle this well at all. Fortunately, he did not find Alex. My mom was her usual divisive and calculating self.

Once the initial shock wore off, things got quiet for several days. Then my mom asked me if I wanted to keep the baby. I said I did. She told me I could give it up for adoption and forget this ever happened. I told her that I would never do that. She tried to bribe me with a new wardrobe, while describing a scenario of suffering and torment I was destined for if I went with Alex. I told her I didn't see that; I saw a great future and I was not afraid. I told her I wanted to leave and be with Alex. She asked me what Alex wanted and I said I didn't know because Alex and I never talked about it.

My mother's next step was to have Alex over to talk to him. She asked Alex if he loved me, and he said he did. Then she asked him if he wanted to marry me, and he said yes to that, too. Then my mom told him he didn't have to marry me. Alex said he wanted to marry me, that he had two jobs and could support us. Mom asked about school, and we agreed to continue high school until we graduated.

When I realized my parents were going to go along with our plans, I felt like I had been released from some sort of prison. I was so excited to get out of there that it took everything I had to cover it up. I knew I had to hide my real feelings because my mother would have changed her mind if she saw how happy I really was.

It took a few weeks to arrange everything, and I lived at home while these arrangements were coming together. My mom decided on everything — where we would be getting married, who would marry us, that the parents on both sides had to attend, and where we would live after we were married.

About two weeks before I left, my mother went into her last explosive attack on me. We were in the kitchen and she knocked me down to the floor. Then she started kicking me in the stomach really hard over and over again. I curled over to protect the baby, but she just kept kicking me and screaming at me. Finally, Randy came over and grabbed her to stop her from kicking me.

Once I got my wits about me, I hobbled upstairs to my bed-room, locked the door, and laid down on my bed. At that point, I became very worried about the damage she could have done to the baby.

Later she told me how she felt cheated because I had finally become useful to her by doing all the cooking and cleaning. She said that she felt it was finally her turn to enjoy life, and now I was leaving. She was concerned about enjoying her life; I was concerned about saving mine. She might have been upset to lose her Cinderella, but I was certainly not unhappy about my impending departure.

On the other hand, my dad was sad to see me go and cried. He took me aside and told me to never come back, warning me that Mom would never change.

My mother scowled at me when I left. Randy sided with Mom. Larry asked me to take him with me and begged me not to leave him there. It tore out my heart to leave my little brother alone with her to take the full force of her now heightened rage. I promised Larry he could join us as soon as possible. Alex and I both felt very bad about leaving him behind.

PART 2: EXPLODING INTO MY NEW LIFE

Chapter 8: The Day I Got Out Alive

On December 17th, 1968, Alex and I were married in Reno, Nevada, at the Justice of the Peace. My mom and dad and Alex's mom and dad were present. I was 16 years old and Alex was 17 so we needed parental consent. My mom asked me if I told Alex about my bed-wetting problem yet. Without hesitating, I told her I didn't have that problem anymore — and to my surprise, I didn't. Without any effort on my part, it completely stopped the day I left home, and it never happened again. This was the first time I had solid evidence of just how toxic that environment really was throughout my early life.

 AWARENESS: When words come through without any thought and you just blurt them out, this is telepathic communication direct from your *guides*. Never make the mistake that this came from you...it came <u>through</u> you. In the case mentioned above, I was being notified by my *guides* that this childhood trauma was behind me.

(By my mid-thirties, I would discover that what causes someone to wet the bed is fear of the dominant parent. It's an emotional release. No wonder I couldn't stop it, and why it stopped the moment I got away from her once and for all.)

Alex and I moved to Folsom, and we went to Folsom High School while Alex continued to hold down two jobs. Our honeymoon was a weekend in Lake Tahoe. We took Larry with us so he would understand that we were looking out for him even if he couldn't come to live with us yet.

My life had become fantastic. Independence was the most amazing feeling, and I knew that life was only going to get better from here on out as I recalled my *guide's* words, *"Life will get better for you as you get older if you can make it through childhood." They* were right! I thanked my *guides* for guiding me through the riskiest part of my life, my childhood. Nothing could ever be that bad again.

I couldn't believe I had gotten out alive. I wasn't worried about anything, even when we had no food and I was really hungry because I was pregnant. Alex would always bring me food from work so I could eat. I knew we would be alright. Life was peaceful and happy. Alex had to hitchhike to work about 30 miles each way every day because we didn't have a car, but he didn't mind it at all. Alex did what it took and wasn't spoiled like the other kids I had known.

I wasn't getting the nutritional supplements that I needed, nor did I have the right diet, which only depleted me throughout the pregnancy. My mother told me that the baby was going to be born deformed. To some degree, I was very concerned she might be right from that time she kicked me in the stomach.

Alex was happy to be moving forward with his life, too. We felt strong together — we were in heaven. We both appreciated what we had. Alex loved my dad and did not like my mother. Dad would stop by with Mom to visit every now and then and try to give me money for food, and Mom would grab it back from me. These visits were infrequent, and each time Dad would sneak a $20 bill into something where I would find it later without Mom knowing.

 LEARNING: Getting out of an abusive, repressive life is a real accomplishment. Once you do, you need to revisit your life to put the pieces back together again. That may be the hardest thing you will ever have to do. It has been for me. I appreciate everything my *guides* did to get me this far. It's gratitude that makes my life so special now.

My mother was selfish and abusive, and she was also insanely controlling. An example of that was when Mom decided Alex needed a car to get to work. One day she showed up with a white Ford Falcon and told Alex that this was his car. Then, as our amazement at our good fortune sunk in, she presented a payment plan, with interest, to pay her back. She also told him the type of insurance he would be required to carry. She insisted that this was the best car for us and that we damn well better take good care of it.

Alex immediately became offended and told her he never asked for a car so she could take it and shove it. Mom looked at me and asked if I was going to let him speak to her that way. I said I was.

Alex and I never felt desperate or broke; we were just doing what it took to get on our feet by ourselves, without strings. I knew Mom was concerned and trying to help, but her typical pushy and controlling approach didn't cut it with Alex. He never allowed anyone to push him around, especially her. I was proud of him. Mom, on the other hand, was so angry with him she cut off all visits and communication. She also found a special way to let us know she was angry.

My baby shower had been planned before the car incident. The neighbors and my mom were arranging it. However, on the day of the baby shower, my mom was a no-show. Everyone asked where she was but I shined it on, not saying anything about her and Alex butting heads.

For some reason, I felt really hurt by her abandonment. Maybe it was the final string being cut that made it so painful for me. In any case, the lines were now drawn between us, and there was no longer any question about that. Alex and I were going to be fine without her around. I would miss my dad, but fortunately none of this stopped Larry from coming around.

In July 1969 when I was still 16 years old, Cindy was born. She was perfectly healthy, with no signs of damage from my mother having kicked me. Not only was she healthy, she was beautiful.

However, the first time I held Cindy the worst feeling came over me. I felt that I must have been out of my mind to bring her into a world like this. In that moment, I realized that the world was an awful place for an innocent new life like the one I held in my arms. Here I was, only 16 years old, and I had already learned what a dysfunctional and evil place this world could be. I was shocked at what I was feeling, but it was brutally honest and true. I was sick inside, and I'm not sure anyone can understand what I felt in that moment. I vowed to never have another child.

While I was fine with being a mom, Alex didn't connect with the new baby situation. He was focused on working all the time and going to school. Although he was doing his best, after Cindy was born, something changed with how I saw him. He was not capable after all. In fact, he came up short. For me, having Cindy was my wakeup call; all of a sudden I saw things more clearly than I ever had before. Still a child myself, in just eight months, I had gone from escaping a childhood of persecution to bringing a child into this world.

After Cindy was born, I was seriously depressed. I didn't understand any of this. But with Cindy crying all the time and Alex on edge, there was no room for my problem. Day after day for about six months, I woke up to that same old depressed feeling. I never told anyone about it even though it was an incredible burden. Everything changed after Cindy was born.

Around the time that she was born, Alex managed to get a reliable used car. While it made things a little easier on him, it didn't help much with the situation at home. Alex was still so exhausted that when Cindy cried, he would get mad and impatient. I didn't like it when she cried either, so every time she cried, I picked her up. That was a bad choice because she became very demanding. At my wits end, I spoiled her. I would walk her in her stroller for miles at a time so she would stop crying.

As the months went by, her crying developed into screaming. She would wake up screaming right out of a dead sleep. I took her to the doctor, and he said she had colic. He said there was nothing that could be done and that she would just have to grow out of it. So I continued walking her in the stroller until I literally wore out the wheels.

Even the neighbors said they had never heard of such extreme crying. Finally, at about eight months old, she stopped crying. However, she had become so spoiled from my continually picking her up that it took forever before she would sleep through the night. I held her so much that by eight months old, she would no longer drink from the baby bottle. She had become used to grabbing my glass from me and drinking my water. At night in her crib, she would unscrew the top of her baby bottle and drink it like from out of a glass.

 LEARNING: No matter who you are, having a child changes you. Maybe for the first time in your life the focus is off of you. Once you experience this, you can never go back. This is when many mothers make their initial contact with their *guides*. After all, they just brought someone in from the other side, one of *them*. "Mother's intuition" is really your *guides* helping you.

While I was going to night school, Larry would come down in his dune buggy to babysit Cindy. He loved his niece. Cindy became very possessive of him. He spoiled her rotten. I never had to worry about her when he took care of her even though he was only 15 years old. He was better at taking care of her when I had to go to school than Alex was. Alex didn't understand the father role, since his father hadn't set much of an example for him.

Other than Larry, in those early days when I was going to night school, I had no help raising Cindy. Everything was on me. I took this responsibility very seriously, which caused me to be over-protective and very strict. Since she was going to be my only child, I had to be sure to get it right. Her well-being influenced everything I would be doing going forward. Parenting her was the most important obligation I had. I wanted to do my very best to raise her and be able to give her the things that would make her shine.

When Cindy was nine months old, I started teaching her to swim. She took to it like a fish. She learned to hold her breath and fearlessly swim under water with me. I loved that time with her. She was doing great in every way. She was swimming before she could walk.

Although Alex wasn't very successful as a father, he was doing pretty well as a husband and provider. He had made enough money to buy me a car, but we weren't sure what kind to get. We looked around and thought about buying a Plymouth Duster, but the Plymouth Roadrunner was just a little more money and much more fun. So Alex bought me my first car — a brand new, red-and-black, Plymouth Roadrunner — a 440 cubic-inch V8 muscle car. I didn't even have a driver's license yet or know how to drive. To learn, I got my neighbor to watch Cindy so I could take the car out by myself. I went on roads with no traffic and taught myself to drive that Hurst 4-speed stick-shift. There was a trick to shifting gears in perfect sync with the clutch, and I figured it out and liked it.

Larry loved the new car, and Alex was rightfully proud of it. That car was the second thing we bought on credit, the first being our refrigerator. I drove the car for about six months, then got my driver's license when I turned 18. Life was indeed getting better for me as I got older, just like my *guides* said it would.

Of course, not everything had changed. There was a big Texan girl in my night school class who also had a baby about the same age as Cindy. She was mean and for some reason would always say nasty things about my baby and husband. After a couple months, I told her to stop it. But she kept it up. You can probably guess what was coming.

Finally she went over the line. So, one night I intercepted her as she was leaving class and told her she had dissed my family for the last time. She was a big girl, and I was small and slender. She sneered and asked what I was going to do about it. In response, I showed her what I had learned from the kids in Sacramento.

I hadn't planned to say anything about it to Alex, but the next day she and her husband came to our house. Alex answered the door to find this fellow and his beat-up wife. She looked terrible. The husband said I had done this to his wife. Alex looked over at me, and I told him she had it coming because she wouldn't stop talking badly about him and Cindy. Alex looked back at her husband and said that apparently she had it coming. He suggested that maybe she had learned some manners.

Apparently the husband hadn't gotten the whole story. He shook his head and told his wife to get in the car. They left and I never saw her at school again.

I had pretty easily won the fight, but I realized fighting was no longer the way to handle things. I had a family now and needed to act like an adult. I actually felt remorse because I was going to miss those fighting days. I only fought when it was necessary, but I knew I had to find new solutions. Interestingly, this was almost an exact replay of the situation with the girl who used to beat up Larry. But this time I learned the lesson. I saw it as the karmic cycle of life playing out that I needed to break.

Two years after I left home, I found out that my little brother started using drugs. He just couldn't cope in that environment without me to act as a buffer. He was losing his way. I never went near drugs, but, unlike me, he found drugs enticing. He started showing up at our house high, sometimes on mescaline, other times on other things. We didn't really know what to say to him, so we provided what we felt he really needed – support without judging him.

Meanwhile, at 18, Alex started his apprenticeship program with the carpenters union. He got hired as a laborer on a framing crew. He was exhilarated to have that job. Larry told Dad about Alex's new job and Dad took us out to lunch to celebrate. Dad was truly happy for us. That is when Dad started calling Alex his son. Alex loved it. He had always wanted respect from my dad. Dad really took Alex under his wing, though not always in the best way. For example, he would tell Alex not to do women's chores. That was pretty chauvinistic, but that wasn't my Dad's intent. It was about camaraderie with Alex. That was a real powerful time between Dad and Alex.

TIP: You know when you are on the right track because everything falls magically into place. You are being guided. You will see through reading this story that it's easier to start something new than it is to change. Why is that? It's because people tend to resist the changes, thinking they might lose something. The resistance is what makes change hard. Otherwise, starting something new and change would be equally exciting.

Chapter 9: Success Comes Fast and Furious

In 1970 I started to rack up some dentist bills. It was a little over a year after Cindy had been born, and I was beginning to have severe toothaches. Not just one or two, but almost all my teeth were hurting. I was out of my mind with pain.

Alex had just become an apprentice carpenter so we had dental insurance. And we had been saving money because he was pretty well paid. The insurance couldn't have come at a better time. When I went to see the dentist, he told he that this was caused by serious malnutrition while I was pregnant. He told me that when I didn't get the nutrition and supplements I needed during pregnancy, the baby took what it needed by depleting me. This was the result.

I remember my mother, who was now back in contact with us, laughing at my suffering. She thought I was paying the price I deserved for not having lived my life the way she wanted me to. There was no end to her judgment and pleasure in seeing me suffer.

The dentist told Alex and me that it was going to cost us thousands of dollars, even with the benefits, but I wouldn't lose my teeth if I started getting the work done right away. The dental insurance covered 80 percent. The dentist said we could pay him monthly payments on the rest. It took about six months to complete. My mother told Alex that she knew I needed dental work when we got married. She considered that she had dodged a medical bill by pushing me off on him, which was not what happened at all. Mom loved digging in her knife as some lingering revenge from the car incident. But I got through that hit to my health, and we quickly got back on our feet financially.

With the dental bills retired, we decided it was time for some real furniture. We went to a store that had great values and bought three rooms of furniture, along with a stereo and a TV.

While we were at the furniture store, I started talking with the owner's wife. She told me about the time she had a breakdown. I was fascinated with that and asked her what it was like to actually have a breakdown. She told me that she didn't know she had had a breakdown until she was well again. I asked her if there were any signs that she was heading in that direction, and she said there weren't. She said she didn't remember anything that indicated it was happening. She didn't look like a person who had a breakdown. It wasn't like she went nuts or was unstable in any way. She said she just shut down one day and turned off to everything around her for a while.

After her candid description of her breakdown, I realized that having a breakdown didn't mean the person went crazy. However, she said the doctors put her on drugs of some kind. I couldn't understand why she didn't remember what led up to the breakdown. Then I started wondering why I was so interested in that in the first place. I had a strong sense that what I learned from that lady would be important for me to know someday. My *guides* were showing me this, but why?

TIP: Nothing ever happens by accident. This is an example of how your *guides* will show you things that are important, even though they may not play out for years. Your job is to pay attention and even write things like this down if you are concerned about remembering them later.

When we had everything picked out, the store manager asked us where we got the money to buy all that furniture. Alex and I thought he was kidding, but he wasn't. Alex looked him in the eye and said that he worked for it.

Alex was very proud; he loved putting our life together. Alex would tell me he wasn't interested in vacations when we could use our money to have these great things. We were renting an apartment, and this new furniture was a great fit. However, that was not enough for Alex; he had his eye on getting us into our first home, although I didn't know that at the time.

Alex was only 19 years old but he was already making good money as an apprentice carpenter. He was working on a crew framing new starter homes on half-acre lots in a really good area. Alex asked the developer if he could frame one of the houses in exchange for the down payment on it. The developer agreed, calling it "sweat equity" and said that would require painting it as well as framing it.

Alex came home and told me about it. As soon as we could, we went to the model of our intended 1,050 square-foot-three-bedroom, two-bath home. It was beautiful. We were so excited that we invited my mom and dad out to see the model.

Mom immediately disapproved. Alex and I couldn't believe what she was saying. We had a perfect strategy to make it happen, we could afford it, and it was a perfect fit for our little family. She said we couldn't afford it and that we were overextending ourselves. Dad, on the other hand, liked it, and he also liked our strategy. Needless to say, we ignored Mom's poor advice once again.

Alex's fellow framing comrades all agreed to come out on weekends and help. I painted it, and Alex helped me when he had extra time. While under construction, I decided to have a contractor come out and give us a bid on the cost of adding a pool. The house was $19,000, and the huge built-in swimming pool with decking, a three-meter diving board, a 12-foot deep end, and all the equipment including a heater was only $3,600 more. We had the pool built right after we moved in.

We invited the families of the men who had helped us frame it over for barbeques and swim parties every weekend. It was so much fun. Larry was 17 years old and we could finally have him move in with us. Alex got him hired by the same general contractor that employed him. I was 19 years old, Cindy was two, and Alex was 20.

Though we loved our new home and new neighborhood, we were not welcomed by our new neighbors. We were not their social equals, and the neighbors decided we were trouble the moment we moved in. They all seemed scared of us. We were baffled as to why they were afraid.

Our priority when we moved in was to put in our swimming pool instead of putting in front-yard landscaping like all the other neighbors had done. No doubt we were a bit immature, but treating us like we were troublemakers only made things worse for them because it set Alex off. In his judgment, we had worked so hard to get to that point, so he was offended by their assumptions about us.

He responded to the neighbors' judgments by refusing to put in the front-yard landscaping. In addition to having the Plymouth Roadrunner muscle car, not a family car like our neighbors, Alex also bought a brand new motorcycle. Larry, who didn't like the neighbors either, was living with us and had his dune buggy, and Alex had his work truck. Our house was not the neighborhood showplace.

Only after the neighborhood reaction against us became obvious did we notice that we didn't have anything in common with any of our neighbors. Being friends with them wasn't important because we had our own friends. Of course, these carpenters were a wild bunch. They were funny and were always looking for an outlet to let off the pressure from a hard week of work. They made a lot of money and spent it as fast as they made it. We were the youngest of them, too, but they liked and admired us.

Every weekend the street was full of our friend's vehicles. We played music, and the pool was full of kids and parents having fun. There was also a lot of laughter. The neighbors would call the police, but every time they came, they saw we were doing nothing illegal and would just leave. While it possibly wasn't the most mature response, our guests, the carpenters, would climb up on the roof and collectively moon the neighbors. There had to be ten or more of them, and it was quite a sight.

Despite the disapproval, we saw our life moving forward and were happy with it.

 LEARNING: This is what happens when people live fearful, paranoid lives. They draw what they fear to them. We were too young to understand that at the time. We were just having fun, and unwittingly being agents of delivering to them what they were creating by their judgments.

Even though things were working out well, my *guides* had a surprise in store for me. Out of the blue, I had an amazing realization that things were going to be headed in a new direction. I refer to age 19 as the best year of my life specifically because of this crystal-clear clarity my *guides* sent me.

It was instant insight, and I knew I had to find my own way without Alex. *They* made it clear that we had no long-term future together, but I didn't see why at the time. My *guides* now directed me to focus on my future, and it was my time to go into action. So, from then on out, there was no doubt in my mind that I had to make my own way. Alex had reached his peak, but I had a ways to go.

I never said anything to Alex, or anyone else. He hadn't done anything wrong, but I was being guided in a whole new direction. I knew what it felt like to actively live in two worlds at the same time; I had mastered that early on and never hesitated to take action knowing that *their* guidance always had a shelf life. That meant I had to start now or this particular opportunity would dissipate. But since this was an inner direction, once again, I just kept it to myself.

Alex had become a journeyman carpenter, and I told him I wanted to start working in the home-building business, too. He took me to meet the architect who did most of the plans for the contractors Alex's boss did work for. He was very nice to me but said he was too busy to train someone new. He didn't know what I could do, and neither did I. Although it was good to meet him, it was premature. Even so, I was clear that I wanted to learn what it would take for me to get into the building business as a profession.

 LEARNING: Even with the lifelong training I received from my *guides,* this news was sad for me. However, I knew I was at a major crossroads in my life and once again, I was being guided. Your *guides* don't think about how you may react to the timely truth *they* convey; *their* only concern is you and your wellbeing. That's *their* job.

Interestingly, I got the opportunity to gain some experience when we built our second home. In 1972, Alex told me that the same developer we bought our first home from had another subdivision going about two miles from where we lived. These homes were bigger and more customized, and they were just finishing the model homes. We went to see them and bought one based on the same "sweat equity" arrangement we made with that developer the first time. We built this new one to live in and kept our first home as an investment and rented it. We wanted to keep it because it was appreciating so quickly.

This time I handled things much more efficiently. Once we finished it, I added a swimming pool, outdoor cabana, and landscaping in the front and back yards. It turned out beauti-fully, but I was even more restless than ever.

 LEARNING: This is what it feels like when you're being guided. You feel like a horse at the racetrack, and once they open the gate you're off and running.

At about the time we got our second home, Alex got his gen-eral contractor's license and started his own framing com-pany. Together we got it rolling. I drew the contracts between the general contractors and our framing company. I took care of the accounting, the payroll, collecting the checks each week from the general contractors, and paying all the bills. I also was handling the legal aspects of the employees, union obligations, insurance, and keeping a close eye on the busi-ness profits and losses.

Alex ran the crews and controlled the quality the workers delivered. I also performed the framing pre-inspection walk-through, and once the pickup work was done, I would call for frame inspections from the city or county building inspection department, FHA and VA.

I would meet the building inspectors to walk through the buildings with them and write up corrections that needed to be made to bring them up to code. I was learning a lot and doing so quickly. It got so I would call in a half-dozen build-ings at a time for frame inspections and the inspector would check one. If it had no corrections, he would pass them all because he knew how thorough and consistent I was.

I found it easy to work with all these people. It all came natural for me, and working in a man's world was easy. Until this point, it had felt like someone had been sitting on me. Until now, I had felt totally repressed from my potential. It's not that I knew how to do all these things that became my jobs, I just felt like I could do anything because I was being guided. With *their* support <u>nothing</u> was ever out of reach for me. This is what made it so easy; *they* knew I would love both the work and the challenge.

We started our new framing business in the middle of a terrible recession. It was in 1972 during the Middle East oil crisis, when cars were lined up around the block at gas stations. The economy was contracting, but we were naïve and bold; we weren't afraid of anything. Our timing turned out to be golden because not only did we thrive in hard times, but the second year in business; we got a $30,000 tax credit for hiring so many people in a recession. I told Alex to take that money and go buy the brand new silver-blue Corvette he had always dreamed about right off the showroom floor. And that's exactly what he did.

 TIP: Even when you have no experience and everything appears bizarre to those around you, don't allow that to distract you. Move through it like you own the place because nothing can hurt you, when you have constant coaching from *your guides*.

That same year, in the summer of 1972, we were framing a subdivision of duplexes when *distant visitors* from some other place appeared in the sky. It was just before daybreak and the carpenters were unloading everything from our trucks. Once Alex's truck was unloaded, I got a telepathic message that said, *"Lie down in the back of your truck so you won't blink your eyes when we leave."* At that point, *"they"* hadn't even arrived yet, let alone left. But I knew enough to lie down like *"they"* told me.

Almost immediately a UFO showed up and hovered right over me. *Their* ship was round and silver with multi-colored lights spinning clockwise around the perimeter. Inside the perimeter, a separate set of multi-colored lights was spinning counter-clockwise.

They started speaking to me telepathically, so, I spoke back to *them* the same way. I asked *them* to take me out of here. Even with things going so well, I knew there were better places I could be. *They* told me about certain things that I needed to do and that I couldn't leave because I wasn't finished here. *They* told me not to tell anyone about this encounter until 1986.

As soon as the sun broke over the crest of the distant mountain range the ship took off so fast that I would have missed it had I blinked my eyes. *They* wanted me to see *them* leave, which is why *they* wanted me to lie down in the back of the truck in the first place.

I got up, and all the carpenters including Alex were still looking up, frozen in position. I asked them what they saw, and all of them had seen what I had seen. This confirmed that I wasn't the only one who saw it. Then, like getting a bucket of cold water thrown in their faces, Alex ordered them back to work.

The next day – same place, same time, and the same carpenters – I asked them if they remembered what they saw in the sky the day before. They all looked at me like they should be able to remember something but couldn't. Not one of them remembered anything about what happened the day before, not even Alex. Once again, it was between me and *them.*

Over time I found that when things like this happens, I never forget, but everyone else either seems to, or they never see it in the first place. Based on the guys' reactions, I didn't bring it up again, but I did wonder what 1986 would have in store.

 TIP: As you progress in your relationship with your *guides,* more *helpers* will show up. If there was any danger, your *guides* would step in by warning you or even creating an intervention.

Alex and I had a great thing going. We started getting big framing contracts for single-family and multi-family projects. This was good and bad. The contracts stated that we had to receive payouts from the general contractor every Friday to meet payroll, union obligations, and monthly state and federal payments, along with paying suppliers. All of this came to about $30,000 per week. In the early 1970s, that was a large amount of money. Everything was fine as long as the general contractor (GC) lived up to his agreement with us. But occasionally, a GC wouldn't get his construction draw and would attempt to skip a week.

One Friday I went to collect our payout check, and the GC would not even talk to me. His secretary told me that he would not have a check for us that week, and that was the end of it. That was a first, and I hadn't anticipated it. However, I found the survival skills I had been forced to learn as a child click into gear.

I could see the GC was in his office on the phone because the light was lit up on the secretary's phone. So, to gather my thoughts, I sat down and watched for the light to go out. As I pondered the situation, a solution came through from my *guides.* It was brilliant and would handle any excuse the GC had.

As soon as the light on the phone button went out, I walked over to his office door. The secretary tried to stop me, but I just walked in. The GC frowned when I entered his office and told me he didn't have our check. He angrily told me to get out. I replied calmly, saying I understood, but I was not sure if our 30 carpenters would understand. I told him I'd have them come to his house that night so he could explain the situation to them.

The guy's face went pale and he hemmed and hawed. And then he wrote the check, and we met the payroll without disruption. Paying our people on time was the magic sauce to our success. I was 20 years old, and, with the support of my *guides,* we were getting good at all of this.

Chapter 10: My New Career Surprises Everyone

The framing business was now solid, or at least as solid as any business could be in the building trades. We became the largest framing contractors in Sacramento at that time. I was very comfortable with my responsibilities and was looking to do more. I would design homes on napkins and wonder what they would look like if they were built. I really didn't want to be a builder, I just wanted to see my home designs come to life.

After coming up with a number of imaginary designs, I wondered if they would be desirable to others. I had such a strong urge to do this, and I never questioned my ability to design and build these homes that I saw so clearly in my mind. Like the building blocks in kindergarten, this was a driving passion.

I came up with a design I particularly liked and wanted to build it. So I told Alex I wanted to sell our first home, the one we were renting out, so I could buy a lot I'd found and build my first house. This time I would be building my own custom home from start to finish. He believed in me and agreed.

The proceeds from the rental house covered the cost of the lot I wanted to build on, and I paid for the lot outright. Little did I know that that would turn out to be a big mistake, but that's what I did because I didn't know any better. I went to the architect that Alex had introduced me to a few years earlier and told him I had a lot. I showed him the sketch of the home

I had designed and asked if he could help me do the plans for it. He took me under his wing and set me up in a room in his office so he could oversee me as I drafted the house plans.

This was the beginning of my ongoing apprenticeship program with him. Just like the way I learned everything else that I mastered, I was always self-taught with the keen direction of my *guides*. With *their* support, there was nothing I couldn't do. This was the same feeling I had when I first came into this life — that I could do anything once I got here. Well, now I was here and unrestrained.

Next, I needed a construction loan, but didn't know how to go about getting one. It was especially hard to get one since this was my first speculation home and I had no track record. I found a middleman who liked Alex and me, and he walked me through everything I needed to do to get a loan.

Using him was more expensive than going straight to the bank, but I needed to do it this way the first time out. I was experienced at managing and overseeing the framing business, I had taken an active hands-on part in building our first two family homes, but I had never built a home from the ground up using my own design.

I was now 21 years old. I had my building lot, my custom home design and building plans, and construction loan. I was ready to go.

It was all new to me and very exciting. As I was getting my final bids and contracts together with the subcontractors, my dad surprised me by saying he would provide his labor to put in the foundation if I helped. That was the first time ever that my dad offered to teach me his business.

 TIP: Your *guides* are the best partners you will ever have. *They* are always at work serving your best interest. Because *they* are so loyal to you, you may not appreciate *them* like you should. This doesn't hurt *them*, but it can hurt you. Observe how you treat those who are loyal to you in your life to get a better sense of your worthiness to have your *guides* in your life.

Once we started putting in the foundation, I discovered that, disguised as his offer to help, was a setup to stop me, not support me in my burning passion. Dad didn't understand why I wanted to work since we were making plenty of money in the framing business. He said I should be taking care of Cindy and be there when Alex got home like a normal mother and housewife. I couldn't believe what I was hearing. I'm sure he wanted what was best for me, but he didn't get it. This was the first time I realized that he really didn't know me. It turned out that when he came out to help me, he was really on a mission to convert me. My mother, under the guise of having my dad help me, was really attempting to derail me from my driving passion and repress me once again.

Despite my dad's judgment of me, I loved having the opportunity to learn and be in charge of my life. Then I got a reminder from my *guides* that my marriage was not destined to work out. Even though I was learning and growing, I had to do more to get my own life together separate from Alex. This was not something I could explain to my dad, or anyone for that matter.

About that same time, Cindy said she also thought I was odd because I never wore dresses, or was at home baking cookies after school like the other moms did. She wanted a mom like the other kids had and felt cheated. I told her I could never be like that. I told her I was doing what I loved.

Not surprisingly, Cindy didn't understand and was determined to either see me punished, or manipulate me into doing what she wanted. So, one day she told her kindergarten teacher that I didn't feed her. I got an urgent call demanding a meeting. I met with the teacher, and when she told me what Cindy had said, I asked her if Cindy looked undernourished. She said she didn't, and I pointed out that Cindy had succeeded in manipulating her. The teacher backed off, and Cindy didn't like it one bit.

It seems that the only ones I was making any sense to were Alex and my *guides*. Alex liked my ambition and vision going forward, but told me he had a hard time keeping up. He complained that he didn't have the energy I did and was becoming frustrated with that. But Alex also liked the idea of us becoming builders of our own homes, and he especially liked the idea of us making more money. The stage was set for that new direction in my life. Dad didn't understand, but he went along with it.

As I indicated earlier, it was actually my *guides* who set this new career of mine into motion when I was 19 years old. I loved where I was going, and I had all the support I needed from my *lifelong friends,* my *guides*. Above all else, I followed *their* guidance, regardless of any other considerations.

LEARNING: Once you develop a line of communication with your *guides,* you are set for life. It's not always easy, but there's no struggling when you walk through this life with your *guides.* All you have to do is listen and step into it. No matter who lets you down, *they* never will.

Getting bids together and scheduling were tricky for me since that was the first time I had built a house from scratch. It was a long ranch-style-single-story custom home on a corner lot right next to an undeveloped park. It was a quiet upscale neighborhood. Once Dad and I had the foundation in and ready, Alex brought in some of his framers. I paid the carpenters out of the construction-draw money. At the completion of the framing, I was back on my own to hopefully schedule in the subcontractors (subs) in the correct order and timing. I knew this was my weak spot when building that first home.

Many of these subcontractors didn't know who I was, which made it hard to get them to show up and get the work done in a timely manner. That was throwing off my scheduling of the other subcontractors. Sometimes I didn't know which subcontractor should come next. I got terrible advice from some of them that often made things worse.

I would ask Alex, but he couldn't help me because he was a framing contractor and not a home builder. He just didn't know. The architect I worked under didn't know either. Once again, I had to figure it out on my own with the help of my *guides.*

The subcontractors (subs) lied to me. They didn't show up to perform their work when they were scheduled in, which really drove me nuts. This made scheduling the other subs in impossible. It was at this point that my *guides* made me realize there was a psychology to getting them to perform. Also, the subs didn't know if they should take me seriously because I was new at this, young and female. In the early 1970s, that was a bizarre combination.

Then there were the bank draws from the construction loan to pay the subs. Receiving the bank draws was not in sync with the invoicing of the subcontractors and suppliers. When a subcontractor submits his invoice, he expects to get paid quickly because, just like Alex's framing business, the subs need their money to pay their employees and suppliers each week. I was very aware of how this worked. I also knew the subs showed up on the jobs that paid them as agreed. Slow payers suffered.

Although I had enough money from the construction loan to pay all the costs to build the house, the syncing problem was going to prevent me from keeping the subs happy. I had no choice but to sell the Plymouth Roadrunner so I had the added capital between draws to pay the subs. Even after doing that, I barely had enough reserves to cover the dry spells between draws. Paying the building lot off at the start had depleted my float capital. I saw how that had been a serious mistake. But I was learning.

Despite the mistakes and the bad judgment calls, I completed the house within budget and on time. But building that house really wore me out. Alex and I decided to sell the home we were living in, which was our second home, and move into this new one. I wanted to experience what it would be like to live in a home I had designed and built to see if I really liked it, as well as to learn what I would do differently the next time. That's exactly what we did.

Building this house had been such a traumatizing experience for me that I felt like I never wanted to build another house again. This is why I knew I needed to go right back out and design and build more homes as soon as possible. I couldn't let this one experience defeat me. I took it personally that these subcontractors made it so hard for me to get through my first building experience. I had to use that as my springboard and come out even stronger the next time.

That was my secret strategy. I didn't let anyone besides Alex know how those challenges had affected me. What I didn't know at that time was that my career in the building business was going to be the catalyst for me to work through my anger issues. This was the healing my *guides* intended for me even though I was clueless about it at that time. *They* are so clever at bringing us multiple and even limitless achievements throughout our lifetime. This is why nothing you do on your own can ever match the pure intentions your *guides* have for you.

 LEARNING: No one ever said it would be easy. Your life is your life and you came here to do the work. Your *guides* are with you to make your life easier, but *they* aren't with you to do it for you. If that were the case, then *they* would be physically here living *their* own lives, and there would be no purpose in your being here.

While this was going on, Cindy was in kindergarten. I never planned on putting her in the public school after what I had experienced as a kid, but she was nothing like I was. She was meek and loved to draw, which is why I felt that, starting from kindergarten, she would do her best in a Waldorf School. Waldorf offered a creative environment where kids were allowed to learn and approach things as they felt ready to. Their approach was not a strict regimen where teaching academics with an iron fist was all that mattered. Cindy always shut down mentally when she was required to do anything, so, for many reasons; I thought this might be the right approach for her. I was hoping that by having her in a safe and creative place to learn and play, it would mellow out her manipulative tendencies. In the end, I think it might have provided more learning opportunities for me than for her.

As things were changing in some ways, they were the same in others. For example, I was still collecting the payout checks from the General Contractors for Alex's framing work. On one occasion, I went to collect the Friday check and the GC told me he didn't have it. He said he was going on vacation and wouldn't be able to pay us until he got back. I told him okay and left. I drove back to the framing job site and picked out Stan, one of our strongest carpenters. I told him I had a job for him and explained the situation on our drive over to see the GC. I told him to remain calm while I give this guy one more chance to pay. If he still didn't come across, I would look at Stan, and he would know it was time to convince him to pay. To be fair, I told Stan not to hurt him too badly.

The GC was quite surprised when I returned with backup. I asked him if he was going to pay as agreed and he said that he wasn't. So I looked at Stan who just nodded and took a step forward. The GC looked at me, then looked at Stan, and saw the wisdom in keeping his agreement. He even apologized for not paying as agreed in the first place. Alex never knew what I did to collect.

Another of the GCs we worked with had a fancy office in a high-rise in Sacramento. He was a high-powered guy, and it looked more like an attorney's suite than a construction office. As was my routine, I called to let him know I would be coming down to collect the Friday check for our company, and he let me know he wasn't going to pay as agreed. So, when I went, I again took Stan along. I liked Stan because he was not excitable, but he knew what to do and when to do it. On this occasion he wore his wide leather belt with nail bags and his rigging ax.

We walked into this GCs office, and the guy was on the phone at his huge cherry-wood desk. He held his hand over the telephone mouth piece, and he asked me what I wanted. I told him the same thing I told him earlier; that I needed to pick up our check. He said he had already told me he wasn't going to pay that day.

I looked at Stan. Stan pulled his rigging ax out of his belt, and with one powerful swing, he sliced through the guy's fancy phone base, burying the ax into his beautiful cherry-wood desktop. Without a word. Stan backed his ax out of the top of the desk and put it back in his nail bag. The GC looked at the desk, and then looked at the dead phone in his hand. Without a word, he gingerly set the phone down, took out his checkbook, wrote a check, and handed it to me. Not a word had been said. From then on, his checks were always on time.

The interesting thing is that it seemed like we had a reputation that made us look like bullies. But that wasn't accurate. In fact, the GCs were the bullies who constantly intimidated the subcontractors with their flashy offices and authority they wielded. I saw through this because I was a master at dealing with bullies. We never pressured anyone to do anything other than what they agreed to do at contract signing. The fact is, we had obligations that had to be met no matter what. Not only did we have over 30 carpenters to pay each week, but their families also depended on them getting paid. That made me responsible for over 100 people each week. So while we sometimes felt pushed to resort to harsh measures, it was always in support of keeping these guys in line with their agreements, not trying to make them do something they hadn't already agreed to do.

 TIP: When the stakes are high and the pressure is on, you can't afford a glitch in the process. The training from your *guides* will show you that your integrity always exceeds that of others. The reason for this is that others are self-serving and not in service to others. When you have this working relationship with your *guides,* everything you do is bigger than you are.

In addition to collections and payroll, I had the responsibility of drawing up the contracts between our company and the general contractors. There were times when they wanted to negotiate the bid down, but I knew what the margin of profit was. I also knew that our cost projections were accurate only if nothing unexpected happened, so there was no room for negotiations. Alex would start to yield to these GCs beating him down on price, and I would step in and tell them that the contract price was not negotiable. Alex was intimidated by these GCs, allowing them to bully him. Having come from a childhood filled with bullies, I was an expert on how to deal with them. I never let them get away with it.

GCs always accepted our bids because they knew our prices were fair, and we had the best and fastest framing crew in Sacramento at that time. We were in high demand. At signing with new GCs, I always made them understand the importance of the Friday Check Rule, and that I would be personally coming to collect it. I told them that this is one of the primary reasons our company could perform as we did. I emphasized we had a zero-tolerance policy for collecting that check on Fridays — no exceptions, not ever!

This contract signing dance with these GCs let them know that I was a force to be reckoned with, though not all of them understood that at the time. They sure understood it after the first time they tried to miss a payment.

I never questioned my abilities; I just knew what to do and when to do it. I was reaping the rewards from what I learned early in life that I couldn't have pulled off if it wasn't for what I learned from my *guides*.

Once our framing work had been done, it had to be inspected, and I had a system for making sure we always passed. Before the inspection, I would grab a few carpenters and a laborer or two. We would start with the first building and, as I spotted deficiencies, the pickup crew would work together to correct them. I knew exactly what to look for and could see things that needed correcting because I was coming to the building for the first time and was seeing it with fresh, though trained, eyes.

We would go right down the line and get these frames ready. I started choosing the same guys, and over time, I developed a team that was really excellent. They took pride in having these pre-frame inspection walk-throughs with me. They tried so hard to get them right before I showed up that they were beginning to feel like they had personally let us down when I found deficiencies. To show my appreciation for their exceptional work, I gave them bonuses as the pickup lists got shorter. They deserved it, and we were great together.

The building inspectors loved coming out to our jobs. We had the cleanest frames in town. Our reputation was impeccable. The GCs had never seen anything like it. That's why they listened when we had a complaint and demanded the Friday checks. Besides, they didn't want a visit from Stan.

 LEARNING: My formal education and family training did not prepare me for any of this. My self-education and prospering had everything to do with my *guides*. Through the life-coach training I received from *them,* along with the direct line of communication I have had with *them,* it's easy for *them* to reach and guide me. Nothing is impossible when you have your *guides* on your side. Together you can literally pull off miracles.

Chapter 11: Unstoppable Success — First Warning

The framing business continued to grow and so did the challenges. We had to be union compliant, and that made it much more expensive to operate, be competitive, and make a profit. To be able to survive, Alex always had some non-union labor to trim expenses.

The union business agents (BAs) would show up on Alex's job sites unannounced to make sure everyone was a union member in good standing. Our crew members understood the situation and were sympathetic to it, so the carpenters were always on the lookout for the BAs.

The non-union guys (what the unions called scab labor) were trained to run off the job site immediately when a BA showed up. The fine for getting caught would have been thousands of dollars per incident. Alex never got caught, but it was a nuisance.

 TIP: You need to apply yourself in a direction that you are naturally good at and have a passion to do. Add the help of your *guides* to the mix and you become unstoppable.

In spite of being in our early 20s, Alex and I had proven we had what it took to run a successful construction business. At least, that's what I thought until we received notice of a union audit. Alex was instructed to meet the carpenters' union business agent (BA) at a bar to talk about the audit, and I went with him to hear what it was all about.

Alex was scared, which is what really concerned me the most. The BA told Alex that he could get the audit lifted by paying him $10,000 cash. Alex was grateful, but I stepped in and said we'd think about it. Alex was going to cave into this pressure. I told him no way because this guy was an extortionist and would never stop coming back for more. Besides, in his eyes, paying them off just proved your guilt.

I told Alex I would work with our accountant to make sure the books jibed with the union reporting. Our accountant understood, and he worked very hard on it with me. When we were done, we had stellar books and were ready for that union audit. Alex was still scared, but I assured him that I had it covered. Then along came the auditors.

They spent a week at our accountant's office going through everything. It was a nerve-wracking month before we got a formal response to their fine-tooth-comb audit. We were informed that we had no violations and not only did we not owe the carpenters union any money, we received a refund for over-payment. This was unheard of — no one ever got a refund from a union audit!

Around that same time, our union agreement came up for renewal. I informed them that we would not be renewing it. After seeing Alex almost agree to the extortion demands of that BA when we met him at the dark creepy bar, I was concerned that the union BAs might show up on the framing job site and pressure Alex to sign back up again. There wasn't anything I could do if he did, so I told him I had gotten him out of trouble with this union audit, but I couldn't do anything if he signed up with them again. He promised he wouldn't sign.

No more than a week later, the union BAs showed up on the framing job site and Alex signed back up. I was totally disgusted with him — I lost respect for him. Alex had lost touch with his personal power and everything it took for us to achieve the successes we had. There was nothing I could do about it, and, as a result, I was losing interest in helping him. His weakness was putting more pressure on me.

I didn't understand what was wrong with him because he had been so strong and focused. I felt like he was leaning on me more instead of holding up his part. It appeared that the stress was getting to him. I already had more than I could handle, so I really resented him for that. Even so, I wasn't going to let him derail my ambitions to continue to design and build my homes.

In one of our conversations about our businesses, Alex told me that he was envious of my high energy. He said he couldn't understand why I had so much energy and he didn't. He felt like he was struggling just to keep up. Alex wasn't the only one telling me this. Everyone I worked with in the business either called me a speed freak or a slave driver. They actually accused me of being on cocaine, which was something I would never use. Everyone had a hard time keeping up with me and would tell me my expectations were too high. But that's what made them respect and believe in me. Everything I promised I delivered, and they knew they could count on me.

LEARNING: This is a perfect example of people working without a compass. Their *guides* are the compass, and they aren't using *them* — they don't even know *they* exist. These people think that life is supposed to be hard and that you are on your own. That's just not true. They claim they lack energy, when that's not the problem at all. It's like they're struggling against the current. So, no wonder they feel like they are missing something when they encounter someone who relies on their compass, their *guides*. This is when jealously starts to surface.

In addition to all the ongoing and increasing demands of the framing business, I was determined to continue my home design and building businesses. As soon as I got the second family home sold and recovered from building my first custom home, I took some of the profit and bought three more lots nearby. I designed three different custom homes under my mentor architect's supervision.

This time I went directly to the bank to get my construction loans. I had learned my lesson. I didn't deplete my reserves by purchasing the lots outright. I had the seller of the lots subordinate to the construction loans. That meant the lot owner got paid off for each lot when the completed home was sold and closed escrow. That gave me the float capital (money) I needed between draws to keep the subs paid so they remained loyal to me. I was driven to design new homes and see them materialize, something like having to have those building blocks every day in kindergarten. This drive was so strong, it was like I was possessed.

LEARNING: This is what it feels like when you are being guided. You always have more than enough energy. You're always right where you should be at just the right time, doing the right thing. By this point, I had come to realize it wasn't all about the money. I was living an unstoppable life because of all the passion that fueled me, backed by my *guides*. With all that happening nothing could stop me, I was on fire.

This time when I started building these homes, I knew how to schedule in the subs without guessing. They were getting to know me and were much more cooperative. In addition to already having built a custom home, I also was able to capitalize on my reputation from my years in our framing company. Plus, building three houses at one time gave me more leverage with the subs. They knew others were bidding against them, and they wanted the work.

Everything was different this time around. For one thing, the homes all sold at the frame stage. For another, I made a very good profit on them, and the bank was eager to loan me more to build my next set of homes. I was really on my way.

With the completion of these three homes, I thought my dad had begun to recognize that I was actually going to be successful in the construction business. So, one day, he asked me to give my older brother, Randy, a job. Randy was a foundation subcontractor, just like my dad. Randy was also whiny and spoiled as a result of my mother's coddling. He was definitely not my favorite person, but I gave him a job because of my dad. I would do anything for my dad.

Despite it being a favor, Randy was disdainful about the job. His resentment toward me was obvious. He tended to be a victim, and he complained a lot. For some strange reason he felt like things had always been given to me whereas he had to work hard for what he got. I have no idea why he thought that since I had to make something out of nothing, while thanks to my parents, he got a free college education, a free car, and a house Mom and Dad built for him.

When Randy grudgingly finished the first job, I paid him and never hired him again. My mom took issue with that, which revealed it was she who had made my dad ask me to give Randy work in the first place. Then, to my surprise, she told me to take care of family because family comes first. I couldn't believe what she was saying after her non-stop abuse and doing what she could to make my childhood a total hell and attempt to derail my every success. If this is what taking care of family is about, then count me out.

Since I would not hire Randy again, Mom was, once again, angry with me and built more resentment against me. Dad understood why I did what I did and that I wasn't going to be manipulated.

 LEARNING: There is nothing a bully hates more than losing control. If a bully does lose control to someone, getting even becomes their obsession. So, if you best a bully, expect that they will take another shot at you. In the meantime, do your best to stay away from them.

Even while I was managing my own building projects, I kept up my responsibilities with the framing business. I never let

Alex down, and I always used Alex's framers to frame my houses.

Before my second project even closed escrow, I had reservations on five more lots in a nearby subdivision. I was able to arrange the same subordination deal with the land developer because now I had a track record and a great reputation.

I designed those homes and built them in record time. I could have sold them in their frame stage as I had done with the previous three homes, but these were appreciating so fast that I decided to build them out and offer them for sale after completion. This not only made me more money, but it also eliminated the hassles of dealing with homeowners wanting to make changes.

It addition to being a home builder, designer, and running the framing business, the subcontractors were always confiding in me. Sometimes their personal needs would take up more than ten hours of my time in a week. I didn't feel like I could just ignore them because they were sincerely looking for answers. In many cases, I was as young as their kids, so I was surprised they would look to me for advice.

It turned out that this would be my next calling in life, although I didn't recognize it at that time. This is how our *guides* work with us as *they* prepare us for what's next – whether we're aware of what's coming or not.

 TIP: Many times you will be sought out for something that has nothing to do with your current career. Pay attention when this shows up. This is what others really value in you and need. You have many talents, so follow the ones that have the strongest pull at any given time because you are being guided in that direction, and that's where your strongest supporters can be found; your *guides*.

While I was in the middle of my third project, a man that came to visit with me at my building site asking me if I would build one of my floor plans on his Folsom Lake home site. This is called a build-to-suit house. I was warned by many in the business to never build-to-suit. I was told it would be a losing proposition because you could never make the home-owner happy no matter what you did. I was aware of build-to-suit, and hearing this advice made me curious.

I met with the man at his lot. The terrain was very steep, and the lot fronted Folsom Lake — what a view! He told me that he was going to import dirt and create a level pad to build the house on. I told him that would take a lot of material and compaction would be a problem, no matter what he used or how well it was compacted. It was just going to take too much material and that drilling pylons deep into the natural soil was the only way to go, which would be very expensive. He tried to assure me that it would be a stable building pad. I told him I would only build his house if he signed a "hold harmless" agreement releasing me from a building pad failure. He agreed.

I built the house for him, and the experience turned out exactly as I was told it would – problem after problem. The guy tried to avoid releasing my final draw by nitpicking me about everything. He laughed at me like I was an easy tar-get. Then, no surprise to me, about a year later, the house started to have settling problems: the doors wouldn't close, and the drywall and stucco were cracking as were the driveway, patios, and walkways.

The owner called me and told me about the situation, which he called structural failures. I told him these were all signs of an unstable building pad showing early signs of failure. I told him to have an engineer evaluate the situation. Indeed, the building pad was settling, and soon after that, severe erosion set in. Nothing could save his house.

For safety reasons, his house was condemned by the county, and the owner was ordered to vacate. Thankfully, I was clearly not liable. What an experience. To me it was more about the challenge because doing the same thing over again was like torture to me. I wasn't afraid of anything, but I sure was glad to have some of those challenges behind me.

 LEARNING: Just because someone tells you not to do something doesn't mean you should not do it. Even if what they say proves true, it's not useful to you until you have your own experience.

Throughout the time I was working on the homes I was building, I was also working at being a mother. I had always loved ice-skating, but with work and all, I didn't have the time to pursue it. Eventually I bit the bullet, though, and took Cindy to the ice arena.

The rental skates were awful, but it was our first time and just a start. Cindy really fought it. She pitched a fit, throwing herself down on the ice, kicking and crying and insisting she couldn't do it. I just let her work through it while skating by her. She had so much frustration and anger, and I thought skating would be a way for her to channel that energy in a beautiful, self-confident way.

It wasn't looking like my idea would work, and then I got another idea. I took Cindy to the ice arena's retail shop where they sold beautiful skating outfits and skates. Cindy loved the figure-skating outfits and suddenly, skating looked like it might be fun. She got her first little ice-skating dress, stockings, leg warmers and gloves. Now she couldn't wait to go skating again in her beautiful new getup.

After a few more times ice-skating, she wanted her own skates, so I got her a pair and a beginner teaching coach. She loved her coach and began taking lessons three days a week plus practicing at open skating sessions five days a week. She was really doing well and becoming a beautiful figure skater. I was also hoping that it would help her work through her anger. Hope springs eternal, they say.

As my home building business prospered, I found I had a new situation to deal with: taxes. I faced a big tax bite because of the windfall profits from building and selling so many homes. To shelter some of the profits, I built two custom duplexes to hold and rent.

I also bought 7.5 acres of raw land that I developed into 30 single-family home lots. These were my first production homes. I anticipated that the ratio between the costs of the lot to the house was going to be a lot smaller than what I had been used to.

I built three model homes in a record-breaking 21 calendar days. That included building, full landscaping, and interior furnishings. Some people in the neighboring subdivision were astounded. They left home for a vacation with empty lots around them and returned home to find completed houses.

Every project I did was unique and completely different from the one before. Each was a new experience, which is what made it so much fun for me. But I was beginning to get tired, and I started feeling like a machine.

The times had been on my side because I entered this business during an upswing. But then, I got the first warning from my *guides* that there was going to be a real estate crash. *They* also told me my marriage was going to end, and that Cindy was going to take it personally.

I got that message in 1976, but I didn't know when the crash would show up. I did know it was coming and that it would change everything.

 TIP: When you're guided, the timing of things is no respecter of your convenience. The timing is what it is. Your job is to be open to the truth when it reveals itself and act without hesitation.

One day when I was driving between job sites, an interesting thing happened: I went out of my body, and from high above, I watched myself driving in the traffic like one of the many rats in a rat race doing the same thing and going to the same places day after day. I sensed that what seemed so important and larger than life was really small, and everyone was mindlessly chasing after the same thing. I was beginning to detach from what had gotten me so far so fast.

I kept moving on my projects, and while I was developing the acreage where I was building the production homes, I was also building three large executive showcase homes I had designed. I was building one of them for us to live in. Building these homes received a lot of media attention. My home designs were unlike anything anyone was building at that time. They were ahead of their time, yet timeless.

Chapter 12: Second Warning — And I Listen

By the time I started building the three showcase homes, change was in the air. It was palpable — but only to me.

So many realizations occurred to me in that year. It was made clear to me by my *guides* that the time had come to sell everything and stop planning out into the future before things flip-flopped.

They showed me that things that worked before were no longer going to work. It was just the beginning of the warning signs that I would continue to receive from *them*. My *guides'* timely warnings let me know I had the time I needed to plan and regroup so I would not be crushed under the impending real estate crash, the end of my marriage, and Cindy's reaction to all of it.

It was 1976 when I first got *their* warning. Trusting myself and changing in an instant was what I had mastered in childhood, thanks to my *trusted advisors,* my *guides.* That came from seeing things for what they really were and adapting.

Colleagues, along with my accountants, bankers, and attorneys, watched me sell everything while the market continued to boom. They all told me I was nuts. They even said that I was creating the crash because of what I was doing, treating me like I was a traitor. But I never let what others thought of me, or how they judged me, affect my better judgment. That was another skill I had perfected as a kid. I was used to doing unconventional things based on trusting and knowing myself and my *guides*.

To say that I was operating out of the box is an understatement. There was nothing I could do or say to convince anyone about what was coming. Again I found myself in an experience like the *merry-go-round dream* illustrated – they couldn't be reached.

At this same time, the media discovered me: a young successful woman designing and building homes in the Sacramento area. I was 24 years old and not looking for attention; I really had no time for it. I had my hands full with completing my projects and handling my part of our framing businesses, not to mention a husband who was falling apart. I had always had a lot of energy, and even that wasn't enough to continue doing all the things I did. I was over-extended in every way except financially.

 LEARNING: When your *guides* warn you of some impending danger or change, you need to listen and take action. When *they* warn you repeatedly, you really need to listen, and really need to take action.

We were in the fifth year of building our businesses. I began to see that the success we had gained changed us both. We no longer had time for each other except when it came to business. I managed to take Cindy on trips and get her into sports. Any spare time I had I spent with her.

Alex was becoming cranky and unpredictable. Once we moved into the showcase home I built, living with him became even more difficult. I really didn't understand what was wrong with him and why he was becoming so angry. My way of dealing with it was to steer clear of him as much as possible. As a result, there was no family life in the new family home. Alex loved the new home but had lost his connection to his family. The end of our marriage was coming, just like my *guides* had told me it would five years earlier.

Not long after moving into our new home, one of Alex's carpenters came to me and hit me with a startling revelation. Apparently not only was Alex unfaithful to me, he had a long string of girlfriends. He said that Alex hardly ever showed up on the job site anymore. Alex was treating his carpenters badly, and they saw him losing touch with reality. They resented him and wanted to see him fail.

The warnings from my *guides* that had started coming in about a year earlier were now beginning to reveal themselves on all fronts. It was like dominoes falling. I had already stopped buying land to build new homes. I was now a year into building out and completing my subdivision — the five custom homes and two other showcase homes. I was also selling my rental properties.

No one in my circle saw what I saw coming. When they asked me why I was pulling back, all I could tell them was the same thing I told them before: I saw a real estate crash coming. I was 25 years old and I was really in this alone. I couldn't believe people were so blind to reality. Though no one else agreed with me, I knew my *guides* had it right.

In 1977, I went to my first National Association of Home Builders (NAHB) convention for the Sacramento area. I found it to be a collection of the most arrogant older men I could have ever imagined. I had never made time to go to these events because I was way too busy. Even so, they knew who I was.

Although I was incredibly successful, they treated me like a secretary. They smiled at me and laughed and blew me off. I was of no consequence to them, as they, had underestimated me, like so many others before.

What I was hearing them talk about made me laugh. They believed that their successes were all because of them. I jumped in at one point asking if they really believed that. They said they absolutely did. I laughed out loud, partly because they refused to see what was happening and that it was about to wipe them all out.

There was no reaching these egomaniacs. It was not us who had created the real estate boom; all it took was being in the right place at the right time. Going to this event only reinforced what I knew: that this coming real estate correction was way overdue, and I suspected it would be bigger than just a real estate correction.

 LESSON: This is a perfect example of people taking total credit for the guidance that put them in the right place at the right time in the first place. Other self-help authors have referred to this as the ego: Easing God Out. Ego is self-serving and it weighs you down with your own self-importance. Nothing ever stays the same, and peoples' egos will eventually crush them because the ego does not like change.

Cindy was in the third grade at the Waldorf School she had attended since kindergarten. It was not working out for her. Neither the teachers nor I could figure out why, under these stress-free conditions, Cindy wouldn't apply herself. She was not self-motivated at all. Her grades were suffering, and she was really falling behind academically.

Cindy told me she wanted to be like the regular kids and go to the public school. I was really surprised to hear that. I was obviously over-protecting her. Because her performance meant she probably wouldn't be placed into her grade level at the public school, I enrolled her into another private school designed to catch her up. The plan was that by spending her fourth-grade year in this "catch up" school, she would be able to enter the public school system at her grade level. Her fourth grade year was very stressful for her, but because she chose to go to the public school, she was willing to do it this way instead of being embarrassed later when she couldn't keep up. Happily, the transition into fifth grade at the public school went smoothly.

 LEARNING: Everything that happens in your life happens *for* you and not *to* you. The decisions that people make usually have nothing to do with you, they are just living their lives the best way they can. It will all work out for you if you don't take it personally. Your *guides* see what's going on, so ask *them* for help when you need it. *They* will keep you on track.

The momentum of the real estate boom in the 1970s was what allowed me to get out clean. No one thought it could end — no one wanted it to. They weren't willing to see the signs right in front of them. Not only was I selling every real

estate investment I had, I was planning a divorce and a property settlement. Winding down and severing ties with Alex
took all the energy I could conjure up because, at this point,
I was really tired. All the years of building up what we had
were coming to a close.

This was the conclusion that my *guides* had shown me in
1971, when I was 19, when *they* told me our marriage would
come to an end, and by then, I would be able to make it on my
own. It took seven years to come full circle — 1971 through
1978. But come to pass it certainly did.

 TIP: Many times your *guides* show you the beginning
and the conclusions of an event at the same time, or
in reverse order. That's because there is no time where
they are, so when things happen, it isn't linear for *them*.
Your job is not to over-think it, or inject too much
analysis into it so you cancel out what came through
by second-guessing the direction that you are being
guided to move into. Consider this to be a new language
that you need to learn — open your mind, don't close it.

Bringing things to a conclusion exposed the totality of what
had been building under the surface for years.

I remember driving down to Sacramento to get a final building permit when I saw a homeless man wasting away on a
park bench, and I just broke down crying. In that moment,
I knew my *guides* were showing me the path that Alex was
destined for. I also knew that staying married to him was
not the answer. It was shocking and unexpected. In that
instant, *they* also showed me that Alex didn't cheat on me,

he cheated on himself. Suddenly I was no longer hurt by his infidelity because once again, I was seeing it for what it was. That insight stopped me from taking it personally, thanks again to my *guides*.

Around that time, Cindy came home from school one day saying that almost all her friends' parents were getting divorced. She was bragging that she was practically the only one whose parents were still together. She thought it was funny. After just one year in the new public school environment, Cindy not only adapted, she thrived. She liked the politics and head games that went on. She was a bully and played out her games of manipulation on everyone she could. She fit right in.

She was the exact opposite of me in school. She had become the very thing I tried so desperately to shield her from. She was out of touch and ego-driven. In that moment, I sat her down and informed her that her dad and I were getting divorced. What a sobering moment that was for her.

Cindy was nine years old, and she had pretty much everything she could have ever wanted — except that her dad was never good at being a dad. He never took the time with her growing up, and he was pretty immature. In light of this, I asked her why she was upset that we were getting divorced since she was never close to her dad. She couldn't answer me.

In that moment, I told Cindy that she should consider becoming an actress. I told her that if she didn't direct her natural tendency to manipulate and create drama in her life in another direction, it would turn on her in negative ways later on. She was surprised to hear that. It was the sweet-and-sour moment of truth. It addressed her negative tendencies and showed her how to direct them in a positive way. I knew I couldn't change her, only show her a path that would support her and prevent her from falling into a life of self-created torment. I wondered if she would turn out to be one of those people that couldn't be reached.

 TIP: Being a parent doesn't mean you own your kids. They come in the way they are. It's really that simple. You can try to give them direction, but it's their life to do what they want. If they turn out to be someone you're proud of, you can't take credit for it. If they turn out to be someone who disappoints you, you can't take the blame either. They don't come from you, they come through you.

After letting Cindy know my plans, I began to consider the changes I would be going through. I was going to need to become more than just a businesswoman; I needed to learn personal social skills. I had gotten married at 16, had a baby, became a skilled businesswoman, and built our businesses. But I had no idea what it was like to have friends or go out on a date. I had no reference for what was supposed to happen when you agree to go out to dinner and a movie with someone. I was 26 years old and only just discovering how uncomfortable I was in personal social settings.

The support I got came directly from my *guides. Their* intuitive messages showed me what to do and when to do it. In hindsight, I might have made a good undercover agent or something like that. I could keep secrets, had a well-developed line of communication with my *guides* who provided me with timely insights, I never let anyone get too close, and because of my *guides,* I had a great sense of timing. My *guides* always showed me when to take action and when to retreat. But socially, I had a lot to learn, and that made me very uncomfortable.

Until now, my work had served me well. I used it as a total outlet, completely bypassing the need for personal social interaction. Work was my safe haven. The divorce and change in the economy had placed a spotlight on this deficiency, and it was embarrassing.

The changes happening for Alex really surprised him. In his mind, his girlfriends weren't acting right. He couldn't understand what was wrong with them, because if they were his girlfriends, they shouldn't be looking at other men and going out with them. This was his reasoning and something he wasn't used to dealing with. They reminded him of his alcoholic mother who slept with anyone and everyone. Alex ended up beating up every girlfriend he had.

None of that type of behavior had gone on in our marriage because I was the opposite of those girls. He assumed that everyone would be like me. What he didn't realize was that I knew his hot buttons and deliberately steered clear of setting him off. I mastered this when I was growing up, thanks to my *guides* and my mom. Alex never had a long-term relationship again.

Because I wasn't distracted with personal relationships, I had valuable quiet time to detect the subtle messages that came from my most *trusted advisors,* my *guides. They* had always pointed me in the right direction at just the right time, making my life spectacular. *They* skillfully guided me through the successes while steering me clear of dangers. *They* walked with me as I experimented and learned. It felt like I was cheating because I got to do what I wanted the way I wanted with *them* by my side. Everyone else always complained and struggled. I didn't have to.

However, I could feel I was about to go in an entirely new direction. My *guides* were making it clear that the home building business would be a shadow of what it used to be, at least for me. I became aware that I had gotten what I needed from it. To my amazement, viewing it in retrospect, the experience included resolving my anger issues, something I completely didn't see while I was going through it. This is how brilliant your *guides* work to bring you into wholeness.

I only saw it when I was on the other side of it. It was like finishing a book: suddenly that part of my life was over. It was more of a success than I realized. However, part of me wished I could go back to prepare better, because I had no other skills; or at least nothing that I could identify as a skill. I became very concerned about where I would go from there, but it was crystal clear that I could never go back.

 TIP: When you experience so much success, it's a good thing until you get a message from your *guides,* as I did, that it's time to change. Now what do you do? What you do is let go and move into new directions that interest you. Who knows how different my life would have been had I just done that at that exact moment. Again, as I said earlier, change is only difficult when you're focused on what you might be giving up. The greater and longer the successes were, the harder it is to let go and step into change.

I was trying to see what was coming after real estate, but nothing was showing up. I'd always been able to see what was next, but this time I felt like I was in the ocean without a paddle. I started to realize what other people must feel like most of the time without the support from *trusted advisors* like I always had. It was a very humbling feeling, but I knew there was a reason I wasn't getting any guidance on the matter, so I just shrugged my shoulders and got moving with my life. I felt tired, but I couldn't let anyone know because I wasn't quite through it all yet. As much as I wanted this to be over, I needed to stay more focused than ever to bring everything to completion.

Chapter 13: Everyone's Reaction to Change

Moving on and out of the real estate phase of my life became harder than I thought it would be. The divorce was dragging on because Alex would not let me go. He would not sign the divorce papers, the escrow papers on the houses I finished and sold, or the settlement agreement.

I discovered he was having me followed, and I had to hire a private investigator to find out why. Just before the settlement agreement and divorce were finalized, I discovered through the private investigator that Alex was dealing drugs. Apparently he had been doing it for years. I had filed for divorce because of his infidelity. That was small potatoes compared to this! What I couldn't wrap my head around was why he would do this when we had all the money we needed. I came to the conclusion that, for him, it was about power. He was able to control people through the lure of drugs.

I had to take Cindy out of school and get her a private tutor because Alex threatened to kidnap her. At one point, the guys Alex hired to follow me shot bullets through the back window of my car when Cindy was with me. That was surreal, and things were becoming much worse than I ever thought they would.

After the shooting incident, I had a restraining order placed against Alex. Then I was contacted by the police Victims of Crime division who offered me protection. My freedoms were threatened because everyone wanted me to crawl into a corner and hide. That was not for me, and it really angered me.

I told my private investigator I refused to allow my life to be restricted like that. So he took me to buy a gun and get a permit to carry it. I also went to school to learn how to shoot it. I knew Alex wasn't doing what he did because he loved me, it was because I provided the only stability he ever had, and I made lots of money. I learned that not only was Alex selling drugs, but was taking them, too. Upon reflection, I finally understood why he had been so erratic over the last several years. I over-estimated Alex. I thought he was smarter and stronger than he really was.

It turned out that my achievements and my making more money than Alex did make him feel inadequate. He always told me that he was envious of my high energy. It turns out that he was serious about that, and his solution to getting more energy was to take cocaine.

While I was going through the divorce, my mother told me how I made my dad feel inadequate. I was shocked to hear that. Dad was always my hero; why would he ever feel that way? According to Mom and just about everybody else, I made everything look so easy. She said I made more money in one year than Dad did in his best five. All this was just an echo for me, hearing this time and time again in one form or another. How did I do this all on my own? I didn't. I had help all along the way — I knew I was being guided. I had fun doing it, I was successful doing it, and that's what made it look easy.

She said Dad told her that what he learned from me was that he didn't take enough risks in his life. I never talked to Dad about it, but I didn't agree with his reasoning.

The times Dad lived in would not have supported the way I did things. Timing is everything. Add to this the heavy load my dad had to carry supporting the family as the sole provider. What Dad could have said that would have made more sense is that he wished he could have been born in a different time. It's all about timing, no matter how good you are at what you do.

 AWARENESS: This is what regret looks like. For my dad to perceive me the way he did was evidence that he had regrets in his life. He was not living in the flow with the help of his *guides;* instead, he was making decisions based on lack and fear. Of course, this just draws those negative qualities to you as it compounds.

Though I was on the verge of being completely clear of the threat of the real estate correction, the divorce was dragging dangerously out and keeping me in the market. Then my private investigator informed me that Alex was being watched by the police narcotics division. He said they were planning a sting to take him down, and they were going to do it soon. Time was short if I wanted to finalize things.

The last group of homes was finished, sold, and ready to close escrow, but I needed Alex's sign-off. With the impending real estate crash that no one believed was going to happen, and discovering Alex's drug dealing and coming bust, I had no more time to wait for Alex to comply. It was now or never! I was not scared because I was not alone; *they* were with me.

The first thing I did was notify the private investigator that I was going to call Alex and inform him that we were going to meet to sign the divorce papers. I would meet him in a public place, breaking the restraining order. I was going to bring my loaded gun, and I would tell Alex to do the same. I knew things could get messy and possibly only one of us would walk away from the meeting. I know this sounds extreme, but I felt it was absolutely necessary. Before the private investigator could object, I hung up the phone.

Then I called Alex and set up the meeting. As soon as we met, I put the divorce papers down on the table, turned them around facing him, laid down a pen, and told him to start signing. Before he signed, he smiled at me and said that this was what he always loved about me. I just shook my head and pushed the divorce papers closer to him. He asked me if everything was split equally and I told him it was. That's when he started signing. He never read the documents, contracts, escrow papers, or tax returns. I had always handled that so why would he start questioning me now? Besides, he knew he could always trust me, even in this situation.

We met at the escrow office the next day to sign all the papers so we could close the remaining home sales. That was the end of our marriage, our business together, and my contact with him. It was also my ticket to escaping the coming housing crash. In hindsight, he delayed everything because he wasn't accepting reality. When he realized it was over, it ended on mutually good terms.

TIP: Keeping a cool head will allow you to achieve things and handle them quickly. Don't get caught up in the what-ifs and drama. Your *guides* are masters at keeping it real.

After we finalized the paperwork, Alex left me alone. About two weeks later the police busted him. They found what they were looking for, and after a long trial that depleted Alex financially, he went to prison. Because they were watching him for so long, they knew I was never a party to his drug dealings. They never bothered me or questioned me at all. Like in the bubble dream, I was protected.

Three months after the divorce was final, the real estate market started crashing. I was completely cashed out, but everyone I knew was affected. Many went bankrupt and lost everything, including their superficial marriages, partnerships, expensive exotic cars, and mansions. The few that got out before the crash continued thinking they were hot stuff. I told them what I thought of them. I just didn't care what anyone thought of me. I finally stopped going to places where I might run into them.

I was concerned about how all the changes, turmoil, and violence was affecting Cindy, so I found a psychologist she could talk to because I was too close to it. Cindy was now ten years old. These sessions went on for about three months, and one day she told me she didn't want to go anymore. She said she wasn't learning anything. I was talking to the psychologist periodically, but the counseling sessions were private between Cindy and the psychologist.

When Cindy said she didn't want to go anymore, I spoke to the psychologist about it. She was completely brainwashed with all of Cindy's manufactured lies and manipulations. Cindy just got bored with her. I surmised that she was no longer a challenge. I told the psychologist that she had been conned by a kid just like the kindergarten teacher had been. That was the end of that. The only thing Cindy learned from that was how easy it was to con people, even trained and educated professionals.

From the time I was first forewarned by my *guides* about the real estate crash in 1976, it took me about 18 months to finish all my projects, sell all the houses and rental properties I had accumulated, and get out of my marriage. Selling everything just before real estate crashed was good and bad because cutting it that close made the last home buyers angry with me. They realized they bought at the peak and didn't like it.

Several of them sued me, asking for their money back. Of course, they had no grounds, and every case was thrown out of court. Still, I learned to never cut it that close again. Everyone I knew in the business got caught with lots of inventory and was hit hard. Of course, these were the same guys who thought they created their successes in the first place and who had ignored my warnings. They had also ignored the warnings from the best advisors: their *guides*, the *ones* who originally brought them all that success.

About six months after I had resolved all the issues pending with my life and business, I found myself between exhaustion and feeling lost. Since I didn't know what else to do other than real estate, I just treaded water. I was very selective about properties and just built a few houses at a time, working on a much smaller scale than I had been used to, but it wasn't fun anymore. For the first time in my life, I was working to make a living not because I liked it.

Despite this, I decided to buy some undeveloped land in a great location in the nearby city of Carmichael. It was zoned for duplexes, so I had the engineering done and submitted plans to the county for approval. While that was pending, I took a vacation — a cruise through the Caribbean for two weeks by myself. It was 1979, and I had just turned 27. I realized I had already lived a whole lifetime and was not even 30 yet. It all happened so fast that I felt out of sync.

I also noticed that slowing down was painful. It was easier and more exciting in the fast lane. It had been much simpler working at something I loved and being supported by the boom times. The *merry-go-round dream* that I was still having came to mind, and I saw that the faster the *merry-go-round dream* went the better I felt. However, just like with the real estate correction that no one wanted to believe was coming, I saw that the people in the dream couldn't be reached.

Returning home from the cruise, I was hit with two shocks. The first was that the interest rate on my new subdivision was 21.5 percent. The other was a very powerful intuitive message from my *guides*. I was shown a future where I would no longer be able to be the recluse I had been. As a professional, I always knew what to do and how to act. But, as I indicated earlier, in my personal life, I didn't have a clue about what to do since I had never had a personal life. I felt an immediate hit to my ego – fear — something I didn't even know was there.

In an instant I was scared, embarrassed, ashamed, and confused. I was always sure of myself and felt I knew who I was. But this powerful moment of truth made me instantly doubt all that. This was a great humbling, and in that single moment, *they* showed me what was to come.

For the first time ever I was scared of what was to come for me personally.

 AWARENESS: There are times when you get an instant knowing. It's always from your *guides. They* see something coming that needs your attention. The stronger the feeling, the more you need to take heed.

The real estate crash put my little brother Larry out of work, so I had let him live with Cindy and me again. When I returned home from the cruise, I found him very unstable emotionally. He was angry that he didn't have work, and his anger hadn't resolved itself as mine had over the previous seven years. His had continued to build, and I had to find him another place to live because I was concerned for our safety.

In the meantime, I started building the duplexes in my new subdivision. That was a nice project that made me money even in a terrible recession. It was the perfect location and product for that time. It also gave Larry work, which mellowed him out. This subdivision kept me going for the next few years. Little did I realize that I was given the project as a time-out to work through my personal life-skill deficiencies that I hadn't previously had an opportunity to develop. That was all the doing of my *guides*.

 TIP: Even though I felt like a bomb had been dropped on me when my *guides* first let me know that I needed to tend to my social and personal life deficiencies, *they* supported me in moving in that direction by having the duplex project. *They* gave me the time I would need and a project that provided financial support to work on this. The lesson here is that your *guides* never just tell you what you need to do, *they* also provide the support you need so you can achieve it. This only works if you are listening and then act on it.

Despite things going well financially for us, Cindy was becoming more and more insecure. She was drawing pictures of herself crying and me with bloodshot eyes. Her perception of me was bizarre. When she drew pictures of the family, I was always the big person in the picture.

The divorce brought out abandonment issues in her and a need for approval from men. The poor father role that Alex had played was now affecting her. It came up because it was over, he was gone, and there was no "dad" for her. She was clinging to anyone she could, especially men.

Cindy didn't know her dad had gotten busted for drugs and was facing a prison sentence. That didn't come out until much later when my mother presented Cindy with a news story about Alex's bust and prison sentence. Cindy was in shock. My mom loved dropping that bomb on her.

I was very concerned about Cindy. I let her know about the times before her dad lost his way that he tried really hard and was smart. I also told her that him selling and using drugs were some of the reasons I had to divorce him. She was beginning to understand.

I would have made a shift out of the building business sooner if I had known what to shift into. But I didn't have a clue, and I felt frozen, like something was holding me back. That was the first time in my life that I didn't have a clear direction — or at least I didn't recognize one.

Now that I was on my own, my mother started telling me to send Cindy to a boarding school. I thought she was way off base suggesting this and told her I would never do that. I warned her to never bring it up again. (I would find out years later that what she told me to do with Cindy was what happened to her when she was about the age Cindy was.)

As I was bumbling around trying to figure things out, I became friends with a woman from the neighborhood where I had built our last family home. Mary was going through a divorce, along with a bankruptcy. She became the first real female friend I ever had.

I had always been careful not to let anyone get too close to me, especially women. It had always been men who had helped me; generally women didn't like me. But Mary was outrageous and funny. She and I would smoke cigarettes and drink coffee as we worked through what had happened in our lives. We were both very intense and confused at that point. We really helped each other.

Mary had just opened a clothing store on a shoestring and was struggling financially and emotionally. Before she got married and had kids, she had intended to be a nun. That pretty much described her reclusive nature. Like me, she was inexperienced about life except for work. Like me, she was a workaholic and had become successful. Her work was also her safe haven, a place where she could control her destiny. So there was a lot of common ground on which we could build a friendship.

I was used to learning from and following my intuition using my *inner guidance system*, so sharing with someone was new and strange. The biggest hurdle was letting anyone that close and then trusting them. From the lifetime of training I received from my *most trusted advisors,* my *guides*, I was very sober about things, seeing them for what they were without drama.

As Mary and I exchanged thoughts and ideas, I started to get a clearer sense of myself. Life was beginning to come into balance for the first time. It was like I was getting my sea legs under me when it came to personal interaction. She challenged me all the time. I would think about what she said and agree with her at times. At other times, I saw things from a totally different point of view. We did a lot of mind-walking together as we puffed on cigarettes late into the evening. We were equally hungry for answers — real ones! I wasn't used to having friendships, but I was used to the intensity that we both had in abundance.

 AWARENESS: When you have a relationship with your *guides,* expect it to be intense.

As things were shifting for me, my dream life was expanding. It was the late 1970s-early 1980s, and I was still having the *merry-go-round dream*. I had dreams that showed me things like money would have no value; owning things would no longer be desirable — rent everything, and many other revelations that are happening even now. *They* continue to show me what's to come with every passing week, month, and year.

Upon reflection, after the divorce, communication from my *guides* had slowed down, resulting in my lack of direction. It turned out that this was exactly what I needed at that time. *They* knew I needed to do the inner work that could not have happened until I worked through the anger issues that had dominated me for so long. As I got on the other side of it, I discovered how the anger that had served me for so long was now a detriment to my moving forward. It was my time to learn in new ways by having personal relationships here in this world.

My real challenges would be with trust issues, especially with women. People usually start out learning these things as kids, but because they never get to know themselves first, most become vulnerable to peer pressure. I bypassed all that, which gave me the capacity to develop the relationship I have with my *guides*. That allowed me, at an early age, to feel what was a good fit and what wasn't.

When I was young, I had the kindest, wisest, clearest *teachers* and *guides*. But after the divorce, *they* were standing back while I "caught up." Since there are no accidents, I know that Mary was sent in at just the right time by my *guides* and hers. We did some life-review heavy-lifting together. We were equally committed to figuring all of it out as we were both catching up in our own individual ways.

Amidst all the changes, many of the people I knew in the building business started confiding in me and asking about what was going to happen next. After the real estate crash happened, they saw that I really was forewarned and (in their words) had some kind of psychic gift. They asked me how I learned to be so intuitive.

I told them it started out as a survival skill, like going to war: soldiers either develop their intuition, or they come home in a body bag. For me, it was a skill that got better with practice. People heard what I said because intuition was sort of a known thing by then, and the survival analogy was easy for them to grasp. But having *guides* wasn't something they could wrap their heads around. They looked past the "*guides*' thing" an just wanted me to tell them what was going to happen next with real estate, the economy, politics, world events, and most importantly, how those events would affect them personally. They wanted to know what I knew without learning how I did it.

It turned out that that was the beginning of where I would be going next, I just didn't realize it then. But it didn't matter because my *guides* knew and were with me every step of the way. Although I recognized that, I just didn't feel ready because I was deficient in my social and personal-life skills. This was also when people first started telling me to write a book to help others with their lives.

I had received guidance my entire life that I had been using for my own benefit. I just hadn't realized that it had any value to anyone else. Protecting myself by not letting others know my way of knowing things had become so second nature to me that openly sharing it would have required a big shift in me. I also didn't want to have to go through the trouble of defending it. To my surprise, this was the shift my *guides* were now demanding of me so when people came to me for answers, I could be of service to them. That was just the beginning of the next phase of my life.

TIP: This is what it's like when you have a connection with your *guides*. You feel like it's too much to explain to anyone else. You don't think anyone else will understand. However, once someone recognizes your abilities and sees your value in this area, people start seeking you out for advice.

While I was actually making some progress with developing interpersonal skills with my friend Mary, the few times I dated were torture. I was so ill at ease that I would have to wear black clothing so my date couldn't see me sweat. At the end of a date I would be drenched. I told Mary I knew I would marry someone who was into computers and lived on the East Coast. But dating wasn't for me, so I quit.

Mary was worse at working through dating than I was. She was so turned off on men, she never dated at all. She was comfortable with her girlfriends and kids. I was learning a lot exploring everything with Mary so that was where I invested my energy.

AWARENESS: Little did either of us know that much more was playing out through our becoming friends.

Chapter 14: Dreading the Personal Relationship Arena

Everyone was struggling to adjust to the real estate correction that was in progress. The entire economy was contracting and reacting to all kinds of other manipulations — the savings and loan scandals, precious metals manipulations, rising oil prices, and a change of presidents from a Democrat to a Republican. Everything was flip-flopping.

In early 1981, my subdivision in Carmichael was about six months from completion. For about six months, Mary's teenage son, Mark, had been spending quite a lot of time around my subdivision. He was kind of lost so I let him hang around at work and at home when he wanted to. I was focused on finishing up the duplexes and coming home to the new townhouse I had just bought in Fair Oaks. It was a very nice place that I had upgraded quite a bit.

Being so busy, I hadn't had much time to hang out with Mary. She was also engaged in expanding her business. Mark showed up every day after school and just hung around. I thought nothing of it and just went about my business.

Meanwhile, in a moment of clarity, I realized that I had been busying my life back up with this subdivision, buying the townhouse, and being in the planning stages of designing the Lake Tahoe house that I hoped to start building soon. Working all the time had been protecting me from looking at personal relationships. Being friends with Mary was about all I could stand.

But now I sensed that I was getting off track when I received the intuitive message from *my guides* following the cruise in 1979. *They* had made it clear that I needed to tend to my personal-life skills. I could feel I was losing my way again, but I just couldn't stop it. That was how much I dreaded the thought of venturing into the personal-relationship arena.

The only difference between this and the past was that this time I was aware of immersing myself in my work to avoid personal relationships. The unsettled feeling was my *guides* letting me know that I was making poor decisions. When I didn't course correct, *they* gave me a nudge.

 AWARENESS: Sometimes what you need to overcome is so difficult that it takes tons of persistence by you and all the help you can conjure up, like from *your guides.*

I didn't want to finish the Carmichael subdivision without having something lined up to do next. So, while the economy was still in a terrible recession, I was hoping I would be granted the sewer permit to start construction on the Tahoe house. To my surprise, on my birthday in August 1981, I was awarded the sewer permit. I thought it was an interesting birthday present. It was a sign of things to come, something I couldn't see coming.

To beat the winter snows, I had to get all the permits, the bids, and the grading handled, and the foundation and framing done by November. Then I could have the subcontractors do the inside work during the winter. The project in Carmichael was coming to a profitable close for me, so I was feeling satisfaction but continued to feel unsettled. It was strange, almost like vertigo, and I didn't know what it was. Of course, it was another nudge from my *trusted advisors,* my *guides.*

 AWARENESS: This is what it feels like when you aren't listening and start going off track. Your *guides* are an energy force that walks alongside you on your path. If you go off course, you have to go out of your way to get around *them,* and everything becomes more difficult. This is *them* nudging you to do a course correction.

Mark continued to hang around after school, so I gave him some work to do on the job site to keep him busy and help him make some money. When I did things like make dinner, go shopping, or run errands, he would tag along. We would watch movies at home, and sometimes he would fall asleep on the living room couch although he would be gone to school by the morning.

He was a sweet boy looking for direction in his life. He had friends and was a wrestler. I let him drive my truck so he could get around. Mary had gone back with her ex-husband whom she had divorced a couple of years earlier. She and I spoke occasionally about Mark because he had become distant from them. He was confused about his mom and dad's on again-off again relationship.

Being focused on her work, Mary was not particularly interested in friendships, and I had no time for social life either. And once she went back with her husband, there was a parting of the ways between us. I didn't really know why, but I respected her decision.

Over the couple of years that Mary and I had been close friends, and even before that when we were neighbors, Mark had seen me around. What I didn't know, and what Mary would tell me later, was that back then he was telling his best friend that he would marry me one day. I was totally clueless; to me, he was just my friend's son.

I pretty much left him to himself to find his way, and that was all there was to it as far as I was concerned. Even when he became very protective of me, I didn't see the signals. But when he started getting into fights when his friends confronted him about spending time with me, I realized this had grown into something much more than a friendship for him.

One day he told me he loved me and he really meant it. This caught me completely off guard. Looking back, I know that it took something like this to reach me. I was really closed down and clueless about the signs of a relationship. Regardless, he was way too young for me to let our relationship be more than a friendship, and I was very clear with him on that point. It was only later that I would discover that he was inserted into my life by a *divine force* — a big one.

In spite of my decision to dig myself deeper into work to avoid developing my social and personal-life skills, the plot was building, all designed by my *guides*.

 TIP: Life is like a movie. There's the plot, the set-ups along the way, the reflections and looking back, the good and bad decisions, lots of "oh-my-gods" and several "oh-shits." You are one of the actors in the script and don't know what other peoples' roles are in your life. Many times they just show up. Your *guides* are the writers, producers, and directors. This is another reason it's vital to build a relationship with your *guides* — *they* see it all.

I did manage to have the outside work completed at the Tahoe house before winter set in. Even so, it was a struggle to get any inside work done during the fall and winter. The snowstorms that season in Lake Tahoe were the worst since the Native Americans had inhabited the land.

There couldn't have been a worse time to have a building under construction than during that winter. The house next door collapsed, and people died right in their homes as their roofs caved in on top of them from the weight of the snow. The Alpine Meadows ski resort was badly damaged, and massive avalanches killed many skiers. All the roads were closed for most of the winter, and I had 30 feet of snow at my house. It was scary, and I was beginning to wonder what I had gotten myself into.

The house I was building was one of the few that were not damaged from the relentless winter snow storms, because I had proper snow removal done so my roof was not put under too much stress. There were days at a time that I couldn't get out unless I skied out. At one point, I crawled through the snow to a neighbor's house and asked them for some supplies to get me by until the storm passed. Believe it or not, they refused. Based on that, I considered selling it as soon as I finished building it.

AWARENESS: This would turn out to be prophetic, but not for any reason I could imagine yet.

Mark would come up to Tahoe with me occasionally, sometimes to work and sometimes just to hang out. In the summer months, he always went fishing. I managed to get the place finished, but it was by far the hardest project I ever built. It went far over budget and was a struggle all the way through. I felt lost and lonely up there where I knew no one and the values and way of life of the locals were so different from mine.

Despite the strangeness of it all, once I was finished, I actually started moving into the Tahoe house. It was the summer of 1982. I don't know why I decided to do that because I was running low on funds. I decided to sell the townhouse I had in Fair Oaks, so I moved into a rental in Carmichael for the transition.

Mark continued to tell me he wanted to marry me. I told him he was too young and to stop bringing it up. If I had any awareness of social dynamics, I would have told him he needed to stop coming around, but I still saw him as a young neighbor kid and didn't see any real problem.

He was disappointed, but persistent. I found out later that he had gone to his mom and asked for money so he could buy me a ring. By June 1982, he was telling me that he was going to be there when I turned 30 in two months. I didn't understand why this was so important to him because I had never said anything about it. My 30th birthday was like some kind of milestone for him. It was a non-event for me.

In the summer of 1982, I felt adrift without a compass because I had no other projects lined up and wasn't looking for any. I was just completing the Tahoe house and moving things up there with each trip from Carmichael. I was tight on cash, and the recession was still relentlessly underway. Not having projects lined up was not on my mind because the Tahoe house was an exhausting experience. I was out of gas. It was like I was on hold, and in some kind of limbo.

 AWARENESS: Doing things that make no sense doesn't always mean that you are not paying attention. In this case I was being moved through the motions like a pawn in a chess game without knowing it. I just didn't feel like myself. I was about to find out why.

The week of my birthday I had a terrible feeling that Mark was going to be in a car accident. I saw it coming and coming soon.

When I brought it up and begged him to be extra, extra careful driving, he just responded that he would be there for my 30th birthday. It sounded like a promise he had to fulfill. It was now getting creepy to hear him say it.

Each day as my birthday approached, my dread increased, but my birthday came and went and nothing happened. I felt like I had been holding my breath, but even as my birthday passed, the feeling persisted.

I had another trip to the Tahoe house planned for August 18th and for no apparent reason, on the evening of August 17, I made a huge Thanksgiving dinner with turkey and all the trimmings. I didn't think about it at the time; I just made it like I was on automatic. Mark arrived late for dinner. When I asked him where he had been, he said he was returning "stuff" he had accumulated over the years from people he knew, keys and other odds and ends he had been given. It seemed a little odd, but I didn't give it a second thought.

Then he proceeded to tell me not to trust his cousin Karen. He was adamant about it and made me promise to never trust her. I didn't understand why he was so concerned. I promised, and once again told him to be very careful driving as fast as he did.

The next morning, I hopped in the car to go to Tahoe. Mark decided to come along so he took the truck. I wanted Cindy with me, but she insisted on riding with Mark. On our way out of town, we stopped at a doughnut shop to get something quick to eat. As we munched our breakfast, Mark announced that he had a plan to get me a ring. He was very sincere about it.

I repeated that that wasn't going to happen and that we both needed to be with people our own age. Mark just shook his head. We left the shop, and he jumped into the truck with Cindy and pulled out ahead of me. All of a sudden, for no apparent reason, I became preoccupied with business strategies for going forward. It was consuming me. In hindsight, I come to realize that I was deliberately being preoccupied by the *divine force*. Something was coming that I was not supposed to interfere in.

AWARENESS: There are times when we are not meant to see the signs along the way. Something bigger is in play. As you look back, you may ask yourself why you didn't do things differently when you knew and felt what you did. The answer is that you were "stunned" with the *divine force* to keep you from interfering with a plan that was bigger than you. Guilt has no place here. In fact, at this point, it's petty. Let all of this "thinking" go and respect this powerful force that's bigger than any of us.

Chapter 15: The Shock That Changed Everything

All the way up to Tahoe, I was crunching numbers in my mind. Like a switch had gone on, I had now become obsessed with what I was going to do once the Tahoe house was done.

I had to stop along the way to keep some business appointments, which put me about 30 minutes behind Mark and Cindy. Once I was back on the road, everything was fine for a while. Then, about 10 minutes before my turnoff, I was overcome with a terrible feeling. In an instant, I knew Mark and Cindy had been in a car accident. It was crystal clear. I shifted out of planning mode and into survival as both of my arms went limp, and it took everything I had physically, emotionally, and mentally to keep driving.

I was in a panic and told myself it couldn't be true. The panic became overwhelming. As I continued to drive, I was getting *guidance* that was telling me that when I got there to slowly turn off the car, pull the brake, open the door, and then get out. These were literally step-by-step instructions telling me what to do when I got "there." At this point, I was so overwhelmed with the information I had already received from this *guidance* that thinking about what "there" was pushed me over the edge. But it was something I already knew.

I continued driving and turned off onto Hwy 89. In desperation, I started talking to myself out loud, telling myself that this wasn't happening! Then all of a sudden, a message came through saying Mark was dead and Cindy was alive. Cindy would live. I was grateful and sick inside at the same time. I already knew what had happened, what to do when I got "there," and the outcome.

I had not yet put together the fact that I had seen this coming for at least 10 days. No more than five minutes after the last messages came through, I heard the sirens in the distance in front of me. I began crying uncontrollably. There was very little traffic, and I just drove up on the accident scene. The wrecked truck was on the side of the highway, another car that had been hit was nearby, and the emergency vehicles were already there.

Everything was happening in slow motion as I turned off the engine, pulled on the brake, and got out of the car. I actually fell out of the car as my legs collapsed underneath me. The people who were standing around the accident saw me fall out of my car and figured out that I was connected to the people in the accident. They came over and grabbed me, asking me who I was. I told them, and they directed me to Cindy who was lying on the ground face up. She was still unconscious. I saw the blood on her face, and it took my breath away.

Then I gently put my hand on her head and she woke up. I told her that I was there, to keep her eyes closed and just relax. She was in shock so she couldn't feel any pain and she wasn't panicking. I didn't know the extent of her injuries. I was doing everything I could to speak in a composed voice so she wouldn't freak out. The paramedics were getting her prepared to put her in the ambulance as I stood up and stepped away to quietly have a moment of emotional release. Then I walked over to the truck.

I was about 15 feet from the truck when I hit a force field. It was an invisible barrier I could not pass through. I tried to go around it somehow but couldn't. The paramedics were right there with Mark, but I was denied access by this invisible barrier. I went back to Cindy. I knew that Mark was not going to make it, because *they* had made that clear to me before I got there. Then I sensed Mark's presence and knew *he* did not want me to dwell on his passing, or see *him* like that. It was clear that my focus was to be entirely on Cindy.

I could feel *Mark's* deep concern for Cindy and me. *He* made it very clear how sorry *he* was about what happened, and *he* was doing everything in *his* power to see me through this step by step. *His* regret about what happened was palpable. *His* presence was with me from the moment the accident happened as it was *he* who first notified me the instant *he* was released from his body; it was *he* who told me what the outcome would be, and what to do when I got there. *He* continued to be with us as a *guide* who was walking me through the entire ordeal.

Although I knew I had been forewarned and assisted by my *guides* and then by *Mark* the instant *he* left his body, there was a part of me that had trouble accepting what happened and how final it all was.

The shock that would change everything was now underway. Leaving the accident scene in the ambulance with Cindy, I was having trouble breathing. But I was holding it together so Cindy wouldn't panic. She was still in shock, and I couldn't tell how badly she was hurt under all the blood on her face. She began asking me how Mark was, and I could only tell her I wasn't sure.

We got to the hospital and they took her into the emergency room to evaluate her condition. I was in the waiting room when the next ambulance showed up with the people in the other car Mark had collided with. They had broken bones and lacerations, but no one had life-threatening injuries. Then the last ambulance showed up. It carried Mark. The paramedics took him through another door.

To keep myself steady, I kept my thoughts on Cindy. The staff was running every which way and had no time to talk to me. Then, one of the staff came out to tell me that Mark was on life support and was going to make it. I cried out loud in relief and fell to the floor.

My relief was short lived. Almost immediately, another person came out looking grave. They had been mistaken; Mark was on life support as they evaluated his injuries, but it didn't look good. I knew he would either die or was already gone.

The fact is, he was gone from the moment the accident happened. I know this because of everything *he* did for us from the other side right from the start of the ordeal. The hospital was just forcing his body to breathe, but he wasn't there.

I tried to see Cindy, but they did not allow me to do so. Then came another message from *Mark* telling me that I needed to notify his family. *Mark* came through and told me that

I wouldn't be the one who told his mother about what had happened; that would be the doctor's job. But I was to call Michael, who was the husband of Mark's cousin, Karen, because Mark trusted him to be the most level-headed person in their family, so, that's what I did.

I was guided by *Mark* to tell Michael not to just call Mary, but to go to her and tell her in person. I got very specific instructions from *Mark* that he was to tell Mary that Mark had been in an accident, and that she needed to call the hospital and talk directly to the doctor. Once I handled that exactly as I was guided, a nurse came to the waiting room and took me to Cindy.

 AWARENESS: This is how your *spirit guides* work; *they* are systematic as *they* make the best decisions and in a timely sequence. *They* are always there when you need *them* — always! Most of all, remember that it's not you, it's *them*. No one in a stressful situation like I was in can make so many precise decisions so quickly — that's *divine* intervention at work. You have help, *your guides*. Everything happens the way it's supposed to no matter what you want, or how you think it should be.

Cindy had a broken nose but didn't appear to have any other injury to her head or the rest of her body. The doctors said they would fix her broken nose, but there were no plastic surgeons at that hospital. I told them to do what was necessary to get her stable, and I would get her to a plastic surgeon in Sacramento.

Once Cindy came out of shock, she was a terrible patient. She was ill-tempered, rude, and screamed at everyone. They couldn't handle her or get her to cooperate. The accident had occurred in the morning, but it was nighttime before they released her to be sure she had no other injuries.

Cindy kept asking about Mark because she did not remember anything before or during the accident. I held off as long as I could, but when they were ready to release her, I had to tell her that he had died. This actually stopped her from focusing on her own pain and suffering for first time since the accident.

It was a tragic day for both of us as we quietly mourned Mark's passing together. By that time, Karen, whose husband I had called to notify Mark's family, showed up. They apparently realized I would be in no condition to drive us home, so she was there to bring us back. As soon as we got in the car, she started talking badly about Mark's mother. I couldn't believe what I was hearing. She was a gossip and, at this sensitive time, was feeding off of a tragedy. I guess she was angry with Mary for some reason and took this opportunity to get her revenge.

I told her to stop it. Apparently she saw that I meant it, so she did. Now I understood why Mark had been so emphatic when he had told me not to trust her just a day earlier at dinner. Cindy and I both fell asleep on the ride home, totally exhausted.

 AWARENESS: It's amazing how life really works when you listen and let it work. You are always in good hands with the support that's always there from your *guides*.

Once we got home, I put Cindy to bed and called Mary. I was very concerned about her and could not put off the call even though I was wiped out. She was very glad that I called; it had been a year since we had really talked.

The first thing she told me was that she had gone back with her husband because she sensed that she was going to lose one of her kids. Having the family back together would be crucial when it happened. She said it was a very strong feeling, so although this was a shock, it was not a surprise.

Then she told me the details of the accident she had gotten from the police. She said that Mark had hit a car head-on as he attempted to speed past the car in front of him. He apparently thought the oncoming car would move to the right so he could squeeze through, but that didn't happen. She told me the other driver was a priest and had admitted that he could have moved to the right, but didn't. He was very remorseful that Mark had died.

Mary said that Cindy was asleep when the accident happened, causing her to be launched right through the front windshield and out of the way. The accident investigators had told Mary that that was the reason Cindy lived — she had been completely relaxed when it happened.

They told Mary that Mark died shortly after they got him to the hospital, but that he had been brain dead immediately. We talked for a long time; she did most of the talking. I felt terrible that she lost her son and a bit guilty that my daughter, Cindy lived, although this was the way it was meant to happen. I could not imagine what that day would have been like had it been the other way around. Mary was actually dealing with this very well, not that it was easy for her.

Hearing that Mary knew one of her kids was going to die and had gone to the extreme of getting the family back together specifically because of it, I was beginning to see that it was Mark's time to leave. Nothing could have stopped it. I got off the phone and finally went to bed.

 AWARENESS: It was no accident that Mary and I hadn't spent time together over the last year. A *divine force* was at work.

A couple days later, Mary called me to talk about the funeral arrangements for Mark. She asked me to help her decide how to deal with his remains. I was not expecting that. I sat with it and got the clear message from my *guidance* that Mark needed to be buried. I believed in cremation, but my *guides* made it clear to me that Mark's family would need to be able to visit him so each family member could work through the loss.

For the funeral, Mary asked everyone to prepare something to say to Mark. So, I sat down and wrote a poem that just came to me as if it were being dictated. It spoke to how he reminded me time and time again to stop closing myself down.

I was really a mess throughout the ordeal. I was in shock and couldn't seem to get past what had happened. Each morning I woke up and shuddered at the thought of facing another day doing things the same way. I was really tired and in terrible emotional pain. I just couldn't accept what had happened.

The only thing that mattered to me anymore was Cindy. We became very close after Mark's death. That would turn out to be our last real shot at a relationship. It was an example of how a tragedy also can create an opportunity.

Chapter 16: A Visitor from the Beyond Returns with a Message

Just a few days after Mark died, he materialized at my place. I was in so much pain and had been incessantly asking why this had happened. *Mark* sat right in front of me, in complete physical form, and told me, "*Please let me go.*" *He* said *he* was in a great deal of pain, and I was holding *him* back. I never questioned how *he* could materialize; I just asked *him* why this accident had to happen. I was in shock and mad at the same time. *He* was so physically present that I could even smell *him* as *he* sat there in front of me. *He* didn't answer, and just left.

He materialized a second time at the exact same location two days later. This time Cindy was there with me and witnessed that second visitation (although, like all the others, when I asked her about it the next day she didn't remember it). Once again, *he* asked me to let *him* go. *He* repeated that it was very painful, and I was holding *him* back. I didn't understand what *he* meant, but I knew this was very serious for *him* to return and tell me this a second time. Without hesitating, I replied by telling *him* I had told *him* not to speed and had warned this would happen. Again, my response caused *him* to leave.

A week after *Mark* died, *he* materialized for a third and final time. Again *he* told me *he* needed me to let *him* go. Then *he* said, "*You will meet someone your age in two weeks,*" and left. For some reason, with that message, I suddenly realized what *he* meant about holding *him* back: the emotional pain I was feeling prevented *him* from moving on. It was like I was in shock, so on that third visit the shock was wearing off so I could comprehend his repeated request.

AWARENESS: This is what can happen when someone dies and exits in such a shocking way. For *their* sake and yours, let go and don't perpetuate anyone's pain. Like in my case, sometimes the shock is so strong that we unknowingly prevent *them* from moving on. It keeps you both frozen in time.

The connection I had over the years with Mary and then Mark turned my life around. I never saw any of this coming, which is probably why it was so powerful in shifting me. It was a major turning point in my life as I turned 30 years old. Mark knew this and stayed; it was his final mission here before he had to leave. The fact that his mother saw his demise coming also, along with everything that Mark was determined to finish before his parting from this world made me realize that we all have a deadline.

It's interesting to note that people who are about to die, even if they're not conscious of it, often return borrowed items to their owners. Apparently that's what Mark was doing the night before he died when he was late to the "Thanksgiving Dinner" I had prepared.

AWARENESS: When it's our time, it's not something we dwell on before we leave, we just do what's right so there are no loose ends and hopefully no regrets so we can have a clean exit.

I resumed my trips to Lake Tahoe to complete the house. On one of the trips, I took Cindy so she could retrace the steps she could remember before she fell to sleep the day of the accident. I knew this would be important for her and me.

We identified a spot where they would have been about 10 or 15 minutes before the accident. She said that was where she had fallen asleep. No doubt *divine* intervention played a part in her dozing off at that exact time. Then I took her to see the truck in the junkyard. She was shocked that she had made it out of that mangled piece of iron. Doing this was all part of the healing process for us both.

As soon as the Tahoe house was ready, I put it up for sale because I couldn't go there anymore. It sold right away. Things work smoothly when you are aligned with what is meant to be.

Two weeks after Mark's third and final visit, I met a man named Steve at the deli just below the hill from where I built my Tahoe house. He was a handsome young guy my own age and was on vacation from New Jersey. He had lived in Lake Tahoe in the 1970s and had come back because he loved it there and was doing some reminiscing. We were attracted to each other, and he wanted to go out on a date. I told him I was only on a quick trip and had to get back to my daughter, so we agreed to meet again in a few days when I returned.

When I got back to Tahoe, we went to the waterfalls he loved so much. It was a really beautiful place. We spent a lot of time together and had a lot of fun, but after a few days, he had to go back to New Jersey. Being across the continent from each other, we stayed in touch by phone and mail. I started looking forward to getting mail for a change.

As our relationship developed, for the second time in my life I was selling everything I owned. Weekend after weekend I held sales out of the large storage unit where I had moved everything. My bankers, accountants, and attorneys thought I was losing it again. I knew that, for a change, I was actually "getting it."

I couldn't get rid of it all fast enough. I wasn't sure what I would do next, but I knew I needed to unload. Between selling my stuff and the proceeds from the Tahoe house, I would have enough money to start over however I wanted to.

 AWARENESS: See the workaholic here? Even with everything I had gone through, I was using my work as an antidote for my pain. Once again, I had to have something to do to distract me from the full impact of it. The layers were coming off, but a lot was still there. This is how it works and why it can take years to heal the stubborn issues.

After I had everything sold and behind me, I bought a townhouse lot and built a custom duplex townhouse. I planned to sell one side and Cindy and I would live on the other. Cindy was 13 years old and had watched me design and build homes her entire life. This time I asked her if she would like to participate in the design. She said she would and actually did a very good job. I built the home just as she designed it, and she loved how it turned out.

I was still processing the accident that had happened months earlier. I was also very sad as I struggled to acclimate to the new me. Building the townhouse helped me get through it; it was a surprisingly easy and fun time with Cindy.

One day, Cindy started telling me about how low her energy was. She said she thought something was wrong with her. She said that when she started working, she would need really good health insurance. I thought that sounded ridiculous, especially at her age. But she continued with harangues about how I had so much energy, which gave me an advantage over others. She said I made everything look so easy when it wasn't easy for other people.

It was like hearing Alex and everyone else all over again. It would turn out to be a resentment she would hold against me for the rest of her life. Unfortunately, the resentment was stronger than the love required for our second chance at having a relationship. Her resentment evolved into full-blown jealousy as the years went by.

She also reasoned that my high energy was why my life worked out so well, making what I did look easy. She didn't understand how this really worked. I had the help of my *guides* that developed into a strong relationship over my lifetime. *They* guided me; making everything I did look effortless.

 AWARENESS: This is what it's like when you consciously co-create your life with the help of your *guides. They* don't do the work for you, but *they* do point you in the right direction at just the right time but you need to listen. The next step is to take action, which is where many people fail.

Throughout the construction of my townhouse, Steve and I continued with our long-distance romance. We met in Las Vegas in November, 1982, and won at everything we played. With luck like that, we decided our relationship was meant to be. Our long-distance romance became stronger than ever.

I went to visit Steve in New Jersey a couple months later. I met his family, and I learned about his work and more about him. While I was there, I got a phone message that there was a structural problem with the Tahoe house I had sold. This was serious, and before I left New Jersey to return home, I called the most reputable structural engineers in Tahoe to go out to the property and evaluate the situation. After the house had survived the record snow storms of 1981-1982 without any damage at all, I couldn't imagine what could have gone wrong.

By the time I returned home, the report was ready. I asked for a copy to be faxed to me and to the owners in San Francisco. The report showed that there were no structural deficiencies; the damage the new owners were complaining about had occurred because of excessive ice dams that built up on the roof and crashed down onto the front covered walkway.

These excessive ice dams were caused by a sprinkler the owners had placed on the roof in their attempt to melt the snow instead of shoveling it off. The reports stated that the weight of these ice dams would have collapsed the roof had it not been built to exceed the building code.

The two people who bought this house from me were a home-builder in San Francisco and his attorney partner. Even after the inspection report, they still sued me. The last thing I needed was to be drawn back into this Tahoe nightmare, but I was. The lawsuit went on for five years and finally ended in Superior Court when they ruled in my favor.

It took the higher courts to expose the lies these new owners committed. For me, it jeopardized my contractor's license, and I was forced to bond around the pending lawsuit so I could continue to make a living. This was a case of David and Goliath: they were the very wealthy powerful Goliath attempting to destroy little David because of their own poor judgment.

I had a great attorney and for the first time I trusted in someone else to go to battle for me. I had always fought my own fights, so this was a new and different way of handling things.

After I had returned home from my visit to New Jersey, Steve called me and told me he had quit his job. He said he didn't like living in New Jersey and was never crazy about his job. He wanted to fly out to California to be with me.

That was all fine with me. I had just bought a Ford Bronco. I sold the townhouses, bought a travel trailer, and he, Cindy and I went to New Jersey to get his things. It was an adventure. I had never traveled like that before, except when my dad had taken us on a summer vacation up to Canada in the early 1960s.

Despite the fun, on the trip Cindy started being difficult. She did not like Steve interfering with our renewed relationship and wanted me to herself. By the time we got to Colorado, Cindy was out of control, so we put her on a plane home to stay with friends and return to school. We had never planned on her being on the entire trip due to school, so it was more of a plan modification than a real disruption.

During the three weeks of our adventure, Steve and I had fun planning how we would live and what we would do when we got back to California. When we got home, I sold the travel trailer for $50 more than I paid for it, and we moved into a rental house with a pool. Life was good.

Cindy liked living in the new place, but she resented Steve. That was a turning point for Cindy. She was resentful of me, too, so there was no way to have a relationship with her that wouldn't require serious changes — and sacrifices — on my part. Succumbing to the tyranny of her desires was never going to work for me; my *guides* would not sanction it. *They* showed me that this kind of compromise always leads to a life of regrets and resentments.

 AWARENESS: People who demand that you lower your standards and live a life of compromise are just looking for company in their compromised lives. The truth is that you can never help someone by joining them in their misery.

Soon after we got back to California and settled into our house, I started looking for a project. I received an offer to build one almost immediately, but Steve felt like I was running over him. He wasn't sure where he fit in. I saw his point and passed on the project. Then I sought and found something he felt more comfortable with. It was a good project in a great area. It involved building moderately priced homes, which was easy for me. It was a new adventure for Steve. Building houses was something he had always wanted to do with the family money, but his mother didn't want to take the risk. We started it in the summer of 1983.

Chapter 17: Dad Dies Mysteriously

One evening, about five months after Steve and I had settled in Sacramento, we were eating dinner when the phone rang. We were just letting it ring, when all of a sudden I got a strong message from my *guides* that I needed answer it. It was my older brother Randy, who never called me. He told me that Dad was in the hospital. Although Randy never said Dad was dying, I told him to tell Mom not to let him die before I got there. I dropped everything, and Steve and I went to the hospital, which took about 25 minutes.

On my way to the hospital, I was wondering why I knew he was going to die. When I arrived Mom, Randy, and Larry were there. I wanted to see my dad, but Mom said he was dead. Defiantly, she said she had pulled the plug on him. Knowing how important it was for me to see my dad before he died, she had made sure it was done before I got there.

Here was the most invincible person I knew, my dad, dead at 64 years old. He came from a family of people who lived well into their 90s and even 100s. His early death didn't make sense to me. My mom had been sick of my dad for a long time, especially after Dad retired about two years earlier. She liked it better when he was at work all day.

I went in to see my dad and put my hand on his head. The instant I did that, I felt a bird flying free. I realized that he actually had waited for me. With my arrival, he was gone. My dad was that bird; he was free and gentle again. I felt him fly away and leave. I was overwhelmed with loss in that moment and broke down crying in Steve's arms.

The next thing I felt was something I didn't expect. It was my own freedom: freedom from Dad's judgment of me. What a strange thing to feel, but a sense of heaviness was instantly lifted from me. Until that moment, I hadn't realized that burden was even there. I realized his judgment of me really bothered me. It didn't prevent me from living my life or being the real me because I stayed away from my parents much of my adult life. I had thought I was only staying away from my mom because she was so blatant about her disapproval. But now I saw they shared a dysfunction, and part of that was how they perceived and judged me in my adult life.

 AWARENESS: The timing for the truth won't always make sense to you. In fact, many times it will make you feel guilty in the instant it appears. That's the wrong interpretation of the information. First of all, it didn't come from you, it was sent to you directly from your *guides*. Second, it's the truth that you are in need of knowing at just that particular time. Forget about reasoning it to death; leave the truth in its pure form along with its timing. In the moment my dad was set free, I was too. Now, that's the pure truth in perfect timing.

After the hospital, we all went to what was now Mom's house. Randy and she were making plans at the kitchen table as Mom explained how dad had died right there while she was making his dinner. She said he fell off the chair and choked on the floor, trying to catch his breath with foam coming out of his mouth.

I remembered the doctor asking if Dad was a drinker because his liver was damaged. That was alarming. Dad would have an occasional drink, but he never overdid it. He was an athlete. He took a great deal of pride in his physical health. Dad was never sick; he didn't even have a doctor.

As I thought about it, I suspected that my mother may have poisoned him over time. Nothing that she did would have surprised me. She did not seem shaken up by Dad's death and in her own words she "pulled the plug on him" as quickly as possible, especially before I showed up at the hospital.

My dad was a tinkerer and builder who made many wonderful things. My mother never let me have anything that Dad made. She was deliberate about that. So, while she and Randy were planning at the kitchen table, I went into the room where Dad made his carvings. I looked through the drawers and found a heart he made for Mom. Dad got sweeter with age, but Mom was done with him. Her heart wasn't just cold — it was dead. She had ignored the gifts he made for her.

I also found a carving I remember my Dad having made. It was small enough to put in a pocket, so I took it. That, along with a necklace of gold nuggets Dad dredged in his gold-mining days that he had given me, are the only two things I have from my Dad. These are two of my most valued possessions.

I didn't stay at the house long. I don't remember what Larry was doing. He had a totally different relationship with Dad than I had. Mom was telling Randy how Dad was losing it at the end, that he was getting dementia. She said she was relieved that she was finally free. I just couldn't believe that my dad was gone. My dad always knew that I loved him, and nothing would ever change that. "Thanks for waiting for me, Dad."

Losing Dad was sad for many people. They called Dad "the leprechaun" at the funeral. He was truly magical. He was looked up to by many. Grown men were crying at Dad's funeral. My ex, Alex, was out of prison by this time, and he was one of them. That was the last time I ever saw Alex.

Never missing a beat, my Mom played the "broke" card, so I paid for Dad's funeral. For my Mom this was a no-brainer, because she knew I would never neglect my dad. Dad deserved a respectable send-off, and no one in the family was willing to make that happen. His two brothers, both older than he, were shocked to hear their younger brother had died. They were devastated. All my mother could say about them attending Dad's funeral was that she hoped they didn't want her to put them up. I got the feeling she was hiding something yet again!

I picked out the most beautifully crafted casket for my Dad. The funeral was very sweet. The only hiccup was the morbid organ music that I told them not to play. The moment they started it, I stopped them.

My mom took all the credit for the funeral arrangements because everyone assumed she would do this for her beloved husband. I saw that as another of her ugly moments where she took pride in fooling everyone. I wondered if anyone besides Larry and I saw this side of her.

 AWARENESS: There are times when there's no way out of being set up by the people who work against you.

These people are in more pain than you can imagine. It's their own negative choices that eventually destroy them. So stay focused on following your own path and steer clear of the negativity of others.

As all this was going on, my boyfriend, Steve, was buying the first computer I ever owned. It was an Apple computer, but he was not happy with it and took it back and got a PC instead. He had gone to the exclusive Choate College as a teenager where he took computer science classes. He was a natural with computers. Interestingly, I had told Mary about four years earlier that I would marry someone from the East Coast who was into computers.

Steve and I had just moved into one of the houses we built in our first project together just before my father's death. Cindy was mad at me, so she moved in with her dad, against my wishes. I told her that I knew she was taking the easy way out because her dad would let her do anything, including giving her drugs. He wasn't a parent; he acted more like a buddy to her. Unfortunately, that approach only works if you have a responsible child. Cindy was far from that.

Cindy took full advantage of that situation by making a number of dark choices. I discovered some of those later. She never knew I knew, and I'm sure I only heard about a small portion of what went on. Seeing this, I started preparing myself for the worst possible outcome. I imagined getting that dreaded phone call someday telling me Cindy had been busted for something, had gotten really hurt, or was dead. She was 14 years old and making all bad choices. No one could stop her.

Steve and I got married in November, 1984, after the Computer
Dealers Exposition (Comdex Show) in Las Vegas. We were
there helping a friend sell his technology product. We got married in our jeans because that's the way Steve wanted it. It
was not much of a honeymoon, and Steve fell asleep as soon
as we got back to the hotel. That night I realized I had made
a mistake.

Steve made it very easy for me to stay detached while in this
arrangement with him – self-preservation was something I
was a master at. When we returned to Sacramento we started
looking for another project to build.

It was 1985 by the time we found it and the investors to back
it. It was a project derived out of hard times. Nothing else
was coming together, and that project was not a sure bet. I
never felt good about it although the homes I designed were
very different and elegant, which brought in home design jobs
from outside the project. At least I was designing homes that
were different from those I had done before and which were
homes I would like to live in myself.

As we moved forward, the subdivision was struggling but
the design business was flourishing. I was really tiring of the
home building business.

It was no wonder I was tired of the building business; I had
been shown years earlier by my *guides* that the building business would never be the same for me again. I had stayed in
it because I didn't know what else to do. That was about to
change, but I still didn't consciously know it.

AWARENESS: Sometimes getting tired is the best thing that can happen because you stop resisting the flow. You get out of your own way and step into what may not make sense, but it leads you in a direction that has been calling you your entire life. The pull is strong — you are being guided.

In 1986, I started taking classes on dreams in the evenings. That turned out to be a major turning point for me. I had had vivid dreams all my life, and I knew they meant much more than I was able to understand on my own. I always recorded my dreams in a journal. The classes helped me decipher them.

My *guides* trained me with precision in dreams. *They* taught me things like how to master my energy and develop the ability to defy gravity. This was very advanced training from the *master teachers*. What I learned in my dreams and from my *guides* surpassed anything I had ever experienced in this life. I thought of it as super-learning. The dream classes helped me to refine my understanding of these dreams and myself.

I was receiving so much clarity and insight from the dream classes that Steve told me at one point to stop taking them because they were going to ruin our marriage. I couldn't believe what I was hearing; it was like telling me to stop breathing. So many things were finally making sense to me. It would take another book just to cover the many experiences that came from my dreams. I told Steve I could never stop the classes.

I'm not sure what he was concerned about because I never let those classes interfere with my obligations to work, or our marriage. As I look back, I sense that he feared that what I was learning would eventually cause me to leave him. He wasn't interested in expanding himself, although it intrigued him. Then, after over 30 years, once I started taking the dream classes, the *merry-go-round dream* finally stopped.

It had been 14 years since my UFO sighting and telepathic communication. At that time *they* told me not to tell anyone about the encounter until 1986. By 1986, I had learned a lot. I had started dream classes and my inner world was opening up like never before, even though I was still not entirely sure what 1986 meant.

 TIP: Try taking a class that resonates with you to learn to contact your *guides*. It could be a dream class, a meditation group, a yoga class, even a music class; do what you are drawn to. Expect the best, and if the class is not a fit, move on to another class until you find the right one. If it makes you feel good then, that becomes the doorway for you to join forces with your *guides*.

After living for close to a year with her dad, Cindy had a falling out with him. I never learned what happened. I do know that during the time Cindy lived with her dad, she had asked him why he cheated on me. He told her it was because he was insecure. Cindy told me he never talked badly about me and defended me when anyone, including her did.

When she left Alex's home, she was 15. She had a job at a grocery store while she continued going to high school. Once she got to know the people at her work, she moved into an apartment with another girl.

I went to her new place to meet her roommate and see where she was living. I knew that this was a major step up for Cindy, and that between work and school, she would not have time to get into much trouble. That impression turned out to be right. She really valued her job because it gave her the freedom she had learned to appreciate so much. She kept that position, advanced in the company, and finished high school. However, being short on money-management skills, having a job didn't include making enough money to pay all her bills. As a result, she got so deep into debt after a couple years that she could no longer pay her part of the rent.

Rather than coming to me or her dad, she went to her grandmother, my mom. Instead of getting a loan, she ended up moving in with my mother.

Mom made Cindy agree to certain conditions before she moved in. Mom always had to be in control and the one who created the rules. On the positive side, Cindy was put on a strict budget with mom taking her entire paycheck, deducting rent, and then using what was left to pay off her debts. Mom as usual controlled everything and got paid first.

Then, about a year after Cindy moved in with her, my mom had respiratory failure. Mom couldn't breathe, so Cindy took her to the hospital. They put her on oxygen as they evaluated her condition. Mom was a heavy smoker her entire life and her diagnosis was emphysema. The doctor told her to stop smoking or she would die. She was upset and said she had ruined her lungs. She actually stopped smoking after that episode. Cindy had saved mom's life.

It was strange when I visited Mom in the hospital because her demeanor was a mix of resentment and avoidance. She actually glared at me when I came in. I could feel that my visit was interrupting some kind of relationship she and Cindy had developed. From what I could tell, the foundation of their bond was grousing about me.

 AWARENESS: Over the years, my *guides* had taught me how to detect peoples' true intentions. In the case of my mother and my daughter, it was obvious that, over the course of just one year, they had developed a common bond and some sort of yet-to-be-revealed plan of attack on me.

In 1987, my younger brother Larry was floundering again. He asked us for some work, but we were already committed to the subcontractors, and they were fully staffed. Instead, we got him a job doing some construction work for our CPA. She needed some sidewalks and driveways installed, and we knew Larry was perfect for the job. About half way through, he lost it and threatened to kill her if he didn't get paid. I had to step in and get him off the job. I paid him what he felt he was worth so he would stop with the threats. He had become very unstable.

I told Mom that I thought Larry needed help. She rejected that and said her job with him was done. She turned her back on him, and that was the end of it. Shortly after that, he met a girl who was also in need of psychological help. They lived together until she died a few years later. Not long after her death, he became a ward of the State of California and was placed in a group home. I expect that losing his girlfriend brought attention to his needs. He was diagnosed as a paranoid schizophrenic and a manic depressive. He remains in that group home to this day. Unlike me, Larry was unable to overcome Mom's physical and mental torment. She succeeded at destroying him, just like when she said to us both, "I'm going to break your spirit."

Larry is one of those people who hasn't completely lost it, so he suffers as he drifts between reality and no-man's land. His moments of lucidity are replays of his younger days as he perceives himself as a victim. The no-man's land moments are populated by demons. His life is filled with wild distortions that keep everyone away from him. It breaks my heart, but there's nothing I can do.

In 1987, Randy and his wife moved to Oregon. Randy said he was tired of Mom asking him to make repairs on her house. He didn't want to be bothered. Mom treated Randy's wife badly, always criticizing her. Randy also was hurtful to his wife, always favoring Mom. It's interesting that his wife's name was Linda because the one time my younger brother had married, his wife's name was Linda as well.

1987 was one of reshuffling the deck for all the families. However, it was just the beginning of even bigger changes to come.

Chapter 18: My Guides Channel Me in a New Direction

By 1988, our struggling subdivision was just about finished. The demands and threats of the homeowners we were building for had reached a crescendo. We managed them as well as we could, but we were getting very tired. Plus, subcontractors were stealing from us at every opportunity. It was overwhelming.

One day when Steve and I went to lunch, I had an anxiety attack. I could not catch my breath. Steve rushed me to the hospital right around the corner, the same hospital where my dad had died five years earlier. They gave me oxygen and told me it was due to stress. The doctor told me to go home and rest for at least two days. This was the first time in my life that I had hit a limit. Could this be the price of my high energy, the downside my dad warned me about?

At that moment on the hospital bed, Steve literally got in my face and told me that this was it — we were finished with building houses. I agreed. After that brief discussion, Steve took me home and told the homeowners what had happened. They backed off with their unreasonable demands and ugly threats. For the rest of 1988, I continued designing homes for clients and Steve finished the project.

The anxiety attack was a nudge from my *guides* that big changes were in motion.

Knowing that we would not be building homes after this project, we took a trip to the Southwest. My friend Mary instigated this when she called and asked if we would like to go to New Mexico with her. I wanted to go to Arizona instead, but Mary had her heart set, so off to the Land of Enchantment we went.

We hit that state in its monsoon season in the summer of 1988. Even so, it was a great vacation that was long overdue for Steve and me. It made us think about moving to the Southwest, but for now it was just a time out and nothing more. Little did we know that this trip was pointing us toward our destiny. It's interesting that Mary played a part in this coming change. Once again, we were being guided.

When we got home, many of the clients for whom I had done custom home designs wanted us to build their new homes. Several million dollars in custom home projects were offered to us. They said they would wait as long as we needed, just as long as we would build their homes. Even though we needed to make money, Steve told them we couldn't do it. He was committed to what he had told me in the hospital.

Life was good at my studio as I received a constant flow of design clients. They all loved me — a total opposite from my building clients. I worked alone in peace and quiet. I was making a lot of money and loving every minute of it. The pressure was finally off. It had been years since Steve and I felt the pressure lift, and life became effortless again. Things were falling into place.

One morning as I was getting ready to go to the office, I took off the top of the toothpaste tube, and just before I put it down to brush my teeth, I did a double take, just to be sure of where I had set it down. I felt that something was up. Then I brushed my teeth. When I finished and went to pick up the top to the toothpaste, it was gone. In that moment I said, "Okay, Mark, you can return it now." It instantly reappeared. I sensed him, or some prankster, was present, which proved to be right. He was playing with me, and it was his way of letting me know that he wasn't gone, that he was everywhere.

 AWARENESS: Probably everyone can remember a similar moment. Yes it's *those* from the other side letting you know *they* are there, *they* are everywhere. *They* also have a sense of humor.

In 1988, I was in the third year of going to evening dream classes. So much had happened, and *those who were guiding me* from beyond this world were more advanced than ever. It turned out that everything throughout the year had been leading up to what was about to happen in December. The anxiety attack I had, the decision to stop building homes, finishing the building project, going to the Southwest, and what I continued to learn in the non-physical worlds through my dreams and from my *guides* were all part of this bigger picture.

That picture started to be revealed when, in December of 1988, the teacher of the dream class invited me over for dinner. That was not like her at all. She was a good teacher, but we did not have a chummy relationship. I was aware she had many insecurities that were in direct contrast to her teaching. In other words, she didn't walk her talk. It turned out that the only reason she had me visit her was because she was faced with an ultimatum from her own *guides* that she and a friend had been channeling using a Ouija Board.

Apparently, several weeks before she invited me over, her *guides* came through one of their sessions and told her *they* needed her to arrange a session with me because my *guides* had something to tell me. She agreed, but never followed through on it. A few weeks later, her *guides* told her that *they* would no longer be coming through for her until this session with me took place. She would be cut off from further communication with *them* until she performed on this.

Of course, at the time I had no idea she was a channel or that she had been cut off from her *guides*. So, I was baffled when, after dinner, she brought out the Ouija Board, tossed a pad of paper and a pen at me, and told me to start writing as she and her friend started channeling the information. She did this strictly out of obligation so she would have access to her *guides* again. The information came through very fast, as *they* got right to the point.

In this session, my *guides* gave me a name to use when contacting *them* in the future — a very unusual name. *They* told me about a job *they* needed me to do and described it in a way so I would understand the importance of performing on it. *They* asked me to create a new talking board, one that did not cause fear and caution, so people would have a way to contact their own *guides* as their lives became more uncertain in the years ahead. I realized this was something that had been shown to me right from the start of my life in the *merry-go-round dream* – that my job would be to reach those who could be reached. The new board would be how they could reach their *guides* without fear.

Then *they* told me that I would be leaving the Sacramento area. *They* suggested that I move to Colorado but also told me that I would decide to move to a neighboring state instead. *They* told me about an earthquake that was coming that would devastate Northern California. *They* said that my thriving architectural practice would be coming to an end because of a recession that would start at the end of 1989 and would continue through 1991.

They also told me to leave Steve. *They* said our marriage would not work out. Steve was present at this channeling session and heard every word. After hearing that, he laid down on the floor on his back and went right to sleep. He simply couldn't handle what he had just heard or anything else *they* were about to say.

After the session with my dream class teacher, I started having dreams showing me the details of what *they* needed me to do to create *their* version of a talking board that would not perpetuate the fear and concern attached to Ouija Boards. By March 1989, my board was designed, the trademark was filed, and it was scheduled for production. Between December 1988 and March 1989, I honed my channeling skills by observing and practicing with my dream teacher and her friends. Doing that also allowed me to test the prototypes of this new talking board, which everyone loved.

Throughout this learning and discovery time, we all made contact with many *benevolent groups of beings*. It would take an entire book to cover what happened in these channeling sessions. Let's just say that I was well prepared for what was coming. I had a direct line of communication with my *guides* and *many others* any time I wanted to contact *them*. My world really opened up.

 TIP: Do you see how fast things can change when you let go? It was less than a year earlier that I had the anxiety attack which resulted in my no longer building homes. We just have to be willing to let go and trust. Stay open and pay attention to the smallest events because your *guides* are always working on what's best for you, and *they* will never let you down.

Unlike other people I knew, including Steve, I was never scared by any of this *other-worldly* communication because I had been groomed for it throughout my life. I was thoroughly prepared for all of it. These *benevolent beings* were not new to me because I always had access to *them*. Now, I had a direct line of communication with *them* through this new talking board device and could reach *them* on command. To me, this was second nature.

I expect that this was why *they* came to me to join forces with *them* in developing the project. *They* knew I had what it would take to see it through: the design ability, the organizational and teaching skills, and a deep rapport with *them* from a lifelong relationship.

The dream class teacher and her followers who became channelers on this new talking board were invested in having the smartest *guides* — *guides* that only they had access to. They were ego-driven and domineering. Of course, this was self-defeating because that approach was in complete opposition to what is necessary to access the *highest sources*, and bring through unbiased information. Nobody owns those *beings* on the higher levels.

I just let those people go on thinking they were superior. They never understood what was really happening. They showed me the ugly side of this precious communication with *higher intelligence*. I used the time with these amateur channelers to work through my learning curve and perfect the performance of this new talking board.

It took me eight months, from January to August, to complete all the learning I would need, along with finishing the refinement and production of the new board. The learning was easy. It was the interaction of the egos that jostled for the highest position as they competed in the "*My guides* are better than *your guides*" power play that made this tedious. As ridiculous as this was, it was just as important for me to experience it as anything else.

That behavior was childish. I thought I would see the last of it once Steve and I left for Arizona. Little did I know that this ego-driven competition would be a common shortfall with almost everyone I would train. People who could master the skill of channeling higher information almost always polluted it with their egos. I seemed to be the only one who understood that it was the value of this information, and not who brought it through that mattered.

Over time, I found that in the very beginning, new channelers tended to be open and humble, though not gullible. That's a perfect attitude for working with *guides*! However, once they became proficient at using the talking board, they almost always fell into the trap of self-importance. They acted like it was they who were bringing the wisdom and timely information through. When that happened, they were no longer channeling *higher intelligence* from *others*; they were channeling their egos. This came from their need to be right, to dominate and control.

 AWARENESS: Be aware that this also happens a lot when people get intuitive messages. They instantly think it came from them when it came from their *guides*. It always comes from your *guides*. It's important to recognize that so you can begin to open up your line of communication with *them*. *Their* job is to guide you so you can lead an authentic life. *They* are not interested in the superficial.

PART 3: GUIDED TO LEAVE CALIFORNIA

Chapter 19: The Connection to my Guides Shifts into High Gear

In March of 1989, Steve and I went back to the Southwest to investigate a possible move. Our strategy was to get the talking board finished and ready for sale, complete with the instructions on how to use it. That way, we would have something with which to start our new life. Of course, we were clueless about marketing, or how a project like it would even work out.

We took ten days off and flew to Phoenix, then drove up to Sedona, which is where I had told Steve we would be moving before we ever went there. We drove all over Sedona and the Verde Valley, and then we went to Lake Powell and rented a pontoon boat. To make it fun as well as business, we pulled a fishing boat behind so Steve could do some fishing.

It was a magical time, especially at night as the stars reflected on the glassy water. There were shooting stars and other interesting night sky life. We stayed up late into the night drinking coffee and watching the night sky show. So far, Arizona was a good experience for us.

Next, we went to Colorado, the state *they* told me to move to in the first channeling session in December 1988. We went to the southern border towns, and then Pagosa Springs. We must have hit six or seven little towns. Our big question was how to make a living with no large city nearby.

We found a lot of tension between the white people and Native Americans in Colorado. In Pagosa Springs, it was especially noticeable. Something was way out of balance there and I got really sick. We couldn't stay and left the next morning on our way to New Mexico. We went to Taos, then Santa Fe, then Albuquerque. The energy in New Mexico was similar to that in Colorado, except that New Mexico had more poverty and crime — so that was out.

We drove back to Sedona and looked for something to rent. We found a place in Cornville just outside of Sedona that had a large, detached metal building. We needed that for the development and storage of our new product.

 AWARENESS: Your *guides* will orchestrate the perfect setup every time. Everything will turn out to be perfect, including dealing with the dysfunction of others. Had I followed *their* earlier advice, what was about to happen next could have been avoided. *They* are always truthful and trying to make our lives easier, but we are not always ready to follow *their* advice the first time *they* present it.

Once we returned from this trip, Cindy, who was 19, came to tell me that one of her regular customers at the grocery store where she worked had made her an offer. Apparently, this woman saw the same potential in Cindy that I had seen years before. She was from New York City and had connections in the acting community. She offered to take Cindy to

New York, provide a place to stay, and introduce her to the right people, making a career in acting possible. Cindy was very excited about it and asked me what I thought.

I told her it would only be offered to her this one time, and if she turned it down, the course of her life would be changed forever. However, Cindy had just met her new boyfriend, and because her insecurities were stronger than her ambitions, she chose to turn down the offer. In that instant, she missed a calling I believed was in alignment for her – a calling I told her about when she was nine years old.

 LESSON: There's a point in everyone's life, around the time you are in your late teens, when you have the most powerful energy you'll ever have. It's at this critical crossroads when you are presented with the choice to direct that energy one way or another. It's that once-in-a-lifetime decision where you make a choice to listen to your *guides* who will be presenting you with an unexpected opportunity to go forward, or to surrender to your fears and succumb to a compromised life that ends in regret. In Cindy's case, her insecurities were greater than her willingness to take that chance. You will see how this fateful decision works against her throughout the rest of this story.

After we rented our new place in Arizona, I stayed in California for another four months finishing my design jobs. Day after day I went to my design studio, which was a very peaceful place for me. I started to think that it was crazy to be leaving when everything was going so well. I reasoned that I was making very good money, I was happy, everyone loved my designs; things were perfect. I was beginning to feel torn.

About a month before my jobs were due to be completed and shortly after I started feeling regrets, I got a message. I was working at my desk and my *guides* said, *"Nothing is as it appears to be, everything will change by the end of the year. Stay on course!"* Receiving that, I snapped right out of my wishful thinking. I was left with a sad feeling because, in that moment, I realized that my entire life had been a series of highs and lows. As soon as I got something working and life was great, something else came along to change it all.

Success was easy. Listening to a *greater wisdom* and acting on it was what always separated me from everyone else. I had become a master at both receiving *their* messages, as well as acting on them on time, at least most of the time.

 AWARENESS: The reason most people don't act on the guidance their *guides* provide, even when it's strong, is because it usually involves changes. These changes may not appeal to them or to those they have made promises to, like family. However, if they don't follow their *guidance*, their safe, compromised lives eventually wear them down.

My *guides* told me that the move to Arizona was going to prove to be more important than I realized, even if it was not obvious at first. *They* said that everyone I knew in Sacramento would fall away for one reason or another.

Because Steve had moved our things to Arizona almost everything had been moved out of our Sacramento house so life was simplified now. I would go to my design studio in the daytime and go home at night and read books about channeling.

One night, while I was lying down reading one of these books, I had a seven-inch crystal that I had gotten on the New Mexico trip laying across my stomach. Suddenly there was a loud snap and the crystal cracked right in half. At the sound, in my mind's eye, I saw a rocket being launched into space. It used up the fuel in its first stage, releasing that stage of the rocket, which fell back to earth. The front half sped forward. I saw that the front half of my crystal was me moving on, leaving the used-up half behind. I left the back half of that crystal with Cindy when I moved.

 AWARENESS: This is another way *they* communicate, and it shows that we're always being guided. We just need to recognize the signs and go with the flow of it all.

When I let Cindy know I was leaving, she became even more distant and cold with me. She had just turned 20 years old and moved out of my mom's place and moved in with her boyfriend. This created a bit of a rift between them. Cindy hadn't liked the rules Mom imposed, although Mom's strategy did work to get Cindy out of debt. Little did I know that her commiserating with Mom about me, which had intensified over the last few years, would gather even more steam once I left.

Cindy continued to tell everyone negative things about me. She had been a liar and a manipulator her entire life, and now she was on a mission to capitalize on it. Fortunately, I was not meant to be a part of that as I was on my way out of her life.

I remember Cindy telling me about the time my mom returned home from the hospital and had confided in Cindy, telling her that she was thinking about getting a job. She never had a job in all her 55 years; she had no skills, no job experience, and she was getting concerned about her finances.

All her life, Mom had treated people who worked in service jobs like they were an underclass. She was disrespectful to them, snapping her fingers demanding their immediate attention. She treated them like her slaves. Going anywhere with her was embarrassing.

Once she decided to seek work, ironically, she got hired as a cashier at a convenience store. Now she got to experience what it was like to be in the shoes of those she had always looked down upon. She could occasionally still be her nasty self with people and get away with it because it was a low-level service job that didn't really attract reliable employees. It was a perfect position for her.

Just before I left, I called my mom and told her I was moving to Arizona. She was a little surprised but that was all.

In advance of my leaving, I went to dinner with my friend Mary several times. She had been going through severe anxiety attacks almost every day. I was really worried about her because it was taking a physical toll on her. Both of her retail stores were thriving, and Mary was living alone, having split up with her husband after Mark died. I spent as much time with her as I could and went with her to her first grief-support group before I left. She really liked it and was now in good hands.

I also visited a few other people we had built homes for over the years. Most importantly, I continued with my channeling partners, testing, learning and perfecting the process. I was writing the guidelines so people could learn to use the talking board the correct way to contact their *guides*.

 AWARENESS: Your *guides* are always moving you into a better life for multiple reasons. *They* work from the big picture and are brilliant planners and strategists. *They* see it all.

I was excited about finally leaving and starting our new life in Arizona with the new project. I was very calm and relaxed as I stepped out of my past and into the future, despite not knowing anyone in the new location. I had just had four months to myself finishing up my design jobs, perfecting my channeling skills, and saying my goodbyes. I felt complete and ready for my new life.

I flew to Phoenix at night and Steve picked me up. He was filled with anxiety and was focusing on everything that was wrong. It was awful driving with him to our new home just outside of Sedona.

Once we got to our house, I started to see what was happening. The first thing I noticed was a horrible smell. Steve told me that our dog, Chu, had gone after a skunk, and the skunk prevailed. He said he had been too drunk to clean her up.

It turns out that he had been spending a great deal of time fishing and drinking at the creek a few miles away. I was surprised at this behavior from him. He had been waiting for me to show up before starting anything. It was like he was completely clueless about how to move forward. I didn't understand it. After I arrived in Arizona, he became very emotionally and mentally abusive, which also surprised me. Everything changed in him; he became angry and mean.

I came to realize he was scared. I didn't understand his fear because we had created a pretty clear plan. I couldn't let his fears take me down, so while he was losing it, I just kept on course, working every day, finalizing our new product, and thinking through our marketing and training plans with the help of my *guides*.

 LESSON: This is what it's like when you have and follow the insights from your *guides* and your partner doesn't have the same awareness. The one who doesn't have a conscious connection to their *guides* is totally dependent on the one who does. This becomes a burden to the one who does. They get blamed when things "appear" not to be working out, and their partner takes the credit when things do. This never holds up over the long run and is designed to help you make better choices going forward. This is what my *guides* saw less than a year before — when *they* told me to leave Steve behind in California.

One day Steve told me that we didn't have the money for rent and asked me what we were going to do. I told him to go to Sedona and do his errands, and I would work on it. I told him all I needed him to do was to avoid thinking about it while he was gone. The fact is, I didn't even remember making that request. That's how *divine intervention* works. *My guides* were fast at work.

Steve went into Sedona, and I focused my intentions on what our moves going forward would look like. With the help of *my guides,* I started to see it and feel it. We were already booked to do an Expo in November. It would be our first big show, so we didn't have a booth setup or presentation for it yet. We would be unveiling our new talking board that, so far, only had a negative reputation from the Ouija Board. My *guides* had charged me with the task of turning this around because *they* saw that people would need a way to contact their own *guides* as their lives became more uncertain in the years to come.

Steve's errands took a few hours, and when he got back, he was frantic. With trembling hands, he opened his wallet and showed me $850 in cash (exactly what we needed for rent) and asked me where it came from. It wasn't there when he left, and he swore he hadn't robbed anyone.

I wasn't surprised at all. I calmly asked him if he had done what I asked him to do when he left — to not think about it. He shook his head up and down. I nodded and told him that that was the reason it worked. He still prodded me for answers because he didn't understand, but that was the only way I could explain it to him. His only job had been to not interrupt the *divine* gift and allow it to manifest. I was making money the old-fashioned way — by manifesting it.

Then I showed him the booth I had designed while he was gone for the upcoming L.A. Expo. He loved it and began to see how things would work out. We went right to work on putting it all together. I was never afraid as he had been because I had my *guides*. Everyone has their *guides*; most just don't know it.

 TIP: When you learn to work with your *guides,* you learn not to panic or be in fear. *They* can't come through when you are filled up with resistance. It's the opposite energy of *them*. It's a life-killer. Don't be naïve and think your *guides* will just stick money in your wallet or purse all the time. But when you are in alignment with *them* and need arises, that need will be met – if you stay out of the way.

While we were preparing for the L.A. Expo, our ads for the talking board appeared in some national publications. A man from Texas bought a board, and he called to tell me something interesting. He said that he contacted a *guide* who told him he was my *guide*. The man told me the name he was given, which was indeed my *guide's* name, a very unusual one. I had never mentioned the name to anyone, so there was no way he could have known it other than getting it straight from the *source*. The call surprised the heck out of me.

He said that he had been told by this *guide* to ask me if it would be okay for him to consult with my *guide*. I realized that the reason my *guide* really asked him to call was to let me know how well the board really worked. In other words, it is energy that draws a *guide* to a person. My *guide* isn't really just *mine*. *Guides* are available to anyone who needs *their* help, has a connection with *them,* and is open to it.

Then one of the predictions my *guides* had told me about just 10 month earlier was happening. On October 17, 1989, the San Francisco-Oakland area was violently shaken by the strongest earthquake to hit the area since the San Francisco quake of 1906. It caused more than 60 deaths, thousands of injuries, and widespread property damage. It took place two months after I left California, and ten months after *they* predicted it in my first channeling session in December 1988. The cofferdam of Folsom Lake did indeed fail, just like *they* predicted it would. And, the Army Corps of Engineers drained Folsom Lake while they rebuilt it, a three-year undertaking — also, just like *they* had called it.

By the end of 1989, just four months after I left California and my thriving architectural practice, the country fell into a terrible recession. It happened just one year after *their* prediction originally came through. Also, when I was having second thoughts in July, just one month before I left, *they* said, "*Nothing is as it appears to be, everything will change by the end of the year — stay on course!*" Once again, *they* were right on the money — even when I wasn't.

Chapter 20: Powerful Forces Amp Up My Energy

Moving to a new state after living in California all my life was pretty strange. I was starting a new business when building and home design were all I had ever done, while dealing with a very different husband — one who had become moody and angry all the time. I was seeing what *they* meant in that first channeling in December 1988 when *they* told me to leave Steve behind. But for the time being, we were doing the best we could with a new life and a new business.

 AWARENESS: Your *guides* are always candid with you. *They* don't consider whether you can handle the truth or not; of course you can. <u>How</u> you handle it is up to you.

We were a big hit at the L.A. Expo. Crowds were 30 people deep at our booth to sample our new talking board and learn to communicate with their *guides*. Most loved it, a few were skeptical, and a few others were afraid because of the negativity associated with the Ouija Board.

For demonstration purposes, I made a transparency of the talking board image that fit on an overhead projector glass. This projected the talking board high up on the wall directly behind us on a 12' x 12' screen. The result was that no matter where you were inside the Expo, you could see us in action.

It was exciting to watch and exactly what my *guides* had shown me a month earlier.

I demonstrated the board's use with each person. I put my hand on the speller (i.e., the planchette) and directed them to do the same. I told them to focus on breathing and let your *guides* come through. I talked to them about what was happening as the speller started moving around the board faster and faster. Then as clear messages were being transmitted from their *guides,* I spoke them out loud.

The people around us were also reading the messages out loud from the overhead screen, which drew even more attention to our booth. Each person received about 10 minutes of messages from their *guides*. I worked without a break for three or four hours at a time. I lost track of time. I didn't hear anyone around me or any other noises or announcements at the Expo — it was just me, the person in front of me, and their first contact with their *guides*. It was good training for me, as I experienced many interesting things.

This was such an explosive demonstration that a Kirlian photographer brought his equipment over to our booth and asked me to put my hand into the photography boot so he could take a photo. I did it in front of everyone waiting in line for their turn with me at the talking board. He immediately displayed it, saying he had never seen so much energy in a photo before. The crowd went crazy with excitement. That just added more fuel to an already roaring blaze of interest. The talking board was a huge success.

After the L.A. Expo, I booked shows for myself in Arizona and California while Steve started his own computer repair business in Sedona and the Verde Valley. I applied the same successful presentation I had used at the L.A. Expo in other shows throughout 1990. More and more people got the experience of what it was like to try the board to make contact with their *guides*. From the exposure I had at these shows, I met many people who wanted training to advance their use of the talking board.

As a result of those requests, I started classroom training lessons. They were filled every time. From that, I chose several people whom I continued to train to be my channeling partners to perform channeled readings for clients and perform at the shows with me. That would turn out to be a real eye-opener for me.

We had been in Arizona for just about four months when Steve's mom came to visit. I was in the midst of a project teaching people to channel their *guides* on the talking board. She was very curious about what this was, so she asked me to take her with me to the event I had scheduled in Sedona that night. I told her it was probably not a good idea and attempted to discourage her from coming, but she insisted, so I told her to be ready for anything, because anything could happen.

I had a sense that she really didn't know what she was getting involved with, and, sure enough, when it was her turn to receive messages her deceased husband came through. He spoke to her saying things only she would understand. She was shocked, and she cried as she asked him questions that he could only answer. That started healing deep-seated wounds. She was grateful and confused at the same time.

She was grateful because she was undeniably in contact with her late husband. She was confused because, being Jewish, she followed a tradition that didn't believe in life after death. She observed for the rest of the night as other people's *spirit guides* and *those who crossed over* came through and communicated with them. The next morning, only a day after she had arrived, she took the shuttle van to the airport and flew back home. She wasn't mad at me; she was torn between her beliefs and her experience.

TIP: It's a powerful experience when you make your first contact with your *guides. They* are straightforward and see things that you don't. *They* also see what's coming. *They* speak to you in an organized way as *they* elevate you to higher understandings. For some, this will be such a powerful experience that it will literally make them dizzy. This is what a shift in consciousness can feel like. For others, it will put them to sleep. Many won't even realize it happened, or will forget it as soon as it does. Your job is to release all resistance and open up to this expanded awareness so you can benefit from it in the here and now.

Training people on the correct use of the talking board was my number-one focus. Unfortunately, most of the people I trained attempted to dominate their channeling partner and even me. Most turned out to be power-hungry, taking credit for the channeled information that actually came from a *higher intelligence.* Their egos took over. The moment they did that, the channeled information became corrupted; it started coming from their own biases, thoughts, and beliefs instead of coming clearly and cleanly from the *source*. They misused their potential to channel greater wisdom for self-satisfying reasons.

Their need to be right was their biggest downfall because it closed down all access to their *guides*. Pure channels, or mediums, get egos out of the way to access the highest quality information from beyond this earth plane to pass that through into this dimension. When performing this way for a client, it allows answers relevant to the client to be transmitted directly from their *guides*. It's always accurate.

I would bring this to their attention, but they would fiercely defend themselves. This was completely unacceptable. From my experience over the years, this is the only problem in using this, or any modality to access information from your *guides*. The charlatans you hear about all the time are people who twist the information because they are coming from their ego. They have their own agenda, and that's where everything goes wrong.

I kept coming across people who were seduced by their egos as they claimed to be in contact with their *guides*. It happened over and over again, channeling partner after partner. It continued to happen as these people with advanced training would contaminate the information. I would cut them loose and move on to others on the waiting list. Just like my mother had demonstrated to me, I was witnessing what power looked like in the wrong hands. There were a lot of wrong hands.

In the summer of 1990, I did a psychic fair with a young girl I had trained. Alisha was in her early 20s. She was one of the few who didn't indulge in self-serving tactics. It was refreshing working with her because she was truly interested in learning what *those wise beings* had to relay to the people we did channeled readings for. Until I encountered her, I didn't know if this cooperative quality could be found in another. I was pleased to see it could be.

We arrived in Southern California the night before the event. Alisha and I stayed with my mother in-law at the home she had rented for the summer. I really liked my mother-in-law, and she was delighted to have us with her since she had come to peace with her experience at the Sedona channeling event.

That night when I went to bed, I closed the door and the heavy wood plantation blinds, making the bedroom pitch black. I closed my eyes, and all of a sudden, a bright blue light permeated the room. I looked at the blinds, thinking it must be coming from there, but they were still sealed shut. This light was not coming through cracks in any window or door; it was in the room.

I tried to keep my eyes open and experience it as long as I could, but I couldn't stay awake. I woke up in the morning with *someone* pulling on my legs. *They* were telling me it was time to wake up and get to the event. I guess *whoever* the *visitors* were from the night before knew I would need help waking up after doing some sort of energy work on me.

At breakfast, Steve's mom and Alisha said nothing about what I had experienced. I asked them if they had seen a blue light the night before, and they said they hadn't. I asked my mother-in-law if she ever saw a blue light in the house, and she said no. I let it go. I felt especially good once I was awake, and I knew it had everything to do with that blue light experience. I knew *they* were up to something.

 AWARENESS: When you work with your *guides* to be of service to others, *they* help you in every way possible. This would turn out to be just the start of more to come.

When we got to the venue, Alisha and I started doing channeled readings for people. Though it started out like usual, all of a sudden my voice turned into what sounded like a computer-synthesized voice. The messages I was speaking out loud were emotionless and very mechanical. I couldn't help it, or stop it. For me, this was obvious, and I was sure everyone else was hearing it. The client didn't seem to hear it, and Alisha only heard it intermittently.

Whatever was happening, it was only happening to me and not anyone else. That's all I knew and all I was allowed to know at that point.

 TIP: As you learn to discover these *unseen forces,* you won't always understand the "when" and "why" of what *they* do. By the fact that you recognize that something is indeed happening, and that you are ready to receive these adjustments, expect more interesting encounters going forward. There's nothing to fear.

Alisha was due to go back to college in the fall. It had been great working with her, and because of her, I finally experienced someone else whose traits made a good channeling partner. Unfortunately, people who possess those traits are rare. When Alisha left, another person from the training class approached me and wanted to work with me. His name was Mike. He was older and was married, so I was okay with trying him out. We started doing events, and things were going fine.

In the summer of 1990, I stayed overnight in a Phoenix hotel after one of my events. That evening I went swimming, and after I got out of the pool, I was *telepathically guided* to lie on the grass on my back. This was similar to the UFO encounter I had in 1972. I did so and instantly started vibrating all over. It progressed into a gentle bouncing of my entire body off the ground. It was like electricity. Then *they* started communicating with me telepathically.

I telepathically communicated back, asking *them* where *they* were. *They* said *they* were on a platform, and *they* were there to raise my energy. *They* asked me to let *them* know if it became too much, and *they* would stop. I told *them* it was okay, and *they* continued delivering *their* electrical charge all through me, as my body vibrated and my teeth started to chatter uncontrollably.

While this was going on, I was transported into a dark, secluded cave where there was a large body of water. I was wearing an electric dress from head to toe. It was a shiny, alive, form-fitting white formal garment. I was lying on my back with my feet in the water and my head in the lap of a Native-American man. The electricity was pulsing throughout my body in this sacred place with the *Native-American guide* looking over me. I don't know how long this went on, but it just stopped when the work was finished.

After the experience, I was physically wiped out. I couldn't walk or talk, so I crawled across the lawn until I stopped vibrating. Once the vibrating and teeth chattering stopped, I stood up and slowly walked back to my room. I was really tired as I fell across my bed. The next thing I knew, it was morning. Apparently I had been ready for an "amping up," and I sure got it!

 TIP: From this, you can see what's possible when you're not afraid so a greater potential can emerge. When you have a strong long-term connection to your *guides,* you are protected, so the key is to not question it because that will stop it cold every time. The effect of this event changed me forever in a powerful and positive way.

The next day, I drove back to Sedona, and the minute I walked through the front door, Steve took one look at me and started crying. That wasn't like him. Then he said, "I'm losing you." He could feel this energy shift in me. I didn't know what he meant. I hadn't told him what happened because I knew it would have scared him. In fact, I never told anyone — how could I? Why would I? For me it was just an ongoing process.

My next event was the Tucson Psychic Faire. To my surprise, the Tucson TV news station showed up unexpectedly with their cameras, lights, news reporter, and microphones. When they entered the room, they came directly to my booth. We were in the middle of a channeling session projected on an overhead screen. The image that bounced off the back wall had created a lot of interest and like always it drew a crowd.

The reporters walked up to me, stuck microphones in my face, and started asking me questions. As this happened, my channeling partner, Mike, came over and literally pushed me out of the way. He positioned himself in front of the cameras, waiting to be interviewed. The reporter asked him to stand aside as they wanted to interview me. Mike reluctantly moved, and the reporters shot a lot of footage and did a short interview with me. It was aired that night on the six o'clock and ten o'clock news. It was great publicity and nice to see that people liked what we did. Unfortunately, I didn't know what to make of Mike anymore.

After this sweet-and-sour moment at the Tucson event, I stopped doing all events and training. Mike said I wouldn't dare stop doing this with the media momentum working for me. I looked him in the eye and told him he sure didn't know me. I also told him I couldn't work with him after what he had done.

I discovered Mike belonged to a spiritualist church where they did amateur channeling contests. I call it "Karaoke channeling." The attendees at this church would recite channeled messages in strange voices as their bodies went into gyrations. They couldn't remember what they did, which is known as trance channeling, so it provided no value to them personally. What was the point? This was like "show and tell," and a B-rated performance at best.

These people had a poverty consciousness, and they actually took pride in it. They followed the false belief that poor is pure. I saw that they were just using spirituality as an excuse for their poverty-filled lives. They were also competitive about who was the best channel, missing the point as they pandered to each other week after week. That sure didn't work for me. I was glad to say goodbye to Mike.

After my disappointment with Mike and so many people like him, I took my project back to the drawing board, to retest it based on what I had learned. For the first time, I realized that this new project had a life of its own, and its timing was not up to me.

I had never owned a project like this before. I saw it was going to take a while to develop it as it moved to the next phase. That was when I made it a part-time endeavor and got back into real estate during the day. I started training and working with people in the evenings. It was never hard to find candidates, because almost everyone I spoke with was fascinated and felt privileged to be invited in.

In the winter of 1990, I started designing a big house for a Phoenix real estate broker who was planning on relocating to Sedona. I needed a layout table to start the job, so Steve built one for me, and I painted it when Steve was away for the night.

The paint I used was oil based so the fumes were toxic. By the time I was done painting it, I was very tired so I went to bed. I knew I should have opened the windows to vent the fumes, but it was cold outside so I hadn't. In my deep sleep, I was dreaming about crawling down the hallway to the big sliding-glass door in the living room and throwing it open. In this dream my *guides* were once again telling me what to do, step by step. I was exhausted and just wanted to sleep, so I found the dream annoying rather than instructional.

Next, I was awakened by a visitation from *them* as *they* blasted a bright light at me through the window on the high part of the bedroom wall. It was as if there was a helicopter outside the window, but without any sound. The light was about fifteen feet outside the window. Since the house was surrounded by pine trees, I knew it couldn't be a helicopter. The bright light was really bothering me because I was so tired, and it kept waking me up. Just like the dream. *They* actually made me act on what the dream had told me to do earlier: *"Crawl down the hallway, get to the sliding-glass door and open it up."* *They* told me to crawl because *they* knew I was so intoxicated by the fumes that I couldn't walk.

Finally I relented. It took everything I had to physically do this. After throwing the door open, I crawled back to the bedroom as fast as I could and passed out. The next morning when I woke up, it was freezing in the house. I walked out to the open living-room sliding-glass door and closed it. That's when I remembered the dream and also the visitation, and realized that if I hadn't gotten the fumes out of the house, I never would have awakened. I realized *they* came to my rescue. I also realized in doing that, *they* wanted me here for some reason. Apparently I wasn't done yet.

 AWARENESS: It's in times like these that you have to ask yourself if you were attempting to devise a way out of here. After all, with my background in construction,

I knew better than anyone to vent the house after painting that table. Again, unconsciously, was I looking for an escape hatch?

When you catch yourself doing something like this, you know that something is wrong in your life. You know you need to make some changes — and they're probably overdue. In my case, my *guides* had warned me just one year before to get out of my marriage. Little did I know at that time how important *their* message would turn out to be, and how much Steve was going to change when we moved to Arizona. But *my guides* knew.

One Sunday morning a few months after the incident with the paint fumes, Steve and I were sleeping when a high pitched sonar-like sound traveled about two feet over our heads. It was like the sound of a whale in the ocean. From all my years of life-coach training from my *spirit guides*, I knew to just lie there, not question it, and just let it tell me what it intended for me to know.

Steve didn't have my experience, so he jumped up and demanded that I tell him what was going on. I tried to stay with it, but he was too loud and interfered with the magic of the moment. I told him he interrupted it so I couldn't tell him anything. Once again, he was really scared. I couldn't believe how he was reacting. And again I saw this as the *merry-go-round dream* showing me how fear would dominate people so that many couldn't be reached.

Chapter 21: My Advisors Mastermind My Next Moves

Having put the channeling project on hold, I took my next step in real estate. As a home builder, an architectural designer, and a subcontractor, I was completing the circle by getting my real estate license. Once I had my license, I began by researching the area to become market savvy before considering myself ready to work with a client.

I found that the real estate brokers were an ego-driven, money-hungry, demanding bunch. Like the channeling partners I had experienced, these people also lusted for fame and fortune. It seemed that everyone expected more, faster. My broker was just about ready to fire me because I wouldn't sell anything until I knew I was ready. I noted that, in my own businesses, I had had the luxury of doing what I loved, which allowed me to always work from the highest integrity.

I knew to be successful I needed to be working pretty much all the time. Working all the time was not what the others around me in real estate wanted; they just wanted fast results and some sort of glorified outcome. They became jealous of me and tried to undermine me on every front. I just kept walking through it, ignoring them.

 TIP: Just because you dread doing something doesn't mean you shouldn't do it, at least for a while. Consider that you weren't quite done, and this is the final step to completing what you needed to learn or do. Hang in there; it's only you who can't see the entire picture. To me, getting back into real estate felt like I was backing up, when what was really happening was that this time, I was just along for the ride.

Meanwhile, life for Cindy back in California was taking on life-changing turns. Cindy married her boyfriend at the start of 1991. Steve and I went to the wedding and found that many of the guests had already formed an opinion of me — and it wasn't a positive one. I had never met these people, so apparently Cindy had been telling her new family members negative things about me to win them over. To top it off, Mom was enjoying how people shared her disapproving view of me. While I took a number of photos at the wedding, somehow, none of them came out. No unhappy Kodak moments for me.

Cindy got pregnant on her honeymoon. In early October, she called to say she was in labor, so I flew to Sacramento to be with her, but it was a false alarm. She finally went into labor two weeks later and I could not afford to fly back out. Of course, my not being there validated all the lousy-mom stories she had been telling about me. I later discovered that that was all part of a web of manipulation and drama she would use later. There went that squandered acting career in favor of a life of self-destructive lies and manipulation. Cindy and her husband were divorced a year after the baby was born.

During and after Cindy's pregnancy, Steve and I had been struggling financially. I finally became fed up with it and decided to take action. It had been three years since we had left the Sacramento area. We continued to pay on a mountain of debt we had brought with us from the California building project.

I looked our financial situation square in the eye. We had paid off everyone except the banks and the interest-gouging investors. I told Steve I was going to see an attorney about filing bankruptcy, and he freaked out. To me, it was just business. Not doing it kept us frozen in time, and I was being *guided* to act on this right now. *My guides* told me that this was the right time.

Despite Steve's fear, I went to an attorney and got an objective assessment of our situation. His verdict: we were definitely a candidate for bankruptcy.

Just before filing, I found a house in the heart of Sedona that the owner would finance. I showed it to Steve, and, again, he fought me. He wanted to live in a nicer property and just keep renting. At that same time, Steve's mom wanted to give us her car. I asked her to sell the car and send us the money she got so we could use it for the down payment on the property. She agreed; we bought the property and were able to close on it before the bankruptcy was filed.

Everything was falling into place; however, starting over meant sacrifices. I was willing to make them, but I had to drag Steve along like a boulder on my back. Little did I know the momentum was building for our next endeavor, and buying this property would play a critical part in it.

Just weeks after closing on the house, Steve, his mom, and I went to Sacramento for Christmas to meet Cindy's new baby.

Steve's mom had never had grandchildren, which was too bad because she had wanted them and would have been a terrific grandmother. I loved that she might experience that through me.

Unfortunately, my mother was there and ruined the whole thing. She was rude and sarcastic to my mother-in-law, which was very hurtful to this lovely woman. Seeing her behavior just made me love my mother-in-law even more. After that episode I told her I was adopting her as my real mother.

When we got back to Sedona, I started working on the bankruptcy in earnest. I filed on April fool's day, 1992, just to put it all into perspective. Steve was so upset about it that he confided in his mother about what I had done, blaming it all on me. To his surprise, his mother told him that his grandfather, the grandfather he had idolized his entire life, had filed for bankruptcy not once, but twice when it was considered a shameful thing to do. She commended me for taking charge and putting this behind us. Steve finally stopped struggling with it.

 AWARENESS: Hard decisions that must be made may distress those around you. They make it harder to move forward. If you find your spouse pulling against you, you may come to realize that you are no longer a fit. If the situation causing the conflict does not resolve itself, like them rising to the occasion, it is likely that eventually your relationship will fail.

Steve continued to build up his computer repair business as I was beginning to sell property. Every month I did better than the month before because I really knew the market. I also understood and disclosed to the buyer the truth about how well or poorly a property was constructed. I showed them how they could change or fix a property to suit them, while producing maximum resale value. The added value I provided was how I grew my business. I also continued my architectural design practice.

Steve, on the other hand, was struggling with his computer repair business because customers were hard to please. One day Steve and I were standing outside on the driveway area of our property next to our cars talking with our friend, Jackie, and her son. Out of the blue, I said, "Watch this!" I walked down into the apple orchard on our property as a spinning whirlwind appeared next to me on my right side. It was like walking a dog; it moved right along with me, turned around when I did, and stopped and started walking again when I did.

Only after my spinning companion and I were at the far end of the property and I turned around and looked up at Steve and Jackie did I realize what had just happened. That's when I recalled when I had said: "Watch this." I was completely "in the moment" with my spinning companion.

It continued to walk with me as I walked back, like it didn't want to leave me. As I got closer to them, my spinning companion dissipated into thin air. They all asked me how I did that. I told them I didn't know. It was years later that, by chance, I ran into Jackie, and she asked me to do that thing again when I walked with my spinning companion. I laughed and told her I didn't do that, it was just there. She thought it was a magic trick.

AWARENESS: Think about the times you have caught yourself "in the moment." It's in that "moment" that you find yourself to be unlimited, and that's when anything is possible. The key is not to interrupt that "moment" by questioning it or having to explain it. Don't expect everything to make sense to you in the moment that it happens.

In the summer of 1993, my mom visited us from California. I took her to the Grand Canyon and through the Indian Reservations and Trading Posts she had always dreamed of seeing. I was surprised at her low energy. She had a hard time getting in and out of my Toyota 4-Runner. Even so, I think she enjoyed herself.

From the time she arrived, true to form, she was very judgmental about the property we had purchased. Before she left, she took lots of pictures of our less-than-opulent living conditions. Years later, Cindy told me that she showed the photos to anyone who would listen, using them to show how I had failed in life. I wasn't surprised and just continued to look past her need to wish the worst for me.

 TIP: Never let people like my mother pull you down. They are disconnected from their *guidance*. They are also in a lot of pain all the time — all of it self-created by their negativity. Hopefully, at some point, they will recognize that something is missing, and they will get it right.

Around this time in 1993, I had a dream where I saw hundreds of volcanoes erupting off the western coastline of the U.S. Then I was instantly transported to Japan and saw even more volcanoes erupting off their coastline. Then I was back on the west coast of the U.S. and saw big earthquakes shearing off the coastal mountain ranges. Thousands of volcanoes were boiling under the water off the coastline, and then came more earthquakes. Next I was back in Japan, and I saw it implode – it was completely gone! When I have dreams like this, my sense is that although they seem out of context, they may be prophetic of things to come.

Despite my mother's evaluation of my life, I was actually doing very well in real estate. By 1994, I had gotten my real estate broker's license, and by the spring, I had opened my own real estate office.

In one of my channeling sessions just before I opened the real estate office, *my guides* told me that our real success would not come from opening this brokerage. It would be from something that had to do with information downloads that would be viewed on what looked like small TVs. I didn't know what this could be at that time, and I was disappointed to hear it because I had put so much into real estate.

I opened the real estate office anyway. Steve's friend, Al, moved to Sedona from California and came to work at my brokerage as an associate broker. I was again off and running.

 TIP: Just because you don't understand the meaning of your *guides'* messages doesn't mean you should start second-guessing yourself. Expect to be confused at times, but don't let it scare you.

A couple months after I opened my brokerage, Steve came to me and said he could no longer do computer repair. He was really tired of ungrateful clients, and I could see that he was truly suffering from it. He told me he wanted to sell the business, but he didn't know what to do next. I told him to sell it and take some time off to recover so he could decide. So, that's what he did.

The Comdex Show, a trade show for the computer industry, was scheduled for November 1994 in Las Vegas. Steve said he wanted to go. I couldn't go with him because of the demands of the real estate business, but I told him to go without me. When he came back, he was very excited. He told me that the Internet was taking off. I instantly felt a bolt of energy run all through me.

The feeling was so strong that I told him to research what it would take to build the infrastructure, operate it, and launch it. We had $50,000 saved up, and I was making about $10,000 a month in real estate. Within a few weeks, Steve had completed the research. When he realized the magnitude of what it would take to get it moving, he choked. He told me he didn't want to work that hard.

I couldn't believe what he said. I told him this had a short window of opportunity, and we were going to go for it. Within a month, almost all of the $50,000 was spent — but we had modems, servers, software, computers, and phone connections. We didn't have a lot of capital left, but we could pull it off.

Interestingly, the property we had bought in 1992 turned out to be perfectly located for our endeavor. This was the same property he resisted buying two years before because it wasn't as nice as the rental property we were living in. It was close to the telephone company's central office, which was important because, back then, modems using phone lines was the way Internet Service Providers (ISPs) connected their customers to the web. Also, our property was not hampered by zoning laws, so there was no trouble having the necessary hundreds of phone lines housed there. The property was a critical part of what it took to launch it. It was perfect synchronicity, and thanks to my *guides*, it was working out perfectly in every way.

 TIP: This is a perfect example of how taking timely action is critical. Hesitating would have squandered the opportunity. Once again, moments of opportunity always have a shelf life.

The year 1994 was also a year when a most unusual thing happened: one of my *"Spirit Guide Angels"* materialized, allowing me to take *her* photograph.

Photograph taken by Linda Deir when her *"Spirit Guide Angel"* materialized

In this photo you can see *her* emerging right out of the TV. *It* is clearly a female form, very tall and beautiful, and *her* presence and energy consumed the room. You can see right through the beautiful, translucent white, blue, yellow, and orange colors that define *her* form (see the front cover of this book). This photograph of my *Spirit Guide Angel* is what *"they"* really look like. *"They"* are energy that use our energy to project *themselves* into our dimension so we can see *them*.

I happened to have my Nikon SLR 35mm camera in hand, and there she appeared in full glory allowing me to take the photograph that would become the cover of this book 20 years later.

The same year I took this photograph of my *Spirit Guide Angel*, in 1994, I had a dream. *They* showed me that I would write a book about relationships that would become a best-seller. This book would turn out to be about my relationship with my *guides* so you could learn how to discover your own. *They also* said that this would become one of many books I would author, and they would all be easy to write. This was one of those dreams that woke me up right out of a dead sleep. I was really meant to remember this one. *They* were showing me my future beyond everything I was doing at that time.

We had started what would be Northern Arizona's first Internet Service Provider (ISP) in December 1994, and it was up and running by February 1995. On March 6, 1995, we went live — exactly one year to the day after opening my real estate brokerage. The technical staff worked out of our property where the infrastructure was housed, and Al and I handled all the on-site customer service at my real estate office. We put up a second sign for the Internet and hosting businesses right under the real estate sign.

I was now aware that the Internet was what *they* had described to me a year earlier, just before I opened my real estate office. That was when my *guides* told me real financial success would not come from opening this real estate bro-kerage, but something else that had to do with information downloads. The things that looked like TVs, of course, were computer monitors. Amazing how everything made perfect sense in hindsight. But then, that's the brilliant way your *guides* work for you.

LESSON: Everything that led up to opening the ISP was already in motion years before. What made it possible was acting on *their guidance* every time it showed up, without hesitation. It's not enough to take action in one place only to miss it in others. To experience real success in your life, you have to be "on" all the time so you are accessible to your *guides*. Are you ready to get to know them?

Our Internet business took off. It was a success from day one. Even though it was doing well, our expenses were greater than our income in the beginning. Steve came to me saying a local stockbroker had offered him $15,000 for a fifty-percent interest in our company. I said that was never going to happen. I sternly told Steve we would make it without investors. I was making enough money in real estate to get us through the lean times. Six months later, the Internet and hosting businesses were breaking even and still growing fast. Based on that, we finally were able to hire help. Our first employee was the administrator. He was a kid still in high school and a rare find. The entire business hinged on him. Steve knew how to put this all together, but he was still scared.

TIP: Once you make a decision, it's best to leave your fears behind. Releasing fear into your endeavor will hinder its potential for success.

Interestingly, Steve found that Internet customers were even more demanding than those he had encountered with the computer repair business. They didn't understand that there would be glitches from time to time. They expected perfection. They screamed and yelled and acted unreasonably when the system when down, reflecting back to Steve the way he had been behaving over the past few years. This had all the signs of karma pointing back at him.

Many of our customers were using the Internet to trade their own stock accounts. If the Internet went down, they would call in screaming at our support team. Everyone tried hard to keep the systems up. Our alarms would sound the moment there was a glitch of any kind, and no matter what time of the night or day, we would get on it.

In those early days, it was the Wild, Wild West for the Internet. I was constantly attending litigation classes to be among the first to find out what case law might affect us and how to mitigate it. Meanwhile, Steve was doing a great job putting the staff together, and I was really good at managing them.

About a year after we went live, we relocated the public office to a larger space. It housed all the support staff and front-counter people. Steve didn't like the public office. He continued to work out of our remote property. From the beginning, I had told Steve we were building these businesses to sell them. In planning that, we now needed to move the phone lines and modems to a commercial location. This location had to be close to the public office and the phone company's central office, and it had to be secure. That was a big order.

By 1996, things were going smoothly. Steve and I knew that the technology was moving toward high speed. The Internet boom was white hot. We had hit it just right, but that would only be a good thing if we had a carefully planned exit strategy.

This time I wasn't going to ride the wave too close to the shore, as I had when I strategically cashed out of real estate in the late 1970s. The business was perfectly positioned, well-oiled and seasoned. It was time to find a buyer. We had to be under the radar, though, because knowing we were looking to sell would have negatively affected the goodwill we had established with our customers. It would be tricky, but I felt I was ahead of the curve this time. I also felt the technology crash coming. My *guides* warned me that it would be a big one.

 AWARENESS: Your *guides* expect you to hone your skills as you learn. *They* are there for you, but you should use your experience to make better decisions the second time around.

We bought a small patio home and moved into it the summer of 1996. Steve wanted to buy a big house instead, but I told him I didn't want to be the one left to have to fix it and clean it. He tolerated the new place but never liked it.

Moving to a new home was not the only change for me in 1996. For whatever reason, when I was talking to people, including real estate clients, the subject of dreams started coming up. When I mentioned I helped people understand the meaning of their dreams, my listeners became very interested.

These people loved this special time I spent with them, and they began to learn to understand their dreams on their own. They also became more skillful at remembering them. These same people turned into channeled-reading clients once they understood they had *guides* who were always there for them if only they were open to it. I showed them that their *guides* came through their dreams all the time and I trained them how to recognize *them*. Many of these clients pressed me to write a book. There's that book again!

 AWARENESS: The reminders never stop. *They* will continue to send you hints and nudges. That's *divine*; that's your *guides*. Like a repetitive dream, *they* intend to get your attention so you will take action. That's why me writing a book kept coming up.

Based on what I saw going on, I secured the Internet domain name, www.DreamHelper.com, and essentially set up shop.

In the summer of 1996, Osaka TV contacted us to participate in a two-week Internet tour throughout Japan. They also invited some of the largest Internet Cafe owners in Los Angeles, and the founder of EarthLink. Our mission was to teach the Japanese to think like entrepreneurs. Each company put presentations together. Steve and I negotiated with the sponsors to bring Cindy along as an educational experience for her, and they agreed.

We went on this tour in November 1996, and the moment we landed, vertigo hit me. Like the dream that I had in 1993, I felt how unstable the land mass was, but I was the only one who did. The vertigo I experienced lasted the entire time I was there, which made me feel sick to my stomach all the time and kept me from eating much.

The Japanese people were very sweet, but they could not grasp the concept of working for themselves. They actually looked down on people who were not part of a large company. However, they were very interested in the channeling and dream work I did and learning about their *guides*.

They were so intrigued by what I was showing them, they wouldn't leave me alone. Unfortunately, both Steve and Cindy behaved like "Ugly Americans" and were disrespectful of their culture. They seemed unwilling to learn from the experience. They were criticizing and demanding. I distanced myself from both of them as much as I could.

From the very beginning, Steve was sick with a fever and stomach pains. That had been a recurring problem since we met, but it increased in intensity and frequency over time. His doctors could never figure out the reason for it, and he was sicker than ever during the trip to Japan.

Steve and Cindy's behavior made the trip very hard on me. I finally stopped covering up for them, so people saw their appalling behavior. Even the tour organizer was having regrets about inviting us.

The trip was a turning point for me. I decided to never take Cindy on another trip again. And, from that moment on, I was focused on getting out of my marriage. It was history repeating itself.

LESSON: There comes a point when you're ready to face reality. You just get tired of trying to fix, change, or cover up for other people. The operative word here is "tired." When you get this tired and finally stop trying to control everything, you become much more accessible to your *guides,* and things begin to work again. You need to be aware of the fact that your *guides* only know how to tell you the truth, and that may be uncomfortable for you from time to time.

Chapter 22: The Consequences of Financial Freedom

After the trip to Japan, my total concentration was on staying the course. I knew it could be challenging, but I had to follow through on everything my *guides* had directed me to handle: the business, the marriage, and making personal changes that were long overdue.

The business had a few glitches that needed immediate attention as soon as we returned from Japan. Otherwise, it continued to grow, get favorable publicity, win awards, and generate lots of goodwill. Our support team handled everything with excellence.

As for the marriage, neither Steve nor I were doing anything to save it. On a personal note, I stopped smoking. I had been doing things for the last year setting the stage to make quitting possible. I created rules for both of us, like no smoking in the new house or in the car, and every time I did smoke, I washed my hands. I also started taking specific vitamins to build up my immune system. I stopped cold turkey, but it took three months for the cravings to dissipate. It was the hardest thing I ever did, but I did it. Steve was a heavy smoker and continued to smoke around me all the time. He would hand me lit cigarettes to entice me to start up again. I didn't take the bait.

While I was quitting this habit I started going to the gym every day and drinking ice-cold water constantly. That was also the year I started ice skating; I really threw my heart and soul into the sport. It was something I always wanted to have time to do, but the demands of work had prevented it. I became addicted to the sport and skated at least four times a week, after work and on the weekends. It was this outlet that made it possible for me to get through the next few years.

Steve's outlets were playing racquet ball with his friends and watching football at home while he drank gin and smoked outside. He was very moody. I hated coming home. I never knew what to expect. If his team won, he was okay, but if his team lost, he was angry and moody for days. He was having more frequent episodes of being sick that would last for days, and he drank too much. He blamed me for everything that didn't work smoothly and took the credit for everything that was successful. It seemed like he was creating reasons to dislike me.

In December of 1997, Steve went to Washington State with his pet employee, a fellow named Rod, to meet with Microsoft. When he came back, he was a totally different person. Something happened on that trip, and Steve returned with a big-shot complex. He apparently had plans of his own.

 AWARENESS: There's a principle that says you become like those you associate with. I have found that the more life-coach training I receive from my *guides,* the more I become like *them.* You learn to contact *them* through your dreams and many other ways, and over time, your intuition becomes razor-sharp. Like *them,* you just know what to do and

when to do it. With this working in your favor, no
one can throw you off track.

By 1998, we were so well known in the Internet world that
we were a target for acquisition. As a result, a business broker contacted us to list the businesses. This guy was experienced in cable technology and knew how to acquire investor
capital to take businesses public. A short time after we listed
with him, he brought us a letter of intent from a locally well-
funded interest. Before we opened the books to them, the
broker got them to sign a non-disclosure agreement so they
couldn't use our intellectual property and accounting information to duplicate what we had done.

Even after all this due diligence, the potential buyers violated
all the rules and immediately started up their own Internet
Service Provider Company in our service area. They had
unlimited funds and were willing to use their stable of pow-
erhouse attorneys to defend them and drag things out for
years should we decide to sue them.

When that company did that, it caused our business broker to
take a hard look at the true value of our business. The closer
he looked, the more impressed he became. Before long, he
put an investor group together that bought us out. It was an
example of how what looks like a problem can turn out to be
a blessing.

While the negotiations for our buyout were going on, Steve
and Rod moved down to Scottsdale where Steve had rented a
house. I encouraged him to go because I saw that he had lost

his focus; all he wanted to do was to party all the time. He was a liability. I handled everything, not bringing attention to our personal situation. It was actually better without him because I did not constantly have to fix the problems he created.

About two weeks after Steve moved to Scottsdale, I had a dream where I was in a big room in a high-rise with large windows that had endless views. The room was furnished with a long, elegant meeting table and plush chairs. In it was the *Council of 12, men* in long robes. This was a very important and formal meeting. *They* asked me one question: *"Are you ready for the consequences associated with financial freedom?"*

I had never thought about this in terms of "consequences" before. *Their* question caught me off guard, and I couldn't answer *them* in that moment, so I told *them* I would think about it and then give *them* an answer. I knew this was a very important question that deserved a well thought-out answer. *They* said okay, and that *they* would return again soon to get my answer.

A few weeks later the same *Council of 12* returned in my dream the exact way as before. *They* asked me the same question: *"Are you ready for the consequences associated with financial freedom?"* I told them I was. In that moment, while still in the dream, a realization came through: If having miserable cutthroat family members in my life required me to be miserable too, then I would pass on both counts. Upon reflection, I realized the lesson here is that in life, there are always consequences, even when good things happen.

AWARENESS: A dream like this requires no interpretation. The information you get from your dreams and from your *guides* is free of lies and manipulation. That's why when you are in a lucid dream, you can ask anything or answer anyone, and it will be the truth.

After having this dream the second time, I realized that the sale of these businesses hinged on my decision. Saying "yes" to the *Council* would allow it to happen. I was also clear that not everything would be peachy once it did happen because, as with any action, there would be consequences.

I saw that these consequences would involve jealousy, potential freeloaders, and other things I couldn't yet anticipate. I was already living in a nice, but very non-conspicuous place that I had chosen two years earlier. I decided not to bring any attention to myself after the sale was done. I would keep the same vehicle I had driven for more than seven years. I would never tell anyone what happened. My plan was to change nothing on the outside so my exposure to negative consequences could be minimized.

Right after this dream, I called my mother-in-law. I always adored her, and I wanted her to know what was going on. I told her what was about to happen, and that I was divorcing her son. I apologized for putting her through this, saying that I knew she didn't need something like this at this time in her life. I didn't tell her any details; I just said I couldn't do it anymore and that she would always be special to me. She didn't sound surprised. It was like she knew her son's shortcomings and that I had had my fill of them.

On August 8, 1998, the businesses closed escrow. On the very same day, all the divorce papers and settlement agreement were signed. It was a good day.

Steve and I met at the attorney's office and completed everything together. When we left, he was so exhausted that he almost fell down the stairs. I don't know why he was so tired — I had done all the work to bring things to a close while he was playing in Scottsdale. I think reality in such a large dose overwhelmed him. As we left, he said to me, "You don't want to go where I'm going. How could I love you when I don't love myself." He was being honest for the first time in a long time, but what he said gave me the creeps.

 AWARENESS: Valuable insights and messages can come from people as well as your *guides*. It happens like a slip, or a thought out of context. It's obvious when you hear it because it's so different from the way that person would normally express themselves.

All this took place three days before my 46th birthday, so by my birthday, everything was done and complete. I guess it was only a couple days later that I was asked out on a date. Without thinking, I blurted out, "I can't go out with you, my wings are still wet." The guy just looked at me, bewildered. I couldn't explain it — it just came out that way.

I did know that I was not ready to go out with anyone. In hindsight, I saw what *they* were referring to when this slipped out of my mouth about "wet wings." The last time I had gone through a divorce, and the few times I dated following that, I sweated profusely under my arms, making it very uncomfortable. Your arms are your wings, and *they* knew I wasn't ready and would most likely feel just as uncomfortable now. This was my *guides* letting me know that I was still lacking the social and personal life skills!

 AWARENESS: The language your *guides* will use to reach you many times won't be what you're used to. In this case, *they* spoke those words "through" me and not "to" me as I blurted them out, i.e., "wet wings." By doing this, *they* say a lot in a few words. In my case, it meant that tending to my social and personal life skills would bring me the freedom I was missing: the freedom to fly. After all, wet birds can't fly. Ah, the universal language.

The month following these completions brought me a new experience. Where I thought I would feel a sense of elation and freedom, what I actually felt was exhaustion. I physically collapsed, and for the first time in my life, I developed gastro-intestinal problems. I couldn't stay awake or concentrate either. I just fell apart.

I went to several doctors, had test after test, and all that turned up was a big question mark. The doctors said it was stress related. The anxiety and stress I had held in for so long had finally taken its toll. I was also having severe anxiety attacks where I couldn't catch my breath for hours at a time. I hadn't experienced anything like that since 1988.

Until these things started taking me down, I had plans to get back to work in real estate, even though that wasn't my passion. My health problems stopped me cold. I found myself really frustrated. My life came to a screeching halt. Could this have been one of those consequences my *guides* had hinted at?

Since I couldn't work — or do much of anything, really — I studied books on self-healing. I read a book on healing remedies by Edgar Cayce, a prominent psychic known as the "sleeping prophet." Since everything else had failed, I tried one of his recommendations to address my gastro-intestinal condition and, what do you know? It worked! It was like magic.

By January 1999, I was beginning to feel a little better when I got a call from Steve. He told me that the doctors finally figured out what was causing those persistent fevers and stomach aches; it was a medical condition he had acquired long before we met.

Then he told me he thought the reason he had had fevers and stomach aches all those years was because I was poisoning his food. What?! I couldn't believe what he was saying, but he was always blaming me for his problems.

The next month, Cindy and her new boyfriend came to visit. I gave them my bedroom because my place was small. I couldn't go anywhere with them because I was still pretty sick, so I gave them money to go to restaurants, spas, and on tours. It was the best I could do, and they were out having fun most of the time.

During that visit, Cindy told me that she wanted her inheritance now because she figured I would most likely outlive her. She also decided to tell me that Mom wanted the life I had and was angry about how hers had turned out. Despite wanting something from me, neither Cindy nor her boyfriend was very friendly toward me. After they left, I discovered that my gold necklace and matching bracelet were missing.

By that time, I had been out of work for seven months, and being idle was really getting to me. All I knew my entire life was work. On the job was where I felt the least exposed and where I always felt my best.

I found myself waking up every morning feeling guilty for not working and making money. It's supposed to feel good to be in a financial position to not have to work, but I was in constant turmoil. I finally realized that I had to face that situation.

My girlfriend Mary had told me she discovered that she wasn't a workaholic; she was a "fearaholic." That made sense to me. I was sick of the compulsion that I now recognized as a limitation and no longer a strength. I vowed to overcome it so I could experience the gems in life. The social and personal life deficiencies my *guides* had been bringing to my attention since the late 1970s now had to be faced.

Working on this was the hardest thing I had ever done, although, on the surface, it looked like fun. I started going out dancing and ice skating every day. I traveled a bit and got lots of sleep. As long as I continued to wake up feeling that anxiety, I knew I wasn't "there" yet. My *guides* made this clear when *they* had let me know my wings were still wet, meaning my undeveloped social and personal life skills were still limiting me. I was determined to heal this once and for all.

AWARENESS: Your *guides* never give up on you. *They* know what you need even when you don't. All you have to do is stay tuned-in to *their* messages, no matter how unconventional *they* seem, or how *they* make *themselves* known to you.

In March and April of 2000, the Internet boom busted. It was called the "tech wreck," and the "dot com dot gone." I had sold the Internet businesses 18 months earlier, so it didn't affect me. Once again, my *guides* had warned me in plenty of time to avoid the disaster, but this time I had the sense to respond immediately, not waiting until the last minute. Also, I was more aware of what I needed to do and didn't fall prey to my husband's fears or insecurities. There were so many parallels and repeats of the previous times I had been fore-warned – as the karmic ride of that *merry-go-round dream* continued to play out.

Steve was resentful of me and my having been right about so many things, including selling our businesses. He joined Cindy and my mother in blaming me for all that was wrong in their lives. He started telling Cindy that I didn't deserve my share of the proceeds from the sale of the Internet busi-nesses. He spun his story and justified his negative attitude toward me while Cindy ate it up.

I spent 1999 through 2000 in my "therapeutic fun" endeavors. I learned to salsa and tango, and continued to ice skate. Through these activities, I overcame my compulsion to work all the time; I was indeed healing my past. Then, at the gym one day when I least expected it, I received a message from my *guides. They* said, *"You had a breakdown."* I was shocked to hear this.

Two things immediately came to mind. The first thing was that *they* said this in the past tense. "I *had* a breakdown," so it was behind me and over now. The second thing was that I never realized I had had a breakdown, just like the woman who described her breakdown to me in 1970. No wonder I had been fascinated with her story back then. It was her candid step-by-step description of what she experienced that helped me understand what actually happened to me.

The difference between her experience and mine was that she could no longer function, so someone took her to the doctor. In my case, I stopped pushing myself and chose to begin a healing process before it happened. I realized that I was under way too much stress when I sold the Internet businesses and got divorced. I had pushed myself too hard for too long. This was what my dad warned me about when I was a kid. He told me to learn to manage my energy or it would be my downfall.

Now that I was aware of what had happened, I was worried that I wouldn't get my full energy back. I was feeling better, but I wasn't running at the "premium Linda energy" I used to have. I started to realize that my healing was much bigger than I imagined. I was healing my entire life, not just something that had happened recently. I saw it was going to be a complete makeover; a new me would emerge from this. And, I saw that this was yet another one of those consequences my *guides* had asked me if I was prepared to accept.

 AWARENESS: This just goes to show you that the setup can happen decades in advance. Time has no relevance to your *guides*. What has meaning to *them* is that you become whole. You came into this life to work out your undeveloped rough edges, and it's *their* job to see that you achieve that. *They* are relentless, and that's a good thing.

In the midst of my healing, I told Cindy I would buy her a car. What can I say – she was my daughter. I had already bought her the car she was driving, so I told her that once I bought her the new one, I needed her to sell the one she had and send me the money from that sale. She agreed, made the trip out to Arizona, and we went car shopping.

We found the car she liked and could afford to maintain. To keep her on the straight and narrow, I kept my name on the title as lien holder so she couldn't sell it and take the money. It also made her judgment-proof if someone sued her.

She went back to California and eventually got around to selling the older car. But, surprise, surprise, she never sent me the money. When I questioned her, she said she figured I didn't need the money, and it wasn't that much anyway. My mom and Steve were supporting her in going in the wrong direction.

 AWARENESS: Sometimes you give your kids way too much rope. I knew better, I really did. It's interesting that my *guides* didn't bring this to my attention as she continued to work against me. *They* just told me that she came into this life sad and sorrowful and that she would always attempt to take down everyone she encountered.

In January 2001, I took a month-long trek through South America. I had always wanted to go there, and the opportunity showed up. I went with a small group and a tour guide. We started out at the Amazon Jungle, then went to Bolivia, Cuzco, Machu Picchu, and to many small towns that were off the beaten path.

The minute we got off the plane in Lima, the air pollution was so bad I had to hold my shirt over my face. We went straight to the Amazon region where we were greeted by natives who called themselves shamans. They were selling the hallucinogenic drug ayahuasca. They weren't shamans; they were addicts posing as shamans.

The environment was beautiful. The tour guide was not. He turned out to be unreliable and actually left us stranded in the Jungle at one point. It was so weird that we started speculating on ways to get out of there on our own. Several days later, he just came walking out of the jungle with no explanations or apologies. This was starting to look like it was not going to be the kind of trip you see on the travelogues.

In Bolivia, we encountered soldiers armed with assault rifles. These young men had the coldest eyes; they were dead inside and would just as soon shoot you as look at you. Seeing that triggered me to recall my mother's assaults on me when I was a child. Like these empty soldiers who saw no value in anyone, she had seen no value in me. It sickened me inside.

So much went on during the trek, it's impossible to cover it all here. But one event, deep in Bolivia, can't be passed over because it was very unique and profound.

We were in an eerily remote place so high in the mountains that some people were having trouble breathing. We were literality in the clouds. Early one morning, we attended a ceremony that was being performed by a shaman named Papa Pablo. This time, it was a real shaman.

It was a straight shot up the side of the mountain, and there was only one way to get there. We left before the shaman did and hiked up the mountain as fast as we could, so we expected to be there before anyone. But, to our surprise, Papa Pablo was already there. I would guess he was in his late 60s or early 70s, and was completely relaxed, with everything prepared for the ceremony, waiting for us! This was becoming very interesting.

As this magical man moved through the rites, my dad kept appearing through him — one moment I saw my dad and then next, I saw the shaman. It had been 19 years since my dad had passed, and nothing like this had ever happened before. I was stunned and mesmerized. In case you're wondering, no, I had not taken ayahuasca. This was happening through the *Spirit*, not through hallucinogens.

The next day this shaman performed coca-leaf readings for each person. His dialect was so old that it took two interpreters to translate his messages. I wrote down everything he told me. He started with childhood and then moved into my future. His predictions have been spot on; some are still playing out.

The interesting thing about this amazing man was that, in everyday life, he was just a regular guy. He worked on the

farm alongside everyone else. But when he stepped into the
ceremonies, something came over him. It was magical and
phenomenal and at the same time, more real than anything
I had experienced.

Papa Pablo never let people take his picture, but he let me.

Papa Pablo, a real shaman

Here are some of the things Papa Pablo told me during my coca-leaf reading on January 20, 2001:

"You work like a man. Your face is sad. You are over your enemies. (He raised his head and looked at me with sadness in his eyes — like I wouldn't really understand what he was about to tell me next). Your parents did not give you the right information and told you the wrong things. You are on the right path. Your work is like a well, a vortex of energy collectively moving together in the right direction. Like getting into a car and starting to drive where you are going. You think a lot. Your health is good. Love is not soon."

What I learned:

I had always worked hard ("like a man") in a man's world.

Regarding my "sad face," as I look back at my childhood pictures, it's interesting that I'm on guard most of the time, so smiling isn't something you do when you're watching your back. Life presented me with enemies at every turn — my family, in school, and in business.

I also recognized in his words that the work I would be doing going forward would be what had been building momentum my entire life. Like the car, it was always moving me in that direction. I've always thought things through and taken care of my health. I understood that a relationship was not in my near future.

As for my parents not giving me the right information and telling me the wrong things, at that time, I had yet to discover what that was all about. But I would, and it would be a real revelation.

Chapter 23: My Wings Are No Longer Wet — I Can Fly Now

I returned from South America ready to jump back into things. So, when one of my old real estate clients called pretty much begging me to list her house for sale, I agreed.

Her house had been on the market for over a year, and she had had no offers. I listed it, and in less than 30 days had an offer that she accepted. Then I got a message from my *guides* that the next property I would be selling would be my place. That had not even been on my radar, so it came as a total surprise. I had been thinking about taking a month to travel through Europe, and my *guides* told me that I needed to go soon or I wouldn't be able to go at all. This time *they* didn't say why.

My client's house closed escrow in June 2001. My *guides* gave me a repeat message that time for my Europe trip was running out. I wasn't at all ready to go, so I took it off my calendar. When I made that decision, my *guides* told me I would eventually go to Europe with my husband. Husband? I figured that the trip was off in the future, way off.

In July, I started writing content for the Channeled Readings website, the project I had been putting off for over a decade. Whatever had been holding me back — my ill health and lack of energy, and healing my life — was no longer blocking my way. The project was my passion: helping people through the challenging times I knew were coming based on what my *guides* had been showing me my entire life. I knew everything about the channeling process and the reliability of the channeled information.

I put my condo on the market, and it sold in one week, the first week of September. While I was very happy about the sale, on September 10, I found myself sobbing all day. I was overcome with an incredibly sad feeling, and I could not shake it. I felt like a pressure cooker, as the feeling intensified inside me. I was baffled; that was not like me.

That evening a friend called, and I blurted out that something bad was going to happen. I said the absurdity would be that it would happen on a day with the most beautiful weather and blue skies. The next morning, September 11, 2001, I woke up to the reports of the first Twin Tower in New York being hit. I watched the second one get hit in horror as smoke billowed up into the crisp blue skies.

With that terrible event behind us, I closed escrow on my Sedona condo, and I left town. I put Sedona behind me and became a wanderer. I went to Colorado for three months, then to Montana for three months. I wound up in Sun Valley, Idaho, for the summer of 2002. I loved Sun Valley. I would go ice-skating twice a day and salsa dancing at Bruce Willis's nightclub, The Mint, at night. I took Tai Chi classes and got massages. It was a great summer.

I continued to write the content for the web site. Pretty much all along, I had been doing readings with my talking board for clients over the phone, and the channeling partner I had been working with stayed at my place in Sun Valley where she got a job in a retail shop selling high-end clothing.

In a private channeling session, Steve's mom, my ex-mother-in-law, came through. I hadn't spoken to her in four years, and I thought she was fine. Imagine my surprise as I heard:

Guides: Steve's Mother would like to speak with you, Linda.

Linda: *Okay, come on through, Mom.*

Steve's mom: *"Hello honey. I never understood what you were doing with this work. Now I see so many things so much clearer.*

I also want to thank you for trying to help my Steven to grow up. I am so happy that you saw the entire picture. You have great days ahead because of your knowledge and preparations.

I willed myself not to be part of your coming days of doom. Of course, I did not have that realization until I was released from my body.

You need to know that Steven was wonderful to me before I passed"

The other Intuitive Medium asked: *"Were your other boys as good as Steve in being there for you at the end?"*

Steve's mom: *"They did not have his insight because they were not exposed to the other side of life as Steve was. Thank you, Linda, for your help."*

Linda: *"You feel great, Mom."*

Steve's mom: *"Yes, young and well. I am no expert on what it takes to do what you both are doing; however, Linda, on your resume you should mention talking to 'us on the other side' as one of your areas of expertise. Many do not understand what is meant by the intuitive psychic medium's guides from beyond. I didn't, but everyone understands what it means when you say, 'those from the other side.' Honey, I also want to say I did not believe in life after death. Now I know I was your mother in another European lifetime. With your abilities on this board of communication, you can also read past lives for others."*

I was surprised to learn of Steve's mom's death, but I was not surprised at the contact from her. We always had a deep affection for each other, and her explanation sure made sense to me.

 LESSON: It's interesting to see how clear people become when they get to the other side. It happens instantly. The illusions are completely released, and they see everything for exactly what it is. Too bad they didn't make the connection with their *guides* while they were here, they could have lived a more satisfying life.

While I was in Idaho, I spoke with Cindy. She was about to graduate from college, and I wanted to attend her graduation. She told me not to come because my mother would be there. I didn't push it, and she went on to graduate, getting a degree in computer science.

As I neared completion of the writing part of my web site, I asked her about building the site. She agreed, so I paid her a retainer to start and bought her the Apple computer she said she would need for the job. Once I did all that, she promptly handed the job off to a web-design company. Frustrated, I asked her why she did that, and her justification was that she had done her part. That was the last straw for me. I had tried to help her time and time again, and she just continued to set me up for her next score.

I considered staying in Sun Valley, but I wasn't finding the people there I felt I needed to build my web site. After a lot of thought, I moved to Scottsdale, Arizona, where I knew I could find the talent to get the work done. The writing was finished, and my channeling partner wanted to leave Idaho before winter hit, so off we went back to Arizona a bit less than a year after leaving Sedona.

Just before leaving Sun Valley, I started feeling a wedding ring on my left hand. I was rubbing my thumb against the wedding finger like a ring was there. I knew something was up, and it was not far off.

 TIP: Watch how your *guides* send you signals. Pay attention because *they* are always doing it and are spot on. Again, time has no relevance to *them,* but the signals are always clear. Many times you will get the answers long before the occurrences. When this happens, these are called predictions.

Once I returned to Arizona, my channeling partner started behaving strangely, acting arrogantly and being rude to my reading clients. I let it ride until one day on the talking board, *they* came through and told me to get a new channeling partner. *They* fired her right then and there! She looked at me like it was my fault and asked me what that was all about. I told her that she knew as well as I did that I have no control over what *they* say, whether *they* were talking to me or anyone else. *They* just say it like it is.

I had more clients scheduled for readings and couldn't replace her right away, so we continued to work together. It was about a week later when *they* came back through and told me *they* were sending me a new channeling partner, and he would show up in two weeks. My current channeling partner was gone in three days, and I never saw her again.

 AWARENESS: Your *guides* know everything, but *they* are not always permitted to tell everything *they* know. *They* will not interfere with who it is you are becoming as you gain new experiences. *They* have a real challenging job.

Two weeks later, I was referred by one of my long-time channeling clients to a fellow who did web design and video production for her. Once the designer saw how I did this work, he immediately became intrigued and wanted to learn. I started teaching him how to use the talking board with me. I was training him to be my next channeling partner. Perfect timing thanks again to my *guides*.

My new channeling partner, Evan, was working out well so far. I continued to build out the website and create the videos. We went to the L.A. Expo and met a marketing agent who worked with people doing something called Remote Viewing — seeing things in places far away. He loved our work of channeling people's *spirit guides* on the talking board. Shortly after our meeting, he booked me for an event in Scottsdale. It was marketed well and was quite a success. This fellow told me to write a book about *spirit guides* and to do it immediately, but I wasn't ready.

Soon after that event, Evan, whom I had such hopes for, started doing the same things my previous partners had done — trying to dominate, becoming argumentative, needing to be right — everything that conflicts with the quality of the channeled information. As a result, I told the agent I would not be doing any more events. Being dependent on another person was an ongoing problem; it was the weak link in my business model and life. I proceeded to focus on getting the web site and videos done so I could go my own way.

In May 2003, I stopped for a latté at a Starbuck's in a town called Cave Creek, Arizona. As fate would have it, one of the customers there was someone who had called me two years earlier, just before my South American trip, asking me to design a home for his parents in Sedona. Since I couldn't do it then, I forgot about it. But there he was, and he recognized my name from that one time we talked on the phone. We chatted, and then we met again about a month later. We started dating and going to Sedona on weekends where I kept bumping into people I had known. They asked me to come back, and I found myself pulled to return.

On my trips to Sedona I started casually looking at houses. I still didn't know what my plans were, but it was interesting to see what was on the market. One afternoon I had a dream that woke me up. It was my *guides* telling me to make an offer on a home I had seen, and *they* said to do it now!

So I got up and called the broker to let him know I wanted to make an offer. He said that he just got two other offers on the same property, and mine would be the third. One offer was higher than mine and another lower. From the logical point of view, it would make sense for the sellers to accept the highest offer. But I was following the direction from my *guides,* so as far as I was concerned, anything could happen.

I waited to hear back, and the next day, the broker called. He sounded a little surprised when he told me they had accepted my offer. I wasn't particularly surprised because I figured my *guides* would not have suggested I make an offer if there hadn't been a chance I would get the house.

I closed escrow in October, two years to the month after I had sold my other place in Sedona, not expecting to ever return.

 AWARENESS: You just have to create enough room in your life to move through the motions, and you will be directed precisely to the right events and the right people at just the right time. You can't chase it. You are always guided. All you need to do is show up, pay attention, and take action.

After buying the house, I became consumed with remodeling. I had no time for anything else, including dating, so the relationship with the guy who was responsible for my returning to Sedona ended. I finished the remodeling and moved in at the end of January 2004.

My new place became the house of music. I installed a state-of-the-art sound system that played throughout the inside and outside. I loved it. This was the first time had I made music the focus of a place I built. Everything had a his-and-hers arrangement, even in the office space. I wasn't sure why I did that because I was not even seeing anyone, but it felt right, and like always, I went with it.

I had left all my possessions in Sun Valley because that was where I intended to end up living. So I returned there, got my things out of storage, and drove them back to Sedona. I spent the next month finishing up the loose ends on my new place and moving in. I didn't know what the future held for me in Sedona, but I had a strong feeling from my *guides* that it was the correct place for me to be right now.

About a month after I moved in, I was in my hot tub, and I had a very strong sensual feeling. It was as if a very passionate man was near me — in my energy field — even though no one was physically present. It was time.

PART 4: A POWERFUL LOVE, A POWERFUL PURPOSE

Chapter 24: *"Their"* Signals and Signs Materialize

It was February 28, 2004, and snowing in Sedona. I was planning to drive up to Flagstaff to go ice skating but Oak Creek Canyon was closed. I was still in the process of moving into my place. I went next door to the Raven Heart Coffee Shop to get my favorite "large Linda latté."

I often went to this place, so all the people knew me, and I knew them. But as I stood at the pickup counter, I glanced to my right and saw a very handsome man looking at me. I had never seen this guy before. He had a powerful energy, and his eyes were very intense as he sent a bolt of his energy right through me. I smiled at him, but his energy was way too intense, so I grabbed my latté and ran out the door. This was one of those "consequences in the works," which may not be a bad thing.

Later that same day, I went to the gym to work out. As I was walking from the ladies locker room to the gym, the same man I had seen at the coffee shop appeared, and he was coming my way. Here we were, the second time in one day.

He pointed at me and recognized me as the girl in the coffee shop. I was very nervous and just smiled as I crept past him. I got on the elliptical machine, put in my ear buds, and turned on my music. He followed me back into the gym, stood next to me, and started talking. Thinking I couldn't hear him, he said, "Take those ear buds out — I might have something important to say!"

I took one out and looked at him. He grinned and said, "Hi, I'm Ray, the Vortex of Fun." This guy was on a mission — a mission to get me. I liked his persistence as I said, "You're not from around here are you?" In response, he gave me his life resume in three minutes.

The first thing Ray told me was that he was married. My number-one rule was to not date married guys, and I never broke it. I just kept this to myself as he continued to tell his story. He said he had a 16-year-old son, told me what he did for a living, said he was spiritual, but not religious, and that he was an animal lover who rescued cats and dogs. He said his passion was playing the guitar, and he had lots of them. He also told me he was a lover of Jazz and movies.

When he was done reciting his resume, he asked if I had ever been to Jamaica. When I said I hadn't, he asked me if I had ever been to Amsterdam. Again, I replied in the negative. Then he said, "How would you like to go there for our honeymoon?" It was less than five minutes since we had met, and the Vortex of Fun had just proposed to me! I was floored. I didn't know how to respond. So I put that ear bud back in and focused on my exercise routine, but not before I gave him my web site address and told him to contact me there by email.

After my boyfriend and I broke up the previous year, I decided that I was no good at picking my life partners. I told my life-long *trusted advisors,* my *guides,* that if I met someone who was right for me to give me a sign. It seemed I picked the wrong people, so it would not be me who did the picking the next time, if there was going to be a next time.

When I got home from the gym that night, Ray had already sent me an email. In it he commented on my salsa dancing and ice skating. Then he mentioned the channeled readings I did and wanted to learn more.

This guy was married so I was definitely planning to keep him at a distance. He wasn't fazed by my attitude. He invited me to go to a short film on salsa dancing in Puerto Rico that was showing at the Sedona Film Festival. I told him I would go but would be leaving right after that to go ice skating. He was okay with that plan, so I agreed to go with him.

A week later he invited me to go with him to Prescott to listen to Jazz. I went but told him I had things to do the next day so he would be clear that nothing would happen later. He was a gentleman. We were becoming friends, and he told me more about himself. He told me he used to be a musician and that he played several instruments. But, he told me, Jazz guitar was his instrument and music of choice. This guy had more music CDs than anyone I had ever met. He loved music as much as I did, except I liked dancing to it, and he liked playing it.

About four days after the trip to Prescott, I was talking to a friend on my cell phone. I told her I had met someone named Ray Holley. She said she knew him from the Sedona Film Festival. All of a sudden, a *voice* came over the phone line, like you would hear on the old party lines. This *voice* spoke over my friends voice saying, "*Lose your rules, he's the one.*" I dropped the phone right there in the driveway. I picked it up and told my friend I would have to call her back later. What *they* meant by, *"Lose your rules"* was the part where he was married.

I wasn't expecting it, but I knew this was the sign I asked *them* to send me if I met the right one. I was scared — not scared from the *voice* that sent me this message, but afraid of allowing myself to become vulnerable to anyone again. I sure hadn't been looking for a relationship, but one had apparently found me.

 LESSON: People spend countless years trying to find someone who satisfies their relationship list of qualifications and demands. You can never chase a relationship. In fact, you have no business picking your relationship in the first place. You don't find a relationship; it finds you like the stray that shows up on your doorstep that you fall in love with. Your *guides* deliver the right person to you at just the right time. Your job is to recognize them when they show up. You will discover that you don't get to pick who loves you.

I let the information settle for several days and then wrote Ray a short email, asking if he would like to go to dinner sometime. Still nervous, instead of sending it, I dropped it into my email tray while I did other things. Then without over-thinking it, I hit the "send" button. In a short time, I got a reply back asking if tonight was good for me. It was.

I met him at his house early that evening. When I arrived, he had music playing and crackers, cheese, and wine arranged on his lanai-style patio. We chatted, and as he was talking, I was overcome with a very sad feeling from him. It was like I felt the lifetime of hurt, disappointment, and lack of appreciation he had experienced hitting me all at once — all while he presented himself with a chin-up demeanor. I saw how sweet he was and had been taken advantage of so many times, yet here he was giving it another shot.

I was being flooded with the real Ray, and it took everything I had to maintain my composure. I recognized him as my kindred spirit. I was caught completely off guard. In an instant, I was feeling an uncontrollable love for him. My heart was totally open. It all had a life of its own. I was being guided and so was he.

Ray and Linda's first dinner date at Pasta Casa, March 11, 2004

As we left his house to go to dinner, he made a romantic pass at me. With some misgivings, I responded. We went to dinner at a little Italian restaurant nearby. This time I didn't have a pre-announced exit plan. After dinner, we went back to his place. We have rarely been apart since.

After dating for a while, Ray asked me about the channeled-readings business and wanted me to show him how it worked. I brought out the talking board that I had created and started teaching him to channel. He was very clumsy in the beginning. I told him that we would do this for about 10 to 15 minutes a day as I helped guide him through the learning curve. Channeling takes a very different energy than people are generally used to using, and in the beginning, new practitioners find it challenging and tiring as they learn to reactivate a primal part of themselves. Ray was no different, but he was determined.

Then one morning, a very strange phenomenon awoke Ray. He was lying in bed when a creature jumped out of his chest and shot up to the corner of the 14-foot high ceiling. He described it as a four-foot-long reptilian-looking grey gargoyle creature with a pointed tail and ears. When it got up to the corner of the ceiling, it looked back at him with a hateful glare, and then shot through the wall, never to return.

Ray told me about the incident, and I surmised that the energy could not live in the environment of love we shared, so it had no choice but to release itself from him. This was the beginning of Ray's being released from the years of hurt and negative energy he had taken on in his life. It was very painful, but finally it was leaving him. The incident never repeated itself, and Ray found he was feeling lighter, as if he had cast off a burden. And he had!

At the end of March, Ray went back to Texas to look after his son while his wife went to Washington D.C., to visit her elderly parents. This arrangement had been made before Ray and I had gotten together.

When Ray left, I thought that it might herald the end of our relationship. I always knew that was a possible consequence of dating a married man. In a way, I was letting go because I couldn't go down the road of being someone's mistress.

Instead of being a separating time for us, the trip turned out to be the last straw for Ray. When his wife returned home, life became worse than ever, so early one morning, Ray and his son packed up his guitars, and he left for good. His only regret was leaving his son, their dog, Charlie, and the cat behind. It just broke Ray's heart, but he knew that's what he had to do.

Ray with his dog, Charlie

Ray came back to me fully committed to us. He was done with that abusive life. He told me he wanted to divorce his wife and marry me. I chose to only listen and refrained from commenting as he processed what he had gone through. When he finally asked me what I thought, I countered by asking him if he really wanted my advice. I warned him that I would be very direct and unemotional about the whole thing. From experience, I knew people weren't ready for divorce until they could think of it as a reorganization — with the love gone, it's just business. I told him if he couldn't see it that way, he wasn't ready.

Ray liked what I said because it made sense to him. So, I took him through the ABCs of this "reorganization." There were times when he had to endure emotional wrath and threats, but all in all, he did well, kept it together, and made it through the divorce process.

 LESSON: From my lifetime of guidance, the #1 rule *they* taught me was to not take things personally and to remain objective. Your *guides* will help you understand how to accept "what is" and not get caught up in "what could have been." In Ray's case, above and beyond what was in it for me — a life together with Ray — it was my responsibility to share what I had learned in order to help him through his life-changing moment, no matter how things worked out between us. This is what loving someone is all about.

Less than four months later, on July 21, 2004 Ray's divorce became final. On July, 22 he took me to get our wedding rings. I told him there was no need to rush, but he insisted.

We went to a gallery in Sedona, and as soon as we made our selections, something hit me. I went outside and sat on a bench to take a breath. I needed to regroup to make sure I wasn't setting myself up to be trapped in a miserable marriage as I had done twice before.

I didn't know how Ray was handling it, but I was glad I had taken a moment to reflect. It all looked positive and clear to me. I went back inside, completed the transaction, and ten days later we picked up the rings. We were officially engaged.

July 31, 2004 Ray and Linda's engagement day

Every day we continued to channel *our guides* on the talking board. Ray was getting more aligned with his *guides,* and the process was becoming easier. While it may be strange to picture, our *guides* were literally dictating *their* messages letter by letter through the talking board. So, in the beginning, *their* messages were static as Ray was working through his learning curve (If you would like to actually see what this looks like, visit our website at: http://www.channeledreadings.com).

They (using the identification of *Seven Rays)* were telling us of things to come and why we were meant to be together. All our channeling sessions were recorded and transcribed. By August, we were channeling full sentences of clear communication. Here are a few excerpts from those early endeavors. Be aware that the communication may seem a bit crude, because Ray was in his learning curve in those early days. But you can see his progression as the messages got longer and stronger.

6-6-2004

Voice of Seven Rays: Marry her, January 1, 2005. U R so in love. Very good timing.

6-19-2004

RAY, you are teacher to both, Rex and Linda. U R starting to move into a time when U will move into great teachings. (Teach what?) *Teach others how to believe in themselves. U will write life-changing books. Word of Seven Rays.*

7-21-2004

Voice of Seven Rays won't be more powerful until you are married. Stronger after 1/1/05. (Why?) *Two spirits united forever. Power will double. All will understand that Ray and Linda "feel loved." Key to romance is feel-*

ing loved. You are not in love....you are feeling loved. Need is greed. Why stay with someone who needs and can't receive love? Trusting that you will be loved and feel loved. Linda — love Ray and you will always be in feeling loved. Write book about feeling loved. Ray, always be funny and you will be happy.

1-18-2005

People wish to be U, they see love, then want love. Teach others what you experience. Teach by example, that happiness can be achieved. Good things will soon happen when you teach what you feel. (It sounds like the world is starving for this?) *Yes, no one can love until they feel love, ask a stray. Ask The Universal Channel to guide you always. We will speak to you when you open the channel. We will speak to others whenever you open the channel.* (In what form will you speak to others?) *Written word. Many written words. Wisdoms flows from Seven Rays to you to the world. Collective consciousness through Seven Rays voice. Are you not hearing our voice now? Try to feel us when you speak. We exist because you exist. You two are the two who will shine the light. Shine the light of love. Love is what you do. Pair of Leo's.*

2-12-2005

Voice heard through Ray's work has power to heal. Any two people who are in love as much as you 2 generate strong message. Couples want to be like you. So much love to teach others, so much to give each other. Time to write best seller. Others will see what they can become when they read the book. Two people who worship each other like you two do won't have to struggle to realize that love is all there is. Return to all there is. Time is all that gets in the way. Once you start to write all will be revealed. Review outline we gave you. Wisdom follows from more thought given to outline. Celebrate the love of others now.

3-10-2005

Photos tell story. Story of true Love. Voice of Seven Rays at your service. Seven Rays Voice of Truth. Seven Rays will reveal all you need to write book. Service to Humanity to start soon.

8-14-2005

Ray, Voice of Seven Rays will guide you writing book. (Book about?) *Feeling Loved. Voice of Seven Rays is voice of Universal Channel.*

7-12-2006

Here we are. Help people ... write the book. Make happiness your goal and ask others for help. Just have faith in yourselves.

8-6-2006

Book comes 1ˢᵗ. Readers are waiting. Book, Love Yourself First. Best seller.

3-13-2007

Seven Rays says stay the course. Love your work. First the Channeled Readings web site, then the CR News Reports, then the Book.

As Ray gained skill, I began to wonder if the power of working with our *guides* would seduce Ray into trying to control things as had happened so many times before with people I had trained to do this. I was more than pleased to find he was not. Ray is the second person I have trained who has stayed clear. In both cases, these people appreciated the channeled information more than how it came through. Neither one of them got caught up in self-importance just because they were able to master it. They realized it was not them but their capacity to "get out of the way" that made it all work. Also, they both personally valued how the information helps others. These are the keys to maintaining a clear line of communication with your *guides*.

 AWARENESS: Here I was sent the right life partner, both a relationship and channeling partner. This was the first time that ever happened. I didn't find it, it found me. This goes way past you. This is where having a relationship with your *guides* exceeds anything you could ever achieve on your own. *They* are the instigators of something this profound. If you think that having a relationship with your *guides* is an option in this life, what do you think now?

Ray and I did lots of fun things together, many of which he had never really done before. We went ice skating, and he became very good at it. I bought him his own ice skates on his birthday. We also went dancing, and he excelled at the cha-cha and salsa. It got so the community recognized us when we went out dancing together. He really won me over and people who watched us loved us too. We spent 2004 listening to Jazz in Prescott, and we took lots of trips to Scottsdale for more Jazz, skating, and enjoying restaurants and guitar stores.

In September 2004, real estate was white hot, so we put Ray's house up for sale. When we didn't get any offers after the first open house, I took a second look at it. I realized that while it was a beautiful property near a creek surrounded by heritage trees, it was in a flood zone, and there was a problem with the floor plan. So, I pulled it off the market and set out to redesign the place to correct the flaw in the floor-plan. At the same time, we proceeded to plan for our wedding.

In the meantime, having fun is what we continued to do. Ray is my dream come true. He's a lot like me, and he likes me just the way I am. That was also a first. Together we are multiples of what we were individually. I finally had my real life partner, and there's nothing we couldn't do as we continued to be guided into our lives together. We continued moving toward our wedding, which was planned for New Year's Day, 2005.

We had invited friends and family from all over the country to join us and celebrate. On December 29, there was a flood in Sedona that virtually closed the town to visitors. Bridges were washed out, and roads were flooded. We couldn't even get to Ray's house. We had to hike through the back of his property so we could inspect it.

Sedona, Oak Creek flooding December 29, 2004, just 150 feet
from Ray's home

The weather was horrendous, and every house in his neighborhood had flood damage — except for Ray's. We were concerned that people wouldn't be able to get to our wedding.
However, our *guides* had told us back in June that January 1
was the right day for us to get married. *They* said the weather
would be perfect, like a warm spring day. It tested Ray's faith
in *them*, but he took a deep breath, and we proceeded as
planned.

Chapter 25: The Wedding

The day of our wedding arrived. We awoke to find it was indeed a perfect, warm spring day just like our *guides* had told us it would be six months earlier. It was like the parting of the seas in the Bible. This one day opened, and it was magical. Ray was beginning to see how these predictions played out against all logic. Just the day before our wedding, the weather started clearing up, and the day after our wedding, the weather completely changed, the clouds moved in and it started pouring down raining again. But on January 1, the roads were all clear, and everyone made it to our wedding. It was like a warm spring day!

Although this wasn't my first marriage, it was my first wedding. To recap, my first marriage was in front of a Nevada Justice of the Peace, a choice made by my mother. The second marriage was at the Chapel of the Bells in Las Vegas, Nevada, where we were both dressed in jeans after a trade show, a choice my husband had made. Neither one was memorable and definitely not special. This was different. It was our mutual choice, and thanks to our *guides,* we already knew it was going to be a stellar day, and it was.

Ray & Linda — married at the Creative Life Center in Sedona,
Arizona, January 1, 2005

And they lived happily ever after

Ray and I found a love in each other that we each had only dreamed of. I was 52 and Ray was 53 years old the day we got married. It was completely out of character for me to marry someone just ten months after meeting him, but Ray and I have that rare connection that transcends reasoning. We both have always relied on our intuition to guide us, and for the first time in our lives, we found our likeness and equal in each other.

Everyone enjoyed themselves at the reception, and Ray's favorite Jazz musicians from Prescott provided the music. We had the wedding planner double the size of the dance floor because many of our friends were serious dancers like us. It was an open bar with good food and an awesome wedding cake. Ray picked the wedding theme, colors, and even my dress.

Dancing the night away

Everyone got a fortune cookie containing messages that Ray and I had channeled from our *guides*:

Love means always looking together in the same direction.

A great marriage requires finding AND being the right person.

The best couples fall in love many times, always with the same person.

There's no perfect couple, only those who are perfect for each other.

Lasting true love includes companionship with your best friend.

Our wedding and the reception had an impact on our community. It seemed to set off a charge of hope and inspiration in those who were sitting on the fence about their own relationships. The result was an avalanche of marriages, just like our *guides* had told us there would be.

 LESSON: When both of you have relationships with your *guides,* everything in your relationship works. It's like nothing you've ever experienced in your life before. There are no secrets, conditions, or hidden agendas. Life doesn't get any better than that. For the first time in your life, you will feel loved because you are appreciated for who you are and not who they want you to be.

Right after we got married, we put Ray's house back on the market. It had been unaffected by the flood, which negated one objection, and the remodel eliminated the other flaw I had identified. I held an Open House in February, got an offer in March, and closed escrow in May.

Living at my place was working out great. As I indicated earlier, I had designed it with an amazing sound system, and here I was married to a former musician who loved music as much as I did. There are just no accidents. Also, once again, everything had a "his and hers" arrangement, even the office space. We did really well together at my house. It became our home.

In June, we went to the high school graduation of Ray's son, Rex, in Texas. His plan was to start college in Arizona in the fall. Ray's mother, who Ray had been supporting since 2002, had Alzheimer's, and handling her care was emotionally and financially draining for Ray, who took care of her every need. Now that Ray was going to have two significant financial obligations for an indefinite period of time, we needed to get serious about making money.

I continued to design and re-design homes for clients, but the real estate market was cooling down. From our channeled readings, we knew it was headed for a crash. Even though I had my real estate broker's license, because I knew what was coming, I couldn't bring myself to represent buyers or sellers. We didn't know what we were going to do for income, but it wasn't going to be real estate.

In July of 2005, just seven months after we got married, Cindy called us to say she had gotten fired from her job because she was sick. She told us she had stomach cancer and needed $1,750 a week for cancer treatments. She said she needed this money immediately because, having lost her job, she no longer had health insurance and needed to start the treatments right away. She also told us she was going for more tests the next day, so we asked her to be sure to have her doctor send us a copy of the results. She never did.

Ray had been an executive recruiter for over 25 years and had a lot of experience with human resources. In an effort to help Cindy, he asked her for everything he would need to investigate the situation because he knew an employee could not be fired just because they became ill. Then we called an attorney in Sacramento who specialized in employment law and made an appointment for Cindy to meet with him.

When we let Cindy know that we had this set up for her, she changed her approach completely. She accused us of butting into her personal affairs and refused to meet with the attorney. At that point, we became suspicious, so Ray called her place of employment and discovered she was still working there. Suddenly we stopped hearing from Cindy.

I called my granddaughter's stepmom and asked her about Cindy having stomach cancer. She said she didn't know anything about it. None of this really surprised Ray or me, and it just confirmed again that, when it came to Cindy, we needed to be extremely cautious. Her manipulation and lying had now crossed the line. What was second nature to her in childhood and as a young adult now apparently had no boundaries. She had become ruthless.

Two months after the incident with Cindy, hurricanes Katrina and Rita became news in New Orleans and Texas. My Uncle Charlie lived in Silsbee, Texas, right in Rita's path. It had been 26 years since I last saw him, but I called to check in on him a day before Rita was projected to hit. He was living in

the house he had lived in seemingly forever, though his sister
in-law and her husband were staying with him because he
was 90 years old and couldn't be on his own. He told me he
was staying put, Rita or no Rita, and invited us to come to
Texas for his 91st birthday in July. We told him we would be
delighted to celebrate with him and asked him to call after
Rita passed through.

Then we waited to hear back from Uncle Charlie. The utili-
ties were down and the town was devastated. We had no
idea how he had done or even if he had made it. Finally, we
got the call. The house had weathered the storm, but Uncle
Charlie had to be relocated to Houston for over a month
while things were restored in Silsbee. Uncle Charlie was
looking forward to seeing us for his birthday. We were very
relieved and went back to pulling things together in our life,
the trip to Silsbee being the only travel on our radar — at
least as far as we knew then.

A few weeks later in a channeling session on September 2,
2005, *they* came through with this message:

> "*Very soon both of you will take trip to Ohio.*"

> (Why?) "*Betty to fail.*"

At the time, Betty, Ray's mom, was not sick, nor had she been
sick.

In another channeling session we did a month later, *they*
told us:

"Ray to become rich when son, a brown tabby, shows up."

We were not planning on getting another cat so that didn't make sense.

 AWARENESS: Sometimes you may not understand what your *guides* are telling you. Don't worry about it. Just keep your eyes open. Sooner or later, it will all make sense.

Uncle Charlie, Ray, and I are all Leos (born in late July and early August). Leos are known to be flamboyant and fun-loving, and Ray always says, "It's not a party until the Leos show up." We had stayed in touch with Uncle Charlie since the hurricane and were very much looking forward to seeing him.

While we were preparing for our trip, some friends told us about a new litter of kittens, thinking that our first cat, Leon, would like a companion. Leon had won my heart when I first saw him, so we adopted him. Then he decided he was Ray's cat (the traitor). Benny, the cat, was born March 15, 2006, and we visited him the first time when he was three weeks old. So, while we hadn't planned it, getting a second kitty had been decided for us. The brown tabby we had been told about five months earlier by our *spirit guides* had shown up.

Our cat Benny three weeks of age, the brown tabby shows up as predicted

In a channeling session on July 12, 2006, we asked about how Ray's mother was doing. *They* came through with this message for Ray:

> "*Slowing down, leg pain, walker needed. Her passing 2007-2008. Betty doesn't know which one* (son) *you are. All at once you see light there, in your dream. Quiet passing.*"

> (See Betty?) "*Yes, go in September.*"

Until this channeling session, we had no idea that we would be going to Ohio, which coincidentally would turn out to be the same time we would need to be in Pennsylvania, but we didn't even know that yet. But with this news, we decided to plan a trip, just two months after visiting Uncle Charlie in Texas.

In early spring, Ray started having dreams about a fire that would come dangerously close to our house. We weren't too concerned about it because our *guides* had told us our property would be fine.

The week we were leaving in July to visit Uncle Charlie, there was a raging wildfire in Sedona so large it made the national news. But, again, our *guides* reassured us that we would be good to go because the air quality was going to be terrible for a while, and that our property would be unaffected.

Photo of the fire taken from the second floor deck of our house the day we left

Before leaving to visit Uncle Charlie, his sister in-law told us he saw my dad walking up to his front door. He told her to open the door and let him in. Then when she told my uncle that Randy had been dead for 30 years, he acted embarrassed. But we knew that Uncle Charlie did indeed see my dad. Things like that often happen when someone's time is getting short.

Knowing that our house would be safe, thanks to the reassurance from our *guides*, we headed off to Texas. It would be Ray's first time meeting Uncle Charlie. After the greetings were over, my uncle suddenly blurted out something about my dad being married to someone named Ann.

I knew my mother's name wasn't Ann. Uncle Charlie looked a little sheepish and mumbled that he thought everyone knew about it. I sure didn't know my dad had been married to anyone but my mom. He wasn't particularly happy about letting this cat out of the bag.

Ray and Linda in Texas with Uncle Charlie on his
91st birthday July 2006

I pressed Uncle Charlie for details. I told him that family secrets left me with a big void in my life, and I had to understand what really happened to get a better perspective on my early life. So he reluctantly said he would tell me what he knew. It turned out that he knew a lot.

He said all three boys — my dad, his brother, and he — were called to serve in WWII. He remembered a letter my dad wrote to him saying he didn't like it in the Navy and wanted to come home and get back to his life. My dad's service in the military took him through northern California, and that was when he decided he wanted to live there.

He said that my dad and Ann were married in 1945 and lived in New Jersey where my dad built their house. Soon after they got married, they came to visit Uncle Charlie in Texas. They were pulling a travel trailer, something very few people had in those days. So it was a big deal. Apparently they were traveling around the country. What an adventure that must have been.

In 1948, Uncle Charlie heard that my dad had moved out to California with a new woman he had met on the Boardwalk in Atlantic City just two weeks earlier. He just left Ann, never got a divorce, and Ann never heard from my dad again. No one knew why he left her. Uncle Charlie said he didn't know anything more until he visited my dad and his new family in California in 1952.

1952 Mom pregnant with me, Linda

Uncle Charlie visited my dad in California in 1952 and met his new family

TIP: The older people get, the less they guard family secrets. They recognize that much of what people are trying to protect in this world, in the greater scheme of things, is essentially nonsense. They're closer to going back to the *source*, which is the truth and love that they came from. That's why many times they will unwittingly provide clarity to those who need it most just before they leave.

Chapter 26: A Lifetime of Family Secrets Unravels

We really enjoyed our three-day visit with Uncle Charlie, his sister-in-law, and her husband. Ray and Uncle Charlie just loved each other. We were both sad to leave because we knew we wouldn't be seeing him again, at least in this lifetime.

With what I had learned from Uncle Charlie, I had more questions than answers about my family's history. Ray and I talked about it and thought we should do our own investigation once we got back to Sedona.

Upon our return home, Ray and I started getting caught up in the usual details of settling back in after a trip. The Sedona Wildfires were contained, the air quality was back to normal, and our home was not affected – just like our guides told us before we left. Then we got a phone call from Cindy. She told us that Mom was diagnosed with lung cancer and had about six months to live. She told us that she had had a recent falling out with my mom and she would not allow her to visit. When we asked her why, Cindy said she didn't know. We asked her to keep us informed.

Knowing that my mom had a short time to live, I went right to work on the investigation into my family. It was no longer a "should do" situation; it was now a "have to do" urgent matter. I just didn't know how revealing it would become.

Ray and I started looking for my mom and dad's marriage license, but no matter how deep we dug, none was to be found. Then we got on the Internet and researched my mom's side of the family. There wasn't much. We had found a lot more on my dad's side because I had more information to go on.

Then I found an Internet phone directory site for Erie, Pennsylvania, where my mother was born. She had a very common last name, so trying to get to her actual relatives was like trying to find a needle in a haystack. Staring at nine pages of people with the same last name as my mom, I became discouraged; I didn't know where to start, so I enlisted the help of my *guides*.

By using the same dowsing technique we use to channel *them*, *they* pin-pointed the key relative who was instrumental in uncovering the mystery. The first person *they* picked was a bull's eye — *they* had led me to a close relative who knew my mom and the rest of her close family. These relatives were shocked when I introduced myself as my mother's daughter. They told me that everyone thought my mom was dead. I told them that she always told us kids that they were all dead. It was the strangest call ever.

I spoke with this person a few times as we compared notes from the past. They recalled what a difficult situation my mom had been in as a kid and felt bad, even a little guilty, for not doing more to help her. They said she didn't have a fair chance, and that she didn't get the right help.

They also knew my mom's brother, Bobby. My mom had told us that Bobby had been a marine and was killed in WWII. It turns out that he was actually alive and well, living in Ohio. I told them that Mom had been diagnosed with lung cancer and only had about six months to live. I asked them if they would contact her brother to pave the way, so it wouldn't come as a shock when we made contact with each other. They understood my concern and agreed to help. From that moment on, everything just took on a life of its own. I sensed that a great healing was about to take place.

When the relatives called Uncle Bob, he couldn't believe what they told him, but, as a result of that call, he decided to contact me. It all had been such a shock to him that he told me he was going to put me to a test to see if I was for real. I told him I was okay with that. I added that Mom had kept her past a secret, and I was only beginning to uncover the truth myself, so I didn't know how well I would do with his questions. When I said that, he recognized it as something my mom would do. That started us off pretty well, and he ended up asking me only a few questions because he could see that I was genuine.

We compared notes about mom's life as much as we could in that first phone conversation. He told me that he had been searching for his sister for 59 years. In future conversations, he told me that they also had a younger sister. I asked him about her because Mom had never mentioned a sister. He said her name was Brenda and that she was still alive, but not in good health. Mom was the middle child, Uncle Bob was the oldest, and Brenda the youngest.

On another call, he told me that he had made arrangements to fly to Sacramento to visit with Mom in September. He was very emotional, both upset and happy at the same time. He was a very level-headed guy, an ex-marine who liked structure and detested not-knowing what had happened. He told me he wanted to meet with Mom first, and then he would like to meet Ray and me later, back in Erie. This trip to Pennsylvania would fit in perfectly with the visit to Ray's mom in Ohio that we had been instructed to make from a channeling with Ray's *guides* the previous July.

Uncle Bob had everything arranged perfectly, and we agreed to cooperate with his plan. I was just beginning to see the magnitude of confusion and open wounds that Mom had left behind 59 years ago.

 LESSON: No matter how much you are hurt, it doesn't give you the right to hurt others. I'm sure you've heard that before. When you have a working relationship with your *guides, they* steer you in an intelligent direction that's not aimed at hurting others. My mother was obviously not connected to her *guides*. She felt alone and angry, and made bad choices as a result. This is not possible when you have a connection to your *guides,* and you act on *their* valued guidance.

Knowing that we were going to be meeting all the relatives that Mom had been telling me were dead for my 54 years, since I was born, I decided I had to take something the relatives could connect with. I put together a chronological photo book of Mom's life. It turned out to be the key component to communicate what words could not. Seeing would be believing.

We met Uncle Bob and his wife in Erie at the end of September. I could sense his lightning-fast mind instantly calculating everything at the moment I opened our hotel door and met him for the first time. Uncle Bob looked nothing like how my mom had described him when we were kids. Mom said her dead brother Bobby was tall, slender, and had dark hair. That would have described my older brother Randy. Uncle Bob was short and stocky with light hair.

The first thing he saw when he looked at me was that I did indeed have the family resemblance. He also saw why Mom didn't like me, which I wouldn't understand until later. Most of all, he was happy to meet me and ready to take Ray and me on an eye-opening adventure into Mom's secret past, starting the next morning.

Just before he left our hotel room, Uncle Bob warned us about Cindy. He said the reason my mom wouldn't see Cindy is because she conned her out of $46,500 by claiming she had cancer. He told us not to believe a word out of her mouth. We thought about the call Cindy had made to us the month before, telling us that Mom had terminal cancer, and that they had had a falling out. We now realized that when Cindy wasn't able to con us, she went to her grandmother and conned her.

The next morning Uncle Bob and his wife picked us up for a day of show-and-tell. They drove us around in their big van while he told me the details of Mom's life. For the first time ever, someone was telling me the truth about it, free of drama and exaggerations.

He told me that when he met with Mom in California, he demanded that she tell him the truth. He said she cried, but he got the whole story as he questioned her about everything she had left undone 59 years earlier.

The last time Uncle Bob saw mom was in 1946, shortly after he was discharged from the service. He had visited her in New York City, and she was dressed to the nines and had lots of money. She took him out on the town to the best places, and he couldn't figure out how she got all that money. He surmised that she was prostituting for it, although he didn't ask her at that time. This time, he finally asked her about it, and she confessed.

My mom said that their dad's sister, Aunt Agnes, had made her a ward of the state of Pennsylvania and sent her to the school for wayward girls. Uncle Bob corrected her by telling her that it wasn't their Aunt Agnes who had sent her away, it was their father. He said that my Mom was in shock when she heard that. She was in total disbelief, but she knew her brother was telling her the truth.

Then she confessed that when she was 13, she started working as a prostitute on the Boardwalk in Atlantic City. It was six months after the war ended, and the Boardwalk was crawling with discharged veterans looking for a good time. She told Uncle Bob it was the easiest way to make money, and at that age, she made lots of it quickly.

When he asked her why she disappeared, Mom told him she had gotten pregnant by one of her johns. In June of 1948, she was six months pregnant when she met my dad on the

Boardwalk. He was thirteen years older than she was. They decided to run away together, which they did two weeks later. My dad was still married to Ann.

When Uncle Bob asked her if she ever got married, my mom said no. She said they had a common-law marriage and that my dad had never gotten divorced from Ann. That was why my mom and dad never answered when I asked when their wedding anniversary was. Now it made sense that my mom had come up with the month of June for their anniversary, because that was when they first met on the Boardwalk. My dad, a married man, ran off with this desperate 15-year-old pregnant prostitute just two weeks after they met. Three months later, Mom gave birth to her first born, my <u>half</u>-brother, Randy. In her attempt to cover up what, in those days was a colossal sin, she named her baby Randy, after my dad.

My mom and dad were on the run. Like James Dean, they were living the fantasy of that time: "Dream as if you'll live forever, live as if you'll die today." That's what it took for my mom and dad to overcome their past. They were both wild rebels running from a past that would become the lifelong secret they mutually agreed to guard and take to their graves. For both of them, that was a better alternative than staying in a place and around people they did not like.

Uncle Bob told me that my mom was always just like their dad, mean and cruel. Also, what he didn't know was that my mom, like her dad, didn't want kids.

When their mother got sick and was put into the hospital at age 33, the kids were handed off to relatives. Their dad was a raging drunk who could not take care of them. He said that he was a rotten person even when their mother was healthy.

My mom, Uncle Bob, their mother and father

Their mother died at age 36 from tuberculosis when my mom was 13 years old. My grandfather's sister, Aunt Agnes, reluctantly took in my mom and Uncle Bob, but my mom and she did not get along. It got so bad that they got into an argument, and my mother threw Aunt Agnes down a full flight of stairs. That's when my grandfather gave up his parental rights, and mom was sent to live in a girl's home as a ward of the state of Pennsylvania.

Learning this, I began to connect the dots in my own life. Finally, someone who knew her was telling me the truth about my mother. The fog was lifting. I was seeing how this all played into the awful things she did to me.

Although it was disturbing, I was relieved to finally put the pieces together. I had always known something was wrong with my mother because of the lifetime of torment she had put me though. She appeared to be replaying her own unresolved life out through me, and even Cindy if I allowed it, which I didn't. Her attempts to get my dad to give me up were just mirroring her own experience in her life. Her attempts to get me to give up Cindy had the same cause.

Uncle Bob took us to the neighborhood where he and Mom had grown up. We saw the old family farmhouse, the bar — now rebuilt — that their dad used to patronize before he burned it down with a careless cigarette. They found him dead on the street right outside that bar in 1976. Uncle Bob told all that to my mom when he saw her.

I happened to mention that my mom used to say that she didn't have a jealous bone in her body. Uncle Bob laughed and said she was one of the most jealous people he had ever known. He said she was jealous of me, and that he had seen that the first time he met me after visiting with my mom in California. He kind of shook his head and said I had everything that she had always wanted. I was taken aback; I couldn't imagine being jealous of your own child.

Uncle Bob took us to a place on Lake Erie where the family used to picnic when they were kids. He took us to the cemetery to visit the family graves and explained who everyone was.

After traveling around for a while, we went to lunch at my Great-Aunt Joanie's house. Uncle Bob said that was exactly what he and my mom would do when they were kids: go to Aunt Joanie's house after school and get fed. Aunt Joanie was known for feeding people, and she continued to tend to her garden and make great homemade food for anyone who dropped by any time. Everyone talked about the loss of Joanie's husband because everyone loved and missed him. Aunt Joanie was in her 90s and sun baked from working in her garden. Her only health challenge was arthritis.

Uncle Bob had arranged a family dinner that evening with the relatives who could make it. There must have been 30 of them attending. We met at an Italian restaurant, the only restaurant, in town that had enough room for everyone. I brought the photo book of Mom's life with me so each person would be able to connect their missing pieces. Uncle Bob did not prepare us for the family other than to say they were simple and not highly educated, but they were very nice people. That turned out to be a very accurate description.

Ray and I walked into the room, and everyone looked at us like we had stepped off a spaceship. Then they all looked down, except for Aunt Joanie, whom we had met earlier that day, and Shelly and Rob, the relatives I had originally contacted. Uncle Bob stood at the head of the table and introduced Ray and me. He announced the theme for the evening; it was "The Evening of Truth." He added that there would be a phone call to my mom so everyone could talk to her. A grand healing was in motion.

After greeting Shelly and Rob, I took the photo book of Mom's life to each person around the long table and explained what had happened to Mom from start to finish during her life. This gave each person an intimate connection with me and a re-connection to Mom's life. They loved it, and many of them cried and told me how sad they were about Mom's early life struggles. Mom's sister Brenda was very sentimental.

It took a few hours to get to everyone, but it was important. I could identify the relatives that Mom would have despised, and I could also see the ones Mom liked. It was about twenty-four likes to six despises. I would say that they mostly liked how Mom's life worked out. Then Uncle Bob got Mom on the speakerphone and those who had something to say talked to her. They were all very nice to her. The connection was weak from Mom's end because she was having trouble breathing, and that made it hard for her to focus. At least the relatives now knew she was alive, though very sick.

I could sense from my mom's voice that she didn't want to talk to these people. The relatives may have been healing some of those hurts, but my mom was not; she remained closed off. And even though Uncle Bob had flown out to visit with her, and they cried and laughed together, I could tell from my mom's voice that she had returned to her cold and closed-off ways.

Because these people were her roots, I knew that they understood that energy. To neutralize the intensity, Ray was fun and funny. He was able to break the tension time after time because he was not a part of the heavy family energy. I was very glad he was there.

The only relative who didn't come to the family dinner was my mother's aunt, Agnes, the one she had attempted to kill by throwing her down the stairs. She was the one relative my mother hated the most. The next morning Ray and I met with Aunt Agnes at her upscale assisted-living community home. Uncle Bob told her what was going on and that we were coming to visit, but he forewarned us that Aunt Agnes still didn't believe that Mom was alive.

Aunt Agnes was in her 90s, well cared for, very proper, and had 100 percent of her mental faculties. When she saw me, she looked up and then looked down, keeping her composure. This reserve was similar to the response we had gotten when we met the relatives the night before.

I could tell she still had doubts that I was really Mom's daughter. Her demeanor was almost defiant, but as I showed her the progression of Mom's life in the photo book, she could no longer deny the truth.

Aunt Agnes also recognized that I was not like her Pennsylvania relatives. That came as the biggest surprise to her. Aunt Agnes was sort of prudish, but when she relaxed and let that go, she started apologizing for not having done a better job with my mom.

We learned that she had been overwhelmed with responsibilities: she already had two kids of her own, was running a farm, teaching school full-time, and had a husband to take care of. She said she felt bad that she couldn't give my mother the attention she needed. I saw that her regret was genuine.

The truth is that Aunt Agnes understandably resented her brother dumping his kids onto her. Besides meeting my Uncle Bob, meeting her was what I needed to put my Mom's young life into perspective. This was the one relative my mom talked about the most with so much hate and anger. I never told Aunt Agnes how my mom felt about her, but I think she knew. Aunt Agnes died the following year.

Uncle Bob did a spectacular job taking us around and telling me the truth about my mom's life. He was instrumental in the family healing. It was Mom's intention to leave the wounds wide open, never to be heard from again. Throughout her life, she always bragged that she would take her secrets to her grave, but that didn't happen after all.

None of this would have happened without Hurricane Rita that threatened my Uncle Charlie, which brought about that visit that started unraveling the family secrets.

LESSON: From the time I was a baby, my *guides* helped me rise above my mother's rage. Discovering the hidden "why's" and the final unveiling of all the secrets lifted this layer of fog from my life. What's interesting is that I wasn't allowed to know about any of this until that point in time. Accumulating a lifetime of tips, learnings, lessons, and awareness from my *guides* was what kept me on my path, but also in the dark. *They are masters at presenting you with events at precisely the right time so you can learn what you came here to achieve, overcome and understand.* Most everything my *guides* have helped me learn is in this book.

Chapter 27: Clarity Brings One Epiphany after Another

We got home from the Pennsylvania trip the end of September. Boy, was I grateful that my parents had taken the initiative to leave that place. My relatives were steeped in religion and tradition. They wanted us to come to their 4th of July family reunions, but, other than a mutual respect, we had nothing in common with them. Over the years, they stopped communicating with us, the trip had been about healing, not reunions. Most of them found healing and peace because they wanted that to. Others, including my mom, chose not to.

After the trip, I was flooded with one epiphany after another. If I were to sum up my mother's life, it would be that her anger and resentments caused her to miss out on much of what was available to her. As a child, she was confined in a religious cloister of simple-minded people who thrived on their judgments. My mom hated it there. Her problem was that, even though she left, she took it all personally and that's what ruined her life. That's one of the first things my *guides* helped me understand – to never take any of it personally. Now I can see from my mother's choices, what it can do to a person when they don't know this.

My dad had his own reasons to run. He always referred to religion as hypocritical. My dad's mother tried to force him into becoming a priest to bring respect to the family. My dad opted out of that, left his wife, and ran off with a pregnant minor to start over in California.

Although my mom and dad did some wild things, it took the rebel spirit they shared to break out of those stifling environments. They built a new life 3,000 miles away, and did their best to run from their pasts. What they did is "out there," even by today's standards, but they did it anyway. Thank you, Mom and Dad, for taking that bold step.

I think Mom's early teenage years of freedom and easy money (as easy as being a prostitute could be) were probably the best years of her life. She had her freedom and control over her life, in spite of her line of work. She definitely didn't want kids. Having control and freedom that the money provided for that short time in her early teens may have largely influenced what set the stage for the negative attitude she had for the rest of her life.

Dad was always worried about Mom leaving him, which I never understood as a kid but can surely understand now. He may have been worried that she would go back to the hooking that gave her the money, freedom, and control she treasured. It didn't require any skills, she had the experience, she was 13 years younger than he was, and they weren't even married. I wonder if the reason my dad didn't stop my mom's abusive behavior was that she was holding the abandonment of his first wife, Ann, over his head. Adding to that is the fact that he also ran off with a minor over state lines. I suspect that was more a probability than a possibility.

I knew my mom's time was short, and I knew the truth, which I was sure my half-brother, Randy, did not. Mom always made it clear that Randy would be the only heir when she passed. This was just the continuation of the ongoing over-protection she extended to him. At this time in his life, Randy was facing some serious challenges. He had a dying mother in California with whom he spent part of his time, and a dying wife in Oregon with whom he spent the rest of his time.

A few days after I returned from Pennsylvania, I called Randy. I told him I had information for him, something I think he would want to know. I told him it was about Mom, and it was something I thought he should know in case he chose to ask Mom about it before she died.

He knew about Uncle Bob's visit because he was there when Uncle Bob visited Mom. Randy told me to go ahead and tell him what I knew because nothing would surprise him anymore. He was half hearing me as I told him that Mom was six-months pregnant with him when she met my dad. I didn't say anything else because the rest was easy to figure out for himself. That was my only obligation to Randy, and it was his choice to act on it, or not.

Sometime later, I called Randy's home, and his wife, Linda, answered. She said Randy was in California with Mom. Then she proceeded to confide in me, telling me that she really resented Randy for choosing his mother over her throughout their marriage. She said she never should have allowed that, and she would have done things differently knowing what she knows now. She felt cheated and said she should have made better decisions in her life — and one of them would have been to leave Randy years ago. She said she would do better next time.

Linda was lucid and clearer than I had ever heard her before. She was also mad, but was in her power and really standing up for herself. She truly confided in me and let it all out. She died two months after Mom died.

Mom called me about a week before she died. She was right back to gossiping and small talk. I asked her if she realized she was dying, and she said she did. She went on to tell me how mad she was at Cindy, making sure I knew that Cindy conned her out of more than $46,000. She said she gave her the money because she had bought the cancer story and felt sorry for her.

Ironically, it turned out that Mom got cancer and not Cindy. The two collaborated against me for 20 years, with mom programming Cindy to take me for all she could financially. Together, they poisoned my granddaughter's mind so badly against me that there could be no possibility of a relationship with her. I had to just shake my head at the irony that it was Mom, not me, who finally got conned by Cindy. But I never mentioned that to her; there was no point. I just let her ramble on like I always did because I believed that even the nastiest person can "get it right" in their final moments. My Mom wasn't one of them; she couldn't be reached.

A few days later, my mom had a stroke and died the following day. Randy was with her, which was appropriate. I had no reason or desire to be there. Randy tried to get me to come by telling me to bury the hatchet. I told him I never had the hatchet; she had it and took it with her. He didn't understand because he was never on the receiving end of the awful things that Mom did to Larry and me.

Randy's paternity was the sinful secret she intended to take to her grave. But just a few months before she died, it was all revealed as she was confronted by those she had hurt the most. Randy never saw the cruel person she really was, simply because he chose not to. He needed to believe that she was a saint, which is what he called her when she died. She was a saint to him because she always protected him. He was her life-long lie and that was what she was really protecting by protecting him. Mom's shame and lie served as their bond in life and into death.

After mom died, I called Cindy and confronted her with everything I had discovered over the past several months. True to form, she saw things from her own delusional perspective and justification. This has been the story of her life. Cindy is caught up in believing her own lies because she can't face reality. In that conversation she told me that Mom gave her the money because she wanted to. I reminded Cindy that Mom wanted to only because she conned her into believing she had cancer, just like Cindy had tried to pull that same con on us less than a year earlier.

I told Cindy that after years of ripping me off, lying, manipulating, turning my granddaughter against me, and constantly colluding with Mom against me, I was done with her. It was the end, once and for all. It had taken me a long time to finally give up on her. I told her that when she was 37 years old.

Randy called to tell me there would be no funeral or memorial, and he would just have her cremated. I asked him if he had spoken with Mom about what I told him. He said he had not. Then to my surprise, he referred to some health problem he was having as something he inherited from my dad. Did he not hear what I had told him; that my dad was not his father?

That mom had been six-months pregnant with him when she first met my dad?

I was so frustrated that I couldn't speak to him anymore. He never could deal with reality. Thanks to the way Mom had fawned over Randy, often at my and Larry's expense, and Randy's own superior attitude toward us, I never had much of a relationship with him anyway. As far as I was concerned, our karma was completed long ago.

However, he did call me one last time complaining about Cindy ripping Mom off. He wanted to get that money back from her. I told him that was his business. I also told him that although I didn't agree with what Cindy did, from a higher perspective, I thought Mom had it coming. She had encouraged Cindy to work against me, and one way of looking at this was that Mom had gotten back what she had promoted.

 TIP: Although you chose that family you came in through to learn some of your most valuable lessons, being stuck with them doesn't have to last your entire lifetime. If you are aware, and if you listen to your *guides*, you can learn what you need to. This gives you the freedom to move on with the rest of your life because you did indeed overcome what you came here to learn from them.

Meanwhile, in a channeling session on December 22, 2006, Ray's *guides* came through with this message for him:

"Very soon feel too bad for mom. Betty will die. Ray good son. Until now she understood nothing (she has Alzheimer's).

At last she will be at peace. Can't see so feels you are there.
(She was now blind.) *This winter will be too cold to for her
to bear. Wrong way to interpret who you are* (Ray's relatives judged him for his decisions regarding Betty's care).
*Relatives ... brother has to find out for himself what you
already know. Not this lifetime."*

In January of 2007, Ray had a dream where he was standing on the edge of a cliff looking out into bright light; refer
back to Chapter 25 and the channeling session of July 12,
2006, right under the cat photo, to see *their* prediction of
this event. From behind him, on the right side, his mom
came walking up out of the haze with her suitcase. Then
behind him on his left side came his Aunt Jean, who died in
2003, with her suitcase, telling Ray she was there to take his
mom to Paradise. That was the way they used to talk about
the Hawaii trip that Ray sent them both on in 1974. The
meaning was pretty clear.

One month after Ray's dream, we got a call from the
Alzheimer's home where his mom lived. They said that she
had gotten the flu and wasn't getting better. She was in the
hospital with pneumonia. This was in line with what Ray's
guides had told us in the December channeling session.

From Arizona, Ray was in contact with the doctors and
nurses while the local relatives started going to her bedside
at the hospital. These relatives were unhappy that Ray wasn't
there, and apparently there was a lot of judgment about that.
However, the doctors and nurses told Ray that there was no
reason for him to be there when she could hold on for weeks
or perhaps even get better. But as the days went by, she didn't

improve, so the doctor asked Ray about her medical directives. Being her medical power of attorney, Ray told them she did not want procedures done just to keep her alive.

The relatives who pined daily by her bedside, preventing her from leaving peacefully, were the same relatives who had criticized Ray for the decisions he made regarding his mother's care, despite the fact that Ray had found for her the most progressive Alzheimer's facility in the country at that time.

One morning, just before dawn, we got a call from the nurse telling Ray that his mother was lucid and wanted to talk to him. One of the first things she said was that her sister Jean, who had died four years earlier, had come to see her to bring her home to paradise. Ray told her that it was okay for her to go now, and that he knew Aunt Jean was waiting for her. Ray told her he loved her and to close her eyes and go to sleep. In that moment, she did exactly that and never woke up. She died peacefully.

This is exactly how and when Ray's *guides* said she would pass: "*when winter is too cold to bear, she won't recover from being sick and she will pass peacefully.*" It's interesting that Ray's mom and my mom died within two months of each other. My mom was 75 and Ray's mom was 85 years old. Ray and I are indeed kindred spirits.

We flew to Ohio to deal with Betty's funeral. Ray had arranged things years earlier, so it went off smoothly. We stayed with Ray's high-school friend, Joe, and his wife Diane in their big Victorian house in Toledo. We had a lot to talk about because they were very interested in spiritual stuff. They especially loved the channeling sessions that we did for them on our talking board while we were there.

In one of the sessions, Joe's *guides* answered questions about his health. *They* told him to get his head examined. Joe laughed, thinking it was a joke, but by 2010, they would both recall that session when Joe did actually have his head examined, which revealed the source of his health problems — a pituitary tumor. They were blown away!

Diane's *guides* came through and told Diane about her teeth in detail. She hadn't asked about it, and we didn't know about her ongoing dental challenges. She was really amazed at the accurate information her *guides* brought through to her.

The first time Joe and Diane had experienced a channeling session with us was December 2004, when they attended our wedding. Our sessions were still in their infancy and crude compared to what they had become. Joe and Diane were really amazed at the speed and accuracy of our sessions now, especially Joe.

After we returned home, Ray's mother came through during one of our channeling sessions to tell us, "*I have my mind back and feel good again. I'm in paradise now and I don't want to come back.*" We asked her if she had any regrets, and she said, "*The only one is that I was a burden.*" (She believed she had become a burden for Ray after his father died, and then she got Alzheimer's.)

Now that we were home from the funeral, I decided to stop putting energy into my real estate businesses. With all the information we had been getting from our *trusted advisors* in our channeling sessions, we knew that real estate was once again heading for a serious crash. I had been designing homes for clients for the past few years, but had not been active in sales. I just couldn't do it knowing what I knew. For me, it was morally wrong to put people in situations I knew would be financially devastating for them. This decision really hurt us financially. I could have done it, and nobody would have known, but I would have been a hypocrite. Thankfully, Ray supported me in my decision.

I started dedicating all of my energy to the Channeled Readings, LLC web site and its monthly CR News Reports. This is where we could make a difference in helping people to avoid pending disasters and setbacks in their personal and financial lives that we continue to do to this day. I had been doing these readings for people since 1989, and with Ray since 2007. Ray and I had become very fluid together on the talking board, by far the best channeling partner I have ever had.

Unfortunately, many people didn't want to know what was coming because they didn't want anything to change. This surprised us because we found that knowing what was ahead allowed us to prepare for it. We had an analogy for what we were doing: If you are sitting on the railroad tracks and a train is coming, we let you know when it will arrive so you can move yourself off the tracks.

In the case of real estate, one of the hazards for real estate agents was that they were vulnerable to lawsuits. It doesn't matter whether they follow the rules or not, they stand to lose money, time, and their reputation. You only occasionally hear about these lawsuits, but they are just one of those hidden facts of life that are revealed in our monthly CR News Reports — the news before it happens.

Ray continued to work in his executive recruiting business, but that had deteriorated by early 2008. With no money coming in from our former businesses, Ray started selling off our personal assets at weekend garage sales.

Next, we put our townhouse up for sale. But a commercial neighbor had recently started an enterprise that created loud noises early in the morning, which completely destroyed our property value. We found ourselves jolted awake each day at 3:00 a.m. with a noise that lasted until 5:00 a.m. We attempted to take legal action, but municipal garbage service is exempt from City noise ordinances, no matter what time they choose to pick up, and we lost our case. It was pretty apparent that no one in their right mind was going to want to buy our home with that issue, which would have only led to future lawsuits if we did sell it.

 So, not only was our livelihood gone, but our real estate was worthless. However, our Channeled Readings business was building, but the investment in setting it up exceeded our income at that time.

Just when things looked like they couldn't get any worse, warnings started coming through our CR News Reports, that we publish 14 times per month, telling our readers an economic crash was on the horizon. Sure enough, later that year, in September, 2008, the "Great Recession" hit full force.

This crash of 2008-2009 was something we had been warned about and preparing for since 2007, but even with the warning, it didn't mean it was going to be easy. We continued to sell our assets and build Channeled Readings, LLC, and its CR News Reports. After the crash happened, our clients who heeded the predictions and had taken appropriate action saw their assets soar in value. Those who did nothing were devastated and even embarrassed when we would occasionally see them.

Some of these people were even mad at us. That's what denial looks like: blame someone else when you can't face the real source of the problem — themselves.

 AWARENESS: Change is difficult, but not changing is just postponing the inevitable. The reason people don't change is because they are fearful and lack support. There is no reason to fear anything when you have the support of your *guides*. *They* never backstab, lie, manipulate, defraud, misguide, use love as a weapon, or have any personal agenda. *They* are the real thing. When you work with your *guides*, you are not giving something up. You are getting much more than you ever had.

Then, in the afternoon of October 31, 2008, we got a call from Uncle Charlie's sister-in-law telling us that he had died. She said he passed peacefully. He was 93 years old. I was so grateful that a couple years earlier he had unintentionally set a powerful healing into motion throughout the entire family. I loved him and was very glad Ray had met him.

Chapter 28: Gratitude for Our Past, and a Guided Future

After the crash of 2008, our CR News Reports predictions had been validated and were getting a lot more attention. That single event affected everyone, and no one could pretend that things were okay any longer. Unemployment was out of control, the financial institutions were melting down, the auto industry was collapsing, the world governments were under great pressure to meet their obligations, real estate collapsed and the cost of most essentials skyrocketed. Everything our personal readings and the CR News Reports had been preparing our clients for was happening.

Throughout 2009, Ray and I continued building the Channeled Readings, LLC, and CR News Reports project as we continued to downsize our lives and burn through our capital. This was the year Ray's son, Rex, graduated from college so, finally, that expense stopped. We even explored leaving the country, knowing what was coming. Our *guides* told us that we would not be moving to another country, that service to others would keep us here in the U.S.

We realized it was our mission to continue helping people navigate these challenging times. That was also the message we got for ourselves. We were already in the process of becoming truly lean and mean, so we were on the right path as we continued to downsize, becoming liquid and mobile. We were walking our talk.

From 2004 through February 2007, Ray and I had a carefree, magical time together. It was in that time that we were able to enjoy our new lives together while we helped each other heal our pasts. We had to love and heal ourselves first before we could help others. Our relationship was built on a powerful foundation of fun, love, and healing.

Between February 2007 and 2010, we made the bold decisions that would turn our barge around. I say "barge" because it involved a huge releasing of all the things that represented value, which, in hindsight, would only contribute to more depletion of our cash, time, and energy while stealing from our future. It was a releasing of old thinking, priorities, beliefs, values, and stuff.

We were careful not to either act too quickly or wait too long, as our own personal *advisors* helped guide us with perfect timing. Ray was reluctant to act on *their* advice for some time. I realized that he was not accustomed to this kind of help, so I stood back and allowed less positive outcomes to occur so he could learn. I looked at this as an investment in our relationship. It was critical to have him experience the downside of not acting on *their* advice. It would not help him if I just told him what I already knew.

Time and time again, Ray would feel tormented because, although we had *their* timely information, we didn't act on it. That went on for a few years. Although I knew I could have saved us from a number of financial losses, I could not interfere. He had to see this and know it as deeply as I already did without interference from me. This was an investment in us.

By September 2010, however, I knew this could no longer go on. Time now was of the essence. On the plus side, Ray was now ready. He trusted me completely and acted with me without any of his previous fear or hesitation. What I did over the next month saved us from complete and total financial ruin.

Ray was coming full circle by learning how to act on the timely information we had been getting from our *guides* for years. Ray was changed forever. He was now able to receive *their* timely advice and warnings, and act on them with confidence.

This was a big shift we took together. His shift was different from mine, but this investment in Ray was worth it and necessary if we were going to go forward together.

It had become clear that paying on assets that had declined drastically was only prolonging the pain. In fact, we realized that anything with debt attached to it had to go. We were taking bold actions that others found too difficult, or even impossible to do, let alone to do them on time before it was too late.

The most important part was that we were mutual in our decision making; we were looking in the same direction together at the same time. It was perfect! Granted, we had the advantage of knowing what was coming from channeling the timely information in the monthly CR News Reports for our readership. We also benefitted from the guidance and insights our clients received from what we had channeled for them in their private readings. This constant flow of what was to come gave our clients and us a peek into the future no one else had.

People felt sorry for us when they saw us selling our possessions and walking away from everything we had spent our lives accumulating. They saw us as victims. What they didn't realize was that they, too, soon would be facing hard choices.

We knew what was coming and had already made the bold moves to position ourselves for it. We were positioned to help others so when "it" did start to hit, we could show them how to walk through it like we already had. Our advice would have genuine substance for people because we had already experienced it ourselves.

 LESSON: People who don't have a relationship want one, and people who have one want out. To have a relationship that's worth having requires an investment in each other, just like your *guides* make an investment in you. If you don't appreciate each other, you won't have what it takes to mutually rise above life's challenges. Again, having direction from your *guides* is invaluable.

From 2010 to 2012, our lives were like the movie *Groundhog Day*: a "nose to the grindstone" repeat of the days, months, and years before. We were living as frugally as possible while staying the course with our timely projects.

By June 2011, the income faucet was completely turned off. People stopped spending money on anything that wasn't necessary. We spoke with many people who all told us the same thing, although the news mentioned none of this. Lack of reporting makes what's really happening even more confusing. That is the reason we do what we do. We keep people informed about what's really going on so they can make reliable and timely decisions based on the truth.

In 2012, I started writing this book, and at the same time, we began a wellness business. We were inspired by our *guides* to start both at that time.

Having Ray, the right partner, to do all this with is the best part. He was that critical missing piece that showed up at just the right time, handpicked and delivered to me by my *guides*...my perfect partner on the *merry-go-round* for what's yet to come for all of us.

A Closing Message to You from Linda's *Spirit Guide Angels...*

"We speak for our Infinite Legions. You are never alone. Just as we saved an unwanted, unloved, and abused little girl, we bring hope and help to each who asks for our guidance.

Our dedication to you is how we fulfill our soul's destiny. We believe in you so strongly that one of us materialized in front of Linda so you could believe (on the front cover of this book). *By asking for our help, your life will change in an instant.*

We are here. You must ask. Walk with Us."

Afterword

Although I have lived a life of high and low points, never have I felt disadvantaged or accepted defeat. For that, I thank my *guides*. I thank my parents second, especially my mom. While she never intentionally made me into the person I am, she made my life so unbearable that I had no other choice but to walk through it, trusting in no one but myself and my *guides*.

There was no way out, and I couldn't run anywhere (I tried that). I had to let go and not take any of what was going on around me personally and just keep walking through the challenges, allowing what was hidden to break through at just the right time. My strengths magically revealed themselves, showing me the best course of action at any given time, every time. I couldn't have done it without the lifetime of coaching, training and guidance I received from my *guides*.

It wasn't until 2006 that the truth of what really happened in my life was completely revealed it to me. It was not something I was expecting. Hurricane Rita, the trip to Texas, my mother's terminal illness, meeting my Uncle Bob and all my other supposedly dead relatives for the first time while my mother was dying, were all critical to my finally understanding the unresolved pieces of my life. My mother almost accomplished her life-long goal of taking all her sinful secrets to her grave.

Then, there was the economic collapse in 2008. Many people were still thinking we were just in a recession and things would be back to normal soon. However, my *guides* have shown me what's coming. I've come to the conclusion that, for some people, it's more painful to know in advance than to face and prepare for it. Then there are others who are more realistic and can handle the truth, and for these people, their lives will be easier.

I wrote this book for both types of people because I believe that people "get it" in their own timing. I don't force you to get it, although it is easier to get it than not to. It all hinges on your ability to face reality – the truth. That's what the world needs now. This is where your *guides* shine because *they* are the truth. There's no place to run to get away from all this because "it" is everywhere now. No one can escape "it" anymore. When you decide it's your time to make your shift, do it with your *guides* because it's not only easier, it will be the most fascinating relationship and life journey you will ever take.

The biggest achievement in my life is in feeling loved. I've had people tell me they loved me before. And now, thanks to Ray and my *guides*, I know what it means to "feel loved." I learned what people meant when they said they loved me: they loved me for who they needed me to be. Feeling loved means being appreciated for who you are. That's what made the difference.

We are kindred spirits whose lives parallel each other's in many ways. Even so, I have had a different way of living than most people do, and it was challenging to others who had come to share my life for a while. This is where Ray is truly unique and different from the rest. When we met he knew about this difference in me and liked it, but he didn't know what it was like to live it. Being receptive to receiving *their* messages is the first step. Trusting yourself enough to act on *their* guidance is the key. Your ability to take action is equal to how well you trust (know) yourself. That's why learning to know myself was the first part of the curriculum my *guides* required that I learned right from the beginning of my life. Ray stepped on board and joined forces with his own *spirit guides* when he was 52 years old. He now knows firsthand what it's like to live a guided life. He is proof that it's never too late to start this journey.

The biggest disappointment in my life is the rapid decline of society. Too many people are subscribing to selfish, ruthless, bully tactics. Money has become their god, the answer to everything. These people have become increasingly more isolated, distrustful, and paranoid. <u>They</u> are the problem. They distrust people they don't even know, which makes no rational sense. This is not making the world a better place, and that is why it's falling apart- it needs to.

I believe that this is what the *merry-go-round dream* was showing me, with people letting go and giving up. This has not yet happened, but it's not far off. None of this is meant to happen "to" you, it's meant to happen "for" you because the world we find ourselves in is not sustainable for anyone anymore. This is a mess that needs a rebalancing — a shift, a big one.

We find ourselves in a world of lies and manipulation that requires everyone to look for answers in unconventional ways. To me, this has never been unconventional.

Now that you have read this book and understand this valuable relationship, you are well on your way to establishing a life-long connection with your own *Spirit Guide Angels* to navigate you through these interesting times ahead.

Your *guides* are best qualified to walk you through your shift. *They* have no agenda. *They* are your biggest fans and your real *life coaches*. This is why it's the perfect timing for this book to be written for you – for us all. It's important to know that you do still have someone you can trust and depend on, your *guides*.

The truth and love are both painstakingly real. You must be 100-percent present to fully experience them. There can be no distractions, no manipulations or strategies to outsmart them, no pretending, or cheating. You must be fearless; you must be <u>you</u>, pure and simple. Not too many people are willing to do this because, to them, it feels too risky. Only if you have a relationship with *those who walk with you,* your *guides,* your *life coaches,* as *they* navigate you through this life will you have the checks and balances necessary to keep you on course. But you have to be open to this relationship and be willing to act on *their* guidance, and on time. No one here knows you better than your *guides*, nor does anyone here, in this life, know what to do... especially now.

ABOUT THE AUTHOR

Linda Deir doesn't look like the kind of person who has endured all she has. That's due to the lifetime of support she has received from her *Spirit Guides*. She has been able to avoid physical harm and overcome challenges, as well as apply *their* guidance to create success in her business ventures. That success resulted largely because of her uncanny ability to know when to get in and out of projects or even industries at just the right time, despite contradictory conventional wisdom. In a nutshell, Linda has survived and prospered because she has mastered living in two worlds simultaneously.

Following her passions combined the alliance she has with her *guides*, is what has prevented her from struggling no matter what the obstacles. She calls it cheating — doing what she loves while getting rewarded for doing it. As mentioned in the foreword, when you live a guided life it feels like you're cheating because there's nothing you can't learn, figure out, do, or have. All you have to do is step into it. That's the way she thinks everyone should be living, because it's authentic.

In 1994, her *Spirit Guides* came to her in a dream and told her she would write this book. Also in that same year, she experienced one of the most amazing moments of her life — her *Spirit Guide Angel* materialized right in front of her as she had a camera in hand to capture *her* for the world to see and believe. That photograph is on the cover of this book.

In addition to writing, Linda is a speaker, a life-coach, an intuitive counselor, dream interpreter, and teaches individuals how to contact and work with their own *spirit guides*. Together, Linda and Ray have services and products that support people in connecting and communicating with their own *spirit guides*, which can be found at www.ChanneledReadings.com . To learn to do this yourself click on the navigation bar: "LEARN TO CHANNEL your *Spirit Guides*." To schedule a personal session or appearance with Linda contact her at: Linda@LindaDeir.com.

A dynamic presenter in person, Linda Deir brings through spontaneous insights from this *higher source* that reawakens the soul's urge to express itself.

Linda and her husband Ray currently live in Sedona, Arizona with their cat Benny. You can contact them through their website, www.LindaDeir.com and sign up for "Linda's Weekly 'Guided' Insights" direct from her *Spirit Guide Angels* – a weekly gift of guidance from *them* to you.

Made in the USA
San Bernardino, CA
12 November 2014